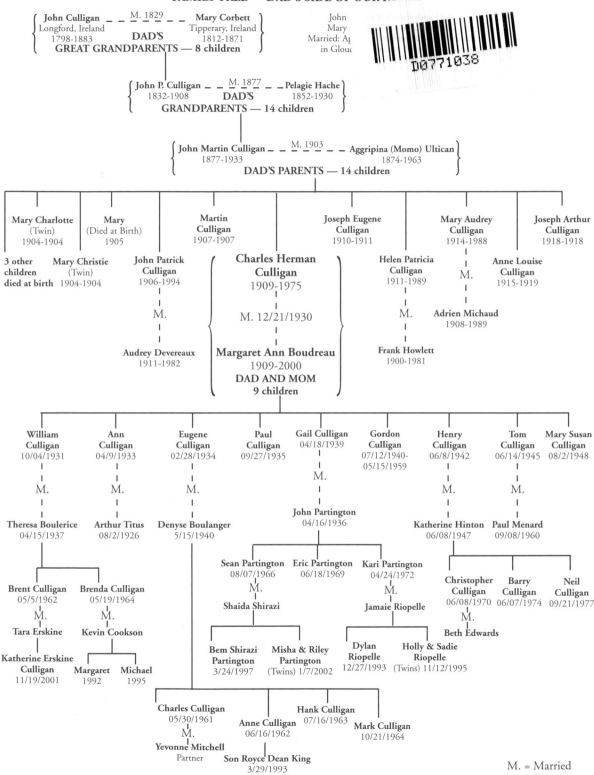

Watching the clouds go by

Teacups &
Sticky Buns

Mom's Story

Tom Culligan

Teacups & Sticky Buns

Mom's Story

Tom Culligan

Paintings by Tom Culligan
Illustration by Paul Menard

Culligan Publishing Limited
Canada

ISBN   0-9730250-0-X

National Library of Canada Cataloguing in Publication Data
Culligan, Tom, 1945-
        Teacups and sticky buns: Mom's story

ISBN 0-9730250-0-X

1. Culligan, Margaret. 2. Belledune (N.B.)—Biography.
3.Women—New Brunswick—Biography. I. Title.

FC2499.B4Z49 2002   920.72'0971512   C2002-900399-7
F1044.G46C84 2002

Development & Book Production: Thelma Barer-Stein, Ph.D.,
Culture Concepts Books. Toronto, Ontario, Canada.

Input Editors: Vicki Hiltz and Louise Amm
Copy Editors: Liba Berry and Wendy Thomas
Cover and Interior Design: Gillian Tsintziras, The Brookview Group Inc.
Paintings: Tom Culligan
Illustration: Paul Menard

Published by Culligan Publishing Limited
55A Old Portage Road, Highway 632
Minett, Ontario, Canada P0B 1G0
Phone: 705-732-1448
Printed and bound in Canada by Friesens, Altona, Manitoba.

Contents

Dedication

To the folks who've inspired and motivated me:

Three nuns in New Brunswick, Sister Florentine, Sister Sophie and Sister Ann, who taught me as a teenager and encouraged me with their loving attention to excel in my studies and student activities.

Ellie Kurtz, Program Director, and Margaret Holland, Vice President, Student Affairs at the University of Dayton, Dayton, Ohio, who provided opportunities for me to develop my leadership skills and generously gave of their time.

Elke Scholz—gifted artist and my art teacher, who guided me to develop my own style of art.

Natalie Goldberg, author and artist—whom I've never met, yet have devoured every one of her many books—exemplified for me that I could both write and paint. I did.

And especially, I dedicate this book to my life partner, Paul Menard, who continues to teach me drawing, perspective, design, colour and appreciation of living.

Acknowledgements

Just imagine being delivered several hundred pages of scribbled-over hand-written manuscript! That's what my editor and book developer, Thelma Barer-Stein, received in a large brown bag from me. A groan escaped from her lips. Got to tell you—that was her first and only complaint. When authors say they would not have gotten their book written and published without their editor, believe me, that's no exaggeration for me. Thelma performed the water-wine miracle with my manuscript.

I suspect that my partner, Paul, knows my manuscript as intimately as I do. He read each of the many drafts, and his thousands of five-cent's-worth advice, together with his loving understanding and encouragement, more than once shifted my pen from being stuck to the paper.

Thanks to all the folks back home on the great ol' Bay de Chaleur in New Brunswick, for your loving and caring support of Mom. Visiting, chatting and enjoying a cup'a tea with each of you meant so much to her. And thanks from my heart and soul for your moving letters, cards and calls with memories of times with Mom.

I especially express my gratitude to my sisters, brothers, aunts, uncles and nieces, nephews and cousins and all the good folks up and down the shore road.

*Tom and his mother, Margaret Culligan,
at the age of eighty-nine*

Tom Culligan, co-founder of The Second Cup was the first to develop a chain of retail stores specializing in gourmet coffee in North America. The first store was opened in 1975 and the 150 stores were sold to new owners in 1989.

Tom grew up in New Brunswick, Canada. He received a degree in theology and philosophy from the University of Dayton at Dayton, Ohio. Aside from his interest in private financial and real estate developments, Tom devotes himself full-time to painting and writing. He lives with his partner, Paul Menard, in Muskoka, Ontario.

Why Write about Mom

How Mom lived her life brings a message of hope for women. Especially for single moms and lonely women raising children with inattentive or absentee husbands. Mom's courage, her strengths, and her determination and faith, provide a powerful example to women everywhere who struggle with a chauvinistic and institutionalized society. Her basic principles of life and her abiding faith are inspirational.

Over a lifetime of faithfully doing all the "little things," Mom demonstrated that an individual really can and does make a difference. She left nobody out in her commitment to care for others. Each person counted as much as the next with Mom. Though she seemed to me an ordinary person, I know now that she truly lived and acted extraordinarily in every action and in every relationship.

Because of her example of "just do it!" I was inspired to develop The Second Cup concept of serving customers in a warm and inviting atmosphere, developing specialty blends of gourmet coffee, studying books, attending seminars and remaining always open to suggestions and ideas in search of success. Through my deliberate efforts to develop a business, a deeper, tenderer understanding of Mom emerged, and I realized that the talents and skills that I eventually developed for The Second Cup concept enveloped the same characteristics of determination and survival that Mom had utilized. In this, her true story, I share segments of her sensitivity to all life, her legendary perseverance, and her selfless caring for others that provided me with unforgettable examples of sensitivity to others while following my vision to the end.

That's why I knew I had to share her life with others, and it was on her eightieth birthday that I decided to collect her poems, to make a point of pulling stories and memories from friends and family, and above all, to tape our conversations and reflect on her gentle but wise responses to my almost endless questions.

Mom sitting in her parlour with painting of her mother, "Granny Boudreau"

One

All in the Name of Love

$\mathcal{M}$om's start to establish her identity was a mixed bag of the best and the worst. She liked to remind me, "I've learned that nothing is perfectly bad. Or all good. Life's somewhat like roses and thorns. So many contradictions that often life seems to make no sense. I had one very miserable life at home with Mama, but on the other hand, I couldn't help but admire how she worked herself to the bone for family and church."

We were spending a quiet day together. It began with us both standing on the back stoop enjoying the grand view of the Bay de Chaleur and the Gaspé Mountains beyond where they gradually disappear into the Gulf of St. Lawrence and eventually into the icy Atlantic waters.

"Mercy God almighty!" Mom was commenting softly on the majestic landscape before us. "Spring's still swallowing up winter's stuff, but deep down the thaw's only beginning and there's nary a hint of bird's nesting. And yet, Tom, can't you just feel the anticipation of bursting life that hangs in midair?"

Mom felt such contradictory feelings. Just like she felt a betrayal to her mama. She never quite resolved this conflict. There was good and there was evil, there were workers and there were shirkers, and there were Catholics and then there was everyone else. If something was not one hundred percent perfect, then it must be bad or wrong. Mom's mother, her "mama," saw the world and all that was a part of it clearly as either good or bad. Period.

We were each deep in our own thoughts, when the dead quiet of the early morning was broken with the heavy thud of a lobster trap hitting the boat's hull getting pulled in to shore for emptying. Two miles over the water and sharp as a whistle we could hear the sound of the crackling short-wave radio and a voice calling out, "Hey! Put her back, that's a young'un!" It was a lobster too small to keep. That was Truman, a young local fisherman from down the road just past Devil's Elbow, that nasty curve in the road.

Mom and I turned our attention then to the sweep of the bare fields and over to Danny's Point, that long sandy rock point that was exposed now by the low tide setting the air adrift with the smell of clams and damp ocean seaweed. This served as breakfast for the screeching mob of seagulls dive-bombing for clams as they popped out of their air-bubble holes in the sand. We both breathed deeply, breaths so deep that it was like drawing the whole landscape with all its sounds and scents into our bodies. This was home. This was New Brunswick.

Mom knew what I was thinking and turned that tanned, wrinkled face and those powerful eyes to me. I thought, even to this day in her ninetieth year, she has the same "straight as a two-by-four" stance and the perfectly fit and trim body I've always remembered. Maybe this was because she ate so many of her meals standing. Mostly moving from the hot cast-iron stove to the kitchen table, always serving others, but never skipping a beat of the talk going on. She always looked tanned, healthy and radiant. The one huge change occurred when the Marilyn Monroe style rage struck Mom. From her natural brunette hair, she turned strawberry blonde. But within months—thankfully—she decided to let the natural roots show.

At five foot five, she always walked with a bounce. No foot-dragging. What simply amazed me was how she could slug and heave the heaviest of anything, like pulp logs or buckets of water, and the next moment appear walking down the steps looking like a movie star, and in my mind, I thought she smelled like one too, all lipstick and powdery feminine.

The Early Messages

"From the earliest I know," Mom recalled, "I accepted that all living was sinful. Except, of course, my music at church, but that became a sin when I thought about how much I enjoyed playing the organ and singing. I remember living under Mama's roof and always feeling a sense of impending doom believing that God would be punishing me. I rarely knew or understood for what reason. It was just that God punished. Mama saw the devil in just about everything. We had a back summer kitchen where I loved to sit and read—but only in the wintertime when that kitchen wasn't used and I could sneak in. All the same, I was certain that reading was a sin. This was because Mama relentlessly reminded us that a resting person is the devil's own handiwork."

Listening to Mom, I guess I kind of wandered off and I could only nod, because watching her face as she spoke, I could only think about how similar my siblings and I are to her. For any one of us, a glance in the mirror reflects chiselled cheekbones, wide mouth, green eyes, high forehead, auburn hair and elephant ears that hint of our dominant family side. Then again, what is inherited often goes deeper inside—like high blood pressure, angina and stomach cancer. Amazingly, what affects us to the core rarely is acknowledged, but it's deep in there somewhere. What we heard, saw and experienced through our childhood sticks like flies to shit, as the saying goes, and profoundly affects our personality and disposition. I've no doubt my own attitudes solidified early in life. This was probably from the daily example of how Mom coped with the challenges and obstacles that came her way. And, too, her disposition seemed, in turn, to be formed by how her folks had lived. Religion dominated the way her parents saw life.

"The early messages taught," Mom said, "were to stuff away, shut down and turn off personal feelings and emotions. They didn't count for anything. Certainly they were never taken into consideration in determining the child's needs. I would not dare to express myself. That wasn't even remotely allowed for a child."

Mom could most easily recall uncomfortable feelings because she never really knew happiness—especially not a sense of contentment or freedom. Later, she identified these same feelings as shame and guilt. No matter what transpired, Mom somehow knew she was not permitted to feel good, especially not good about herself. That would be "a sin of great proportion."

"Comfort and security came only when I attended church. All along both sides of the church hung tall statues depicting the 'way of the cross.' These, together with the burning incense were a comfort to me. I knew these saints had pleased God through their martyrdom. Lingering inside the church made me feel safe. Outside, the devil would tempt my every thought. And I had plenty. Especially I had thoughts of getting away from Mama and finding a new life. But such thoughts only added to my guilt.

"I remember when I was little, it was always the baby that was loved, but that didn't make room for the child. Anything new had to take on the manner and look of the old. Tradition meant the past and the only way to do things. In my time, any idea or suggestion was considered to be a confrontation. And any confrontation got slapped and strapped down.

"Lots of crazy behaviour is done in the name of love, coming from 'I know what's good for you.' These are the childhood events that stay with you forever, like Sister Mary Albert breaking her long black pointer across the back of my hand. Not once, mind you—three times. Each time at piano practice, Sister watched over my shoulder, always at the ready to smack me. The worst would be the difficult classical composers. Only when Mama saw my red and swollen knuckles did she believe what Sister had done to me.

"I cried myself to sleep every night until Mama transferred me out of the Dalhousie Boarding School because of the nun's cruelty, to the Bathurst Convent Boarding School, which I really enjoyed. None of that interfered with my loving family times at the piano and the organ. Probably from staring at the painted pastoral altar scenes, I often imagined myself as an angel playing the church Gregorian organ music.

"Then I'd be feeling guilty all over again, remembering Mama warning me that my church-music playing was for suffering, not for enjoyment or pleasure. Just like doing homework at the kitchen table when she ordered us to keep our feet flat on the floor. No slouching. Our backs had to touch the back of the chair. At home, I often daydreamed to escape Mama."

As I listened to my mom, my own thoughts went back to her mama— whom we called Granny Boudreau—and how severe she always was. Can't say I ever saw her bend either in posture or ideas. She wore only black. What I recall most about Granny is either getting ready for church or sitting in our church pew. Not one memory of her as ever being what I wanted a grandmother to be. Not a single birthday card, certainly no gifts and nothing at all for Christmas, first communion, confirmation or graduations.

I never visited Granny or Grandpa Boudreau. The handful of times I remember when Granny came visiting us, I only recall, in later years, her sour expression of disapproval for my mom's dating a gentleman since her separation from my alcoholic and abusive dad. Granny called it a scandal for us children and for her whole family. I knew even then that there was something wrong with Granny's severe and unwavering judgement. Because, without ever being able to name my feelings, I had been keenly aware of the calm atmosphere in our home since Dad had left. Something like how I felt when Granny Boudreau left us after a visit.

Aunt Maggie's Leather Strap

On another occasion, I was listening to Mom's first cousin Deany remembering Granny Boudreau too, whom she called her Aunt Maggie.

"Aunt Maggie had a leather strap. She kept it close by, so as to grab it anytime. Believe me, it took barely a whimper for Aunt Maggie to resort to slapping. 'Quickly, she'd say, 'Hold out your hands!' Only when she heard the kids cry and yelp was she satisfied enough to stop. Your Mom's Papa, my Uncle Joe, was a quiet good-natured man who never punished the kids. But she believed in religious suffering, so for hours on end, Aunt Maggie forced the kids to sit in a corner on the floor, and ordered them to hold their heads down. No one dared turn around, for the punishment would be even worse. I never understood how they got along, what with your mom's papa, who was my Uncle Joe, being such a quiet, good-natured man who never punished the kids.

"Aunt Maggie carried her rosary beads all the time—tucked into her belt while mending, cooking and even while doing housework. I' d say she was more religious than a nun. That's saying a lot. Aunt Maggie spoke few words other than dishing out punishments, and her praying and singing hymns forever out loud. But what a lovely singer! Mom's family, the Firlottes, were all musical. Your Mom got the good with the bad. Aunt Maggie and your Mom and her sister Tookie could sing and play the church organ better than anyone in the whole province of New Brunswick.

"We were scared of Aunt Maggie. Though not as frightened as her own kids. The Firlottes were fanatical in everything. Even how grandfather pruned the orchard trees. You never put anything out of its place at the Firlottes'. With them, there was only one way to everything—*their* way.

"Tom, Aunt Maggie and the kids practically lived at church. She marched them off every Sunday morning for two Masses where they played the organ, sang the Latin Gregorian Mass with Father Trudel and served as altar boys. At 2:00 p.m. they attended catechism classes, and the Sunday ended with the 7:00 p.m. benediction of the Blessed Sacrament. For your Mom there was plenty more—she played the organ or sang for every first Friday of the month, for the forty days of Lent, for the two-week fall preaching missions and for countless special holy days of church obligation. Since my mother wasn't a Firlotte, we were saved from being trouped to church for every saint or soul.

"I knew better not to show up visiting your Mom after supper, because without fail, they'd all be on their knees repeating the rosary and saying prayers for the conversion of communists, Jews, pagans and sinners. They were definitely the most praying bunch. In the mornings, too, and before bed, they all got down on their knees, with arms stretched out like a cross, to confess their sins, beg forgiveness and pray for family alive and dead. During the month of May, just when winter finally relinquished itself to bright evenings for playing sports, Aunt Maggie dragged them all off to the nightly May Devotions to the Blessed Virgin Mary. The kids had no choice but to take to the pews. Tom, I think your Mom's dedication to burning church vigil lights and the sanctuary lamp took root from a solitude she discovered as a kid."

Despite Deany's memories of the Boudreaus, I know that Mom admired her Grandfather Firlotte, who was a stern man with steely eyes, while Grandmother Firlotte had lovely blue eyes that sparkled with warmth. Mom took every advantage for a visit to their place. That was easy, it being only a two-minute walk away.

Mom told me, "I'd manage to slip away from home early Sunday morning before Mass to spend time in Grandmother Firlotte's kitchen because her front and back kitchens being larger than our entire little brown house, were so grand that I just loved to be there with her. The back kitchen was used during the summer and fall harvest for the worker's meals, while the front kitchen was usually for family.

Grandmother Firlotte had a kind word for everybody, and good principals concerning gossip. There was a very large woman, called Mrs. Paddy Pat, Patrick Dempsey's wife. I suppose poor Mrs. Paddy Pat weighed about four hundred pounds. Well, this Sunday I was over at Grandmother's kitchen when a group of ladies chatting there over tea, started to gossip of Mrs. Pat, saying, 'What a size to be waddling along the road to church!' Well, Grandmother piped in quickly, 'Rather tall she is and a very educated woman as well. Mrs. Pat's such a grand lady that it doesn't look at all bad on her.'"

I asked Mom to describe her Firlotte family as compared to the Boudreau one, and she said, "Clannish, caring, and giving but still fanatical. I loved to go to Aunt Tessie's. She and Uncle Joe were so in love. No such intimacy existed between Mama and Papa. There was always a snag with my father. Always nagging. Mama was never happy with the wages he made. She'd say, 'What's wrong, Joe? You're a first class carpenter, I've filled out forms telling such for you. You're always feelin' lower than someone else.'

"Of course, I wouldn't dare say I heard their conversations, but it made me angry. Mind you, I felt plenty guilty, me thinking, 'Why aren't we better off?' So I'd be on her side, and I'd bite my tongue.

"My sister Tookie would say, 'But, Margaret, it was a dear little home we had.' And I would say, 'Sure a dear little box and speaking of boxes, it wasn't a home.' But Tookie didn't want to be honest in accepting our living conditions. Truth was, you could have cut the atmosphere in our house with a knife."

That First Dance

I think it was when Mom was about eighteen—and anyhow it was just before she left home to work in Boston—that Granny Boudreau gave her permission to attend her first dance with Leslie Doyle. Now *that* was something for Mom!

The dance of course was chaperoned by several adult parishioners and was held in the old small schoolhouse. You can be sure nothing ever got out of order. Even the priest and Miss Dempsey, the teacher, attended. There was no slow waltzing and there was no touching. But everyone had lots of fun square dancing to the local fiddlers. It was over by 10:00 p.m.

"Strange," Mom said, "because Leslie Doyle was my first cousin, the son of our other Uncle Joe and Aunt Lizzie. (There sure were a lot of Uncle Joes in our family!) Now, that Leslie could charm a snake, so he had no trouble winning over Mama to his side. Surely I had fantasized of just such a social occasion. That night, overtop my high shoulder-padded suit of green wool, I dressed in my red velvet coat, and white soft wool tam. My shoulder-length hair turned under and I had a sparkling sapphire-like brooch on the upper lapel. I looked pretty nice.

Who would have known I would never again see my cousin Leslie after that night? But you see, some time later I went to Boston. He went overseas. While living in London, one night in a pub, Leslie went haywire and shot his best friend. Fired bullets right through his face! Completely broke Uncle Joe and Aunt Lizzy's heart. All their family lives were ruined forever. Uncle Joe and Aunt Lizzy packed up, left New Brunswick and never returned.

"You know, Tom, I didn't have the compassion I should have had for my father. He'd break out in eczema that lasted for months. It left ulcerated sores on his arms. His stomach bothered him always. Accidents and injury were common in the lumberyards where Papa worked, and because no health care existed at that time, accidents and injury caused real hardship for the families concerned. And I knew that Mama and her sisters didn't get along. They ribbed Mama about marrying a Frenchman called Boudreau, and they teased Papa even before he married Mama for the Yankee French accent he had picked up while working in Massachusetts."

Looking at Mom now and enjoying her talk of the early years, I realized yet again that I sure do come from hardy stock. Both her grandparents were as tough as nails. They were as determined as they were hardworking. There's no wondering how or where Mom got her work ethic. She's just a chip off the ol' block. Maybe because she witnessed even her Grandfather Firlotte going into the field at 5:00 a.m., driving his horses by hand reins. With the winter thaw, he got two hours of ploughing and cultivating the crops under his belt before he was off to his 8:00 a.m. Canadian National Railroad foreman's job.

"What a worker, " Mom noted, "Like an ox! At 4:00 p.m. upon returning from his railroad job, he'd hitch his team of horses and head to the backfields haying and digging until dark.

"Before bed each night, Grandfather pulled up the root cellar doors to go down for the next day's provisions. I'm reminded of their stock when I shop for produce. The sights and smells bring me into that root cellar with its neatly piled store of potatoes, turnips, carrots, onions, beets and, oh my, that fruit! Grandfather and Grandmother tended their gardens and orchards with the same devotion they gave religion, giving us delicious green, red and crab apples, cherries and plums for those long winters. Those fruits were for eating and making pies, because all the canned and bottled preserves were done from early fall harvesting. I've not seen a grocery store or pantry that could stir your soul with the sight and the smells like my grandparents' root cellar.

"I never saw a day Grandfather and Grandmother didn't work. Including Sunday, when they milked cows, gathered eggs, exercised the animals and cleaned stalls. It had to be only something big like a family wedding for our clan to put aside a Saturday for fiddling and square dancing. On that day, the furniture got pushed back to the walls, carpets rolled up, and china cabinets moved so the fiddlers could take their place.

"Papa's side of the family was French through and through. The Boudreaus lived in Petit Roche, just fifteen miles down the road from Jacquet River. Back in those days, rarely did the English and French mix socially or otherwise. Deep suspicions lingered about the intentions of the English-speaking folks by the Acadian population. Most French people were forced into English education facilities. When I visited Papa's family in Petit Roche, not a word got spoken in English. Just as I didn't speak a word of English until I was about six years old.

"When we were kids, I loved when Papa worked for his mother at their Boudreau Hotel in Petit Roche. His parents and siblings were an interesting bunch. They were no slouches. Did well financially. Uncle Tim went on to make a fortune building and operating hotels in Quebec. I remember Grandmother Marie Alène Boudreau always wore a tightly tied bun on top of her head. She'd sit straight as you may on a large ridged back chair, issuing orders. Always sitting like that in her flouncy dresses, we called her Queen Victoria. Papa's sister, Aunt Amanda, was ambitious. She had no small part in Uncle John Robichaud's rise to power in Ottawa as a Cabinet Minister, Senator and then lieutenant governor. It's said that I'm most like my Aunt Amanda."

Mom placed a lot of emphasis on character and physical attributes in assessing folks. This was confirmed by her constant reminders to every one of us kids on how to stand, walk, sit, eat and talk.

She told me often, "It was the intermediate school years of Grade Seven and Grade Eight with Miss Abby Dempsey that most inspired me to be strong. She had big, strong hands, built tall—not fat, wasn't girlish-looking or petit. Acted like her mother, Mrs. Anthony, the midwife who delivered Dr. Ellis's babies and later delivered mine. What a disciplinarian both were. Miss Dempsey was no sadist as the nuns could be. She'd see us yawning from the ol' red-hot wood stove and immediately opened all the windows. Didn't matter whether snow or flies flew in. It never took long to have us back on track to our multiplication tables. I used to think, now I wouldn't mind looking a bit like her."

Now Mom was making tea, setting the kettle on the stove to boil and placing handfuls of black tea into the white granite mug. Guess I had a happy grin on my face as she quickly hurried out from the pantry with a big plate of warm sticky buns. Of course, earlier when they'd come out of the oven, I just had to scrape up the warm soft sauce that dripped from the buns as she turned them out to a plate. Then, as we enjoyed the buns and the strong hot tea, Mom continued.

"You know, Tommy, Mama was teaching in Jacquet River when she met Papa. That was when he was building a new set of stairs for the little schoolhouse. As was quite normal back then, Mama taught several grades in one classroom. Teaching all curriculum subjects except religion, which was the domain of Father Trudel. Mama mastered mathematics and English literature. She also taught Latin. My lifelong appreciation of English literature and Latin was because of her.

"She could also dance, sing, and play the organ better than anyone I knew. She rarely two-stepped in public view, in fear, I think, that her ankles would show. But I remember her round dancing with Papa, and that was at my Grandmother's for my first cousin's wedding. What fascinated me was how Mama taught my older brothers to square and round dance—but only in the living room, out of sight. 'Step one, two, three. Now slow down, turn around, do it over again.'

"My, how I wished that she'd come to dance with me. To have her in full public view so all could see how wonderfully elegant my mama danced."

We sipped our tea quietly then. I'd already polished off as many sticky buns as I could handle and we both settled back in our chairs. But then Mom set her teacup down and looked earnestly at me.

"Tommy, our roots are cut deep into childhood events. Indeed, there's no escaping the impact of family, including influences through the generations. Whether we like it or not, the past defines much of who we are today.

"But what I can change is me. I can change today—my behaviour, my thinking, my goals and my outlook. What else I can do is to accept whatever happened, be it good or bad. It's the past and yesterday is gone forever. Spending precious time worrying and fretting about yesterday—and even tomorrow—takes time away from this precious moment."

A moonlit "Miss Jacquet River"

Two

Boston, High Expectations and the Contest

$\mathcal{M}$om was telling me, "You could get to the moon faster than it took us driving to Boston in 1927." That didn't matter. She would have walked. Leaving northern New Brunswick's backwoods and gravel roads for the high expectations of Boston was a slam-dunk. But it was a horse of a different colour for her mama. Even though Mom was eighteen then, getting permission from her mother to take leave for Boston struck nerves worse than having teeth pulled. Mom's dream was to work as a nanny while studying to become a hairdresser. Other family members encouraged her to persist. For some time, Mama's three sisters, Lena, Alice and Clara had lived in Boston. They dealt the argument that convinced their sister Maggie to cut the apron strings. The *coup de grâce* was the American dollars that Margaret would be able to mail to her mama every month, which were no small potatoes. In 1927, since times were financially squeezed for her parents, her promise to help alleviate their condition made her trip to Boston a dream come true.

Mom hitched a ride to Boston with the Foley family, folks who were originally from Jacquet River, New Brunswick, and were now returning to their home. Since the Foleys were distant relatives of the Firlottes' and long-time family friends, they were only too pleased to provide Margaret's entry into Boston.

"I rode in a huge black car with side running boards!" Mom said to me excitedly. "I sat high up in the back on a plush leather-padded seat. Next to me was a large apple orchard basket full to the top with homemade cold pork sandwiches, pickles in the bottle, vinegared boiled eggs, apple and rhubarb tarts and green apples, all packed by Grandmother and Mama.

"That morning," Mom continued, "I struggled almost the entire day between an excitement bordering on disbelief that I was really on my way, and then fearful worrying over Mama because of her total sadness with me leaving."

"Because of my being so distraught and distracted, I kept having to say sorry to not hearing the conversation coming from the front seat. The Foleys caught on to my emotional state early on and told me they understood my mixed feelings at leaving home for the first time."

At the U.S.-Canada border, after identifying our national residences, the customs agent insisted on interviewing Mom alone in an office. He began the interrogation asking, "Will you be looking to work or study during your stay in Boston?" Mom could not remember what she was to say.

"I froze and panicked," she said, "while he raised his voice, rapidly firing off questions I could not understand. I cried. He got louder. Then I screamed. Hearing me sobbing, the other agent and Mr. Foley accusingly demanded to know what he was doing to this pretty young girl. That was enough to scare the wits out of the agent. Shaken by the turn of events, he quickly stamped my visitor's visa and meekly let us go.

"I can't remember where, but after we stopped for lunch, and had just settled on top of a blanket with our spread of food, some rustling noises coming from a clump of trees beside the river alerted us to look up, and there directly in front of our picnic stood two car-sized, mud-splattered moose. One antlered, the other not. We froze. They stared us down for what seemed a long silent time, and then they gently galloped in slow motion into the forest. It took us a while before we could eat.

"Nothing living in the little town of Jacquet River, New Brunswick, could have prepared me for our excursion and overnight stay motoring through the state of Maine. The drive, passing by farms each seemingly as large as our whole village, and towns placed on ocean points like postcard cutouts, mesmerized me. The ocean shore along the coast nearing Massachusetts, unlike our Bay de Chaleur coast, had mansions, each with their own piers and yachts. "Summer homes for the wealthy" said the Foleys.

"Later that evening, all I could think as I soaked in the palatial-sized tub of my very own oceanside resort room in Orchard Grove, Maine, is 'Good St. Ann, this cannot really be happening!

"Walking into the candlelit floral-scented dining room that overlooked the ocean, I kept thinking to myself, 'Surely I'm dreaming and will wake up any moment.' The hovering black waiters dressed in stiff tuxedos outnumbered the seated diners."

Laughingly, Mom added, "Though I felt somewhat intimidated and uneasy, I even managed to flirt with a dashing, smiling young man sitting with his parents at the adjacent table. And we even brushed up aside each other walking out to the foyer after dinner. All the while, I watched to make sure my hosts noticed nothing of my fancy, or imaginings."

I tried to imagine the jolt in everyday living circumstances that Mom must have experienced moving from a cloistered village in New Brunswick under the wings of a strict religious upbringing to the crowds of a bustling 1920s Boston! "Who ever really knows how life will turn out," sighed Mom.

In those first weeks, she felt certain that Boston would be home forever. In remembering the Boston days, she never spoke a negative word. She fell in love with the Boston twang, the colourful crowds, cotton and silk dresses, men's top hats, the grand homes with verandas like streets, and the soda fountains and bandshells in parks. Initially she stayed with Aunt Lena who had married Jimmy Rogan shortly after he arrived from Ireland in 1903 .

"That Jimmy was a firecracker," Mom recalled. "Smart as a whip. Within three years over from the 'green emerald' he had dozens of other Irishmen working for his roofing business. As for me, for a few weeks before being hired on for my nanny job, I housecleaned what seemed a castle—Aunt Lena and Uncle Jimmy's house on top of the hill stood high and grand above the entire street. It was expected I pay for my keep. Nobody back home, including even our nearby towns, lived in such splendour. Yet, no matter what our living circumstances, none of us are immune to tragedy. Just when you think you've got it all—how sad for them—their oldest son, Paul, working up high on the Cathedral Church roof alongside his dad, slipped on a rope and fell to his death."

In Boston during the 1920s, Canadian girls received the choice nanny jobs. "My aunts knew of the demand. I was told the American girls could not be depended upon," Mom said, "they not being used to work as the likes of us. My employer, Dr. Garland, was a gynecologist. I was lucky to have the Garland family taking me on as nanny. They doted on me like my parents surely never had. Always looking out for my concern. On my days off, they had me driven to my aunt's. How I looked forward to visits with Aunt Clara and Uncle Johnny. Johnny could have worked for English royalty. He had magnificent white horses for pulling carriages—teams of them. Uncle Johnny and his hired drivers chauffeured wealthy ladies with their ladies-in-waiting around the parks to tea and to Boston shops. Never did I imagine riding the likes of it.

"That was also the time of cast-iron gaslight lampposts in the parks. It was Uncle Johnny and his staff who lit them. Still to this day, on hearing the music of the 'Blue Danube Waltz,' I can see Uncle Johnny—suit, topper hat, and with all the trimmings of white shirt and tails. What an all-out devilishly handsome figure! And that Irish brogue and emerald twinkle in his eyes sure made him the ladies' man. He played his charm to the hilt with those wealthy ladies clamouring for his carriage. My head went dizzy the first time I stepped in his gold-trimmed carriage. A footman placed Aunt Clara and me in our seats. I felt like Queen Victoria and proud as a peacock. Aunt Clara was a wealthy woman after Uncle Johnny died."

That was Boston's heyday of horse and carriage. Fancy, stylish and working their business around the clock, it was Johnny's hard work and Aunt Clara's penny- pinching, that they saved their money and lived well.

Mama's Letters Like Rosary Beads

But New Brunswick was never far in the background. Mom's letters from her mama repeated like the rosary beads, "Margaret, I know you're not praying. All I hear of is pleasure and none of suffering. Pleasure awaits us in the next world and we must earn it. I've said often, pride and vanity were the devil's hold over you. The company of young men is when the devil's temptation takes over. Keep yourself busy with the rosary and daily Mass to resist the devil's work."

It was words like that, that frequently set Mom to reflecting about herself and made her think, "I know I'm bad. I ought not be liking where I am too much. She's right that I've been too contrary and will pay for my sins. I did get to early Mass every morning, but I still felt guilty and shameful, especially thinking of the hard times Mama had in supporting our family. I wished that I could be there to help clean, cook and babysit. Dr. and Mrs. Garland could see my upset and repeatedly said these concerns were not my responsibility, and that I would have my own family caretaking soon enough. Then another letter would arrive giving me a sick feeling just holding the envelope, knowing full well what to expect—preaching and damnation. Of course, the guilt only worsened.

"Even Mama's own sisters had little to do with her. They said that for them she was just far too weird and religious. Aside from them being siblings, they weren't much alike elsewise. Though she was invited frequently to visit them in Boston, Mama always stubbornly refused. My Boston aunts were live wires. Entertaining. Poking fun at everything—even about the priest—unheard of back home in fear of some wicked zap. For sure, Catholic through to the core, yet they used their legs for dancing as well as praying. Aunt Alice loved making mischievous trouble, naughtily teasing Mama by writing her that 'The local boys just can't get enough of Margaret, using every excuse to help out our parish priest, just so they can escort Margaret to church!' "

Lipstick, nylons, nail polish, structured brassieres and high heels were out of the question in Mom's house. "In Boston, on days off, I'd be waltzing with dreamy eyes through the lingerie and cosmetics departments, just imagining the feeling of such luxury. A year passed before I even tried anything on. My God, I thought, after my first purchased pair of black silken bra and panties, surely God will strike me dead."

Mom had set out to the States with a purpose, the goal of one day opening a beauty salon. She often expressed gratitude for her employers who'd allowed time off for her to take classes. That encouragement made the difference. After nearly three years in Boston, Mom earned a beautician's certificate. It would prove to be her future ticket to independence.

"Returning to Jacquet River was never on my mind," she said, "Papa was a carpenter and he owned his own barbershop that also sold ice cream and convenience goodies. From that, after I worked cutting and setting hair for him, I had decided that I would own my own business too. That was the year before going to Boston. I had no doubt I could do it, especially as I became increasingly aware that it was my aunts who stoked the fires of their family business success. They were all like-minded women with both strong mind and hand. Nobody crossed them. And no matter the circumstances, they could right any wrong."

Mom had talked so much about those ladies from Boston—Lena, Alice and Clara—that I could hardly wait to meet them. Eventually I did. Crackerjacks they were. Full of pee and vinegar, as the folks from back home say. Darn good thing Mom returned, or I would never have seen them and would've missed knowing our Boston Irish Mafia. Mom says she herself was most like Aunt Alice. However, I felt that Mom's personality had a touch more variety that included Aunt Alice's exacting and confident voice, Aunt Clara's graceful but determined facial features, Aunt Lena's gait and charm, and her own mama's firm spine.

"A team of horses couldn't have dragged me away from Boston—that is, until a pregnant team did just such," Mom said.

Tugging the Guilt Strings

Her mama, Granny Boudreau, now pregnant with the baby who would be Mom's youngest brother, Stanton, cried out for help. Somehow word got passed on to Mom through the lot of Firlotte visitors returning to Boston from their Jacquet River holidays, that her mama was pregnant and feeling distressed and only Margaret would do to help her. Thus the guilt strings were tugged and off she went to the rescue.

Mom recalled, "All I could think was how could I return to what I remembered as such a miserable life with Mama? But duty called me, and I reluctantly answered the alarm. I returned to Jacquet River with Aunt Alice. We packed a full load. Two trunks just for me. The Garlands had generously laden me down with coats, dresses, skirts, suits and even the latest-style women's heels. Mrs. Garland had collected this storeful of used clothing from her sisters. All this to take back for my siblings. I'll never forget their generosity.

"In the wee hours of the morning, Uncle Johnny piled trunks and kinfolk into his two-seater carriage and trotted us down to the train station. My hope for a future in Boston was lost to a sickened stomach thinking of my miserable mama. The train trip was made through a downpour of sobbing tears, feeling like I was journeying to a funeral—my own. Then, by the time we screeched into the central Canadian National Railway Station under the Queen Elizabeth Hotel in downtown Montreal, my spirits suddenly soared in realizing that I'm now travelling and there'll be more of the same to come in my life.

"From Montreal to Jacquet River, we boarded the CN overnighter, sharing a sleeper suite. At 6:00 a.m. we had a breakfast of poached eggs on toast, Canadian bacon, toasted English muffins and tea, all eaten with the CN-crested silverware, embossed china and white linen, while the train tooted and smoke streamed through the Matapidia, Quebec, mountains. It was a glorious entrance to New Brunswick after nearly three years. During each mile travelled I grew increasingly excited."

What surprised Mom were both her feelings and her rapid adjustment once back in Jacquet River. For one thing, assisting her mother with the chores left no time to dwell on missing anything. But she also commented on other feelings that had surprised her. "Living with my siblings and Mama again gave me something I wasn't aware I'd missed—a warm fellowship of sorts. Also, once I decided to come home, I knew my own way of living would prevail. Yet Mama continued to inflict her guilt on me just like I was still a little girl. This hurt she inflicted annoyed me and my talking back enraged her. But too much had changed for me now, and the maturity I had gained in Boston gave me the courage to tell her straight out that even with her continued onslaught about sin and temptation, I knew that I had remained a virgin and would be to my wedding night! Dancing and dating were now a matter for me to decide."

The Miss Jacquet River Crown

Upon Mom's return, there was big excitement in the air about who would earn the Miss Jacquet River Crown. The event was a community fundraiser with the money going towards building a new Parish skating rink.

"No sooner was I back," Mom said, "when the official Miss Jacquet River Crown Committee asked me to place my name among the contestants. Before Boston I would not have had the nerve, or even the clothes, to consider such a possibility. My sister Tookie and first cousins persuaded me of their support, were I to compete."

This was a worthy cause that got the support even of Mom's mother. The two finalists turned out to be Cecelia Callaghan and Mom.

Mom noted that the race was a popularity contest of sorts, in that the winner was the gal who could muster up the most energy to raise the greatest amount of money. Considering that it was the Depression year of 1930, money was as scarce as hens' teeth. Men were so hard up those days, some jumped on top of the stopped rail cars at the Culligan railroad station—heading anywhere—looking for work. For the fundraiser, lots of card parties, craft sales, bake sales and door-to-door knocking produced the loot.

"It was the backwoods boys who made the difference," Mom said. "There was still money being earned in the logging camps that supplied our local sawmills. Three sawmills were owned and operated by the Culligans. Your grandfather, John Culligan, was the father of my sometimes boyfriend at that time, Charly Culligan.

"I hit gold with an invitation to the logging camp. John and Hilda Audit, owners of the Head of Benjamin River Logging Camp, invited me back to raise funds for the contest. John and Hilda were highly regarded folks. Hilda cooked for dozens of men. You would have died at the sight of the men and team of horses sent to escort me back to camp. Tookie accompanied me. Took quite a few hours of hard hauling, and it being a cold winter, bear-fur hides covered us to keep warm. A howling snowstorm struck up with an hour still to reach camp. Leave it to Hilda, for the sleigh ride she had packed hot tea and cake for us. The Hickey boys, strapping-sized men, reined the horses at a hard clip. Beside us, the sleigh hauled a load of flour and feed for the animals just loaded on from MacMillan Wholesalers where we stopped along the way."

The cut trail through the dense spruce and pine forest had ruts from the morning run, but not in the open fields, which got cut in earlier logging camps. In those areas, the horses heaved and huffed up to their bellies through fresh snowdrifts. The boys stood high in the sleigh, cracking the reins, hollering, "Yee-ha, yee-ha, geddy up your arses!"

The Moon Cast Its Spell

"That night at camp will last forever with me as a Cinderella moment. A magic spell hung over the camp. The everyday stuff of living stopped for a moment. Not only for me, but for the others as well. Hilda walked Tookie and me from the cookhouse out to a frozen pond where the kitchen help fetched pails of water through an axed hole in the ice.

"Maybe it was there and then that the pull of the moon would be with me for the rest of my days. Something I'll carry to my grave. My God, that moon enveloped me into its white-silver and yellow arms, and seemed to pull me inside as it hovered overtop a cathedral of silhouetted dark evergreens, like giants in white overcoats.

"Pure was all I could think. In that moment, I felt myself painted in a landscape, unable to take it all in. The only movement was clouds of falling snow from branches letting go its weight. What brought me back from this reverie was the curling blue-white smoke of the cookhouse. Strange as this sounds, I carry that night's wonder to this day. Tom, when you were young, you'd say to me how you 'loved smelling frozen winter air because it tasted like strong-flavoured sticky pine cones.' Well, standing still outside the cookhouse on that full moonlit night, I'll not forget the stinging cold and the overpowering perfume of pines frozen in the air.

"Hilda had to coax me out of my moonstruck trance. She tugged at my arm, leading Tookie and me back into the cookhouse. We helped Hilda peel extra vegetables for her stewing bouillon.

"Can't say I ever tasted chicken bouillon like Hilda's. God knows, I downed countless bowls, including my own. Hilda's cast-iron pot outsized my bread-making pan (twenty-four inches diameter). The top six inches of her chicken bouillon was afloat with doughboys: round dumplings made with flour, dry mustard, soda, baking powder, summer savory, salt, pepper, water and sour milk. Because of her three layers of doughboys, nobody had to fight for their share. She didn't spare on the chicken either, which she added to the simmering turnips, potatoes, carrots, onions and parsnips.

"Hilda enjoyed having us girls as company. She giggled and joined in with Tookie and my comments as the men arrived for supper. We had something to say about each one. After they ate their bellies full, John Audit requested the men clear the floor. All the tables and chairs were crowded to the walls, leaving the round pot-bellied stove alone in the middle. Six stools were placed around what was by now a glowing red-hot stove."

Mom could not believe what she next saw walking towards the stools: two men with fiddles, two with guitars and two with spoons. The applause started. Stomping followed. What a surprise! For Mom and Tookie had been kept in the dark about the evening's fun. They were beckoned to step dance. John and

Hilda were well familiar with the girl's amateur-hour step-dancing status.

"We were taken by the moment," Mom remembered. "We could not help ourselves while our feet just followed the fiddling tunes. Before long, one by one, the men tap-danced round the stove, shaking the lighted gas lanterns up and down in their cast-iron rings.

"We square-danced to the ol' time Canadian maple leaf fiddling tune, taking partner turns, swinging around till we'd stop from dizziness. But nobody left till the fiddlers hung their bows at midnight. It was time to eat again. A cauldron of tea was brewed. Then out came Hilda's colourful tins full of oatmeal fudge cookies and molasses cookies. John jumped atop a table and stomped for attention. He grabbed the brown Irish hat off his head, and announced to all assembled that he was passing it round for their most generous support of the Boudreau girl in becoming Miss Jacquet River! I tell you, no small amount it was, for it put me over the top."

My dad's first cousin, Mary McCarron, wrote about Mom of that year: "Never forgot when Margaret and her sister Tookie came calling to our place in fall of 1929, just after my mother, your Grand-Aunt Cary died. They walked the several miles to come give us condolences. Margaret was competing for the Miss Jacquet River contest with Cecelia Callaghan. Aunt Lizzy Ultican came by that day to help us clean after the long haul of our mom's funeral and the wake in our house. Instead of cleaning, we got Aunt Lizzy to make us a Washington pie. I baked potato scallops. Margaret regaled us with Boston stories filled with romance and intrigue. They all stayed for supper. There was no cleaning that day. But we had a lot of laughter and fun to help us forget the sadness in losing our mother.

"You know, of course, that Margaret won that contest with flying colours. She was Miss Jacquet River. When I was a young girl, I always admired her looks. She had smiling eyes and teeth as white as pearls. And beautiful. Margaret had personality and charm."

The Rambling Homestead

*(L to R) Dad, Mom (8 months pregnant with first baby Billy), Grandparents
Momo and John Culligan, Great Grandparents Pelagie and John Culligan*

Three

All I Ever Wanted

Charly Culligan had pursued Mom even before she left for Boston. As she told it, that being the late 1920s, the future for a woman meant finding a husband. Getting married was never questioned. So, looking at what was possible and available at that time, the notion of entering into the Culligan family had plenty of advantages. The Culligans were rich. They were considered the wealthiest family in that entire area. The Culligans all lived in huge homes on the ocean, and they drove the latest models of cars. At church, the Culligan women stood out in their fine furs purchased from the best furriers in Montreal.

Yet there was one heck of a downside. Mom knew Charly to be spoiled rotten and with a drinking problem, and his only brother, Jackie, was a double-fisted drinker and gambler, and spoiled just like Charly. So her decision to leave Jacquet River for Boston was as much to get away from Charly as to flee her mother's dominance and discipline. Charly had actually asked Mom to consider getting engaged before departing for Boston, but she told him no because he drank too much.

When Mom returned to Jacquet River after nearly three years, Charly loomed larger than life in his pursuit of her. Right off, on her return, he took a two-year pledge not to drink alcohol—a commitment sworn on the Bible with Father Trudel. Charly was intent on having his way. He told Mom he'd do anything to win her as his wife; a promise carried a lot of weight in her way of thinking. After a couple of months of Charly's staying cold sober, Mom took greater notice of his athletic prowess. He played hockey and baseball better than anyone and he proved to be a skilled athlete. And as she said to me, "There's nothing greater appealing than a man's masculinity taking centre stage in sports. Charly pitched a ball and stickhandled his way to the roars of our local crowds. Every team wanted Charly. In his short stint at university, he became their hero athlete."

Unfortunately, Charly's university days never amounted to much because, as his classmate, Father Miller, said, "Charly'd no sooner be driven down to university, he'd return home by train even before his parents returned home. Charly didn't much like taking exams and especially paid no attention to lecturers."

On December 16, 1930, Margaret Ann Boudreau and Charles Culligan tied the knot with a small wedding party of only family. Catherine Hayes and Jackie Culligan stood up for them. Mom recalled that it was so cold that morning, they took their vows in the church sacristy rather than in the main church—all of them standing with winter coats and boots still on. The ceremony was followed by a breakfast at the Culligans' home. Charly promised a honeymoon in the spring. Like all Charly's promises, "It never saw the light of day."

Even with the worsening economic times, the Culligans were not affected. They had plenty in all essential categories. Just before Mom and Dad's wedding, the Culligans sold their huge forest and the pulp and lumber holdings to International Paper. They had to wait more than a year to receive the money because concluding negotiations involved lengthy inventory and accounting verification. Yet even with all the wealth of the Culligans, Charly couldn't afford to buy Mom's wedding ring. She paid for the ring out of her Boston savings.

They started their life together living with his parents, John and Aggripina Culligan, who everyone called John and Pina. In our family, we called our grandmother "Momo" Culligan.

Charly's university career was cut short a year earlier when he announced he'd rather work for his family at the sawmills. Of course, Charly made few appearances at the workstations. Besides, he told Mom that the business was being sold and he would take over the main farm once his parents resettled. She actually believed that once married, Charly would settle into a farming life. The family farm was massive and successful, so there seemed to be a mighty tantalizing future awaiting them.

A 1930 picture of the Culligan property shows a white picket fence surrounding the entire property of home, barns, orchards and other outbuildings. That picture made anything look possible. Looking at that photograph now, it's hard to believe the "Happy Forever" would not happen. Merrymaking was not to be. Instead, misery and hard times were to bring black clouds to that wonderful picture.

Living with the Culligans

"What was it like," I asked Mom, "those first months living with the Culligans?"

"First of all," she said, "remember, in 1931, I was only twenty-one and living in someone else's home. Sure, Charly grew up there. It was his family's home. But I felt obligated to earn my keep. So mostly I cooked. I wasn't particularly pleased with Momo's hired cooks. Not fussy enough with cleanliness. So I worked hard at baking bread, pies, cakes, sticky buns and biscuits and making soups. Charly's mom loved my cooking. I knew it pleased her. Though there was no shortage of staff at the Culligans,' I worked hard because I knew no other way.

"Behind the home, attached to the ice shed, was a two-storey building to house the farm workers and house staff. The outbuildings went all the way across the front of the property and pretty near reached down to the beach, with the huge piggery, for obvious reasons, being the farthest out, and the large double-tracking floor barns nearby to store hay, oats and barley for cattle and horses. Old Walter Roy milked the cows and did the morning milk and cream separation. You had to keep a close watch on those opened milk cans. More than once Walter had pulled out a drowned cat. The huge silver milk cans were held in the icehouse until delivered to Bathurst for sale and bottling, and even your grandmother took turns at churning the butter. I took a hand in doing just about everything.

"It was February when Dr. Ellis confirmed I was pregnant. All I could think was that my mother had nine children, her mother had thirteen and I would have a lot too. Getting pregnant was everything I wanted and hoped for.

"When I worked as a nanny for the Garlands in Boston, I couldn't understand how any woman would not want to look after her own babies. Those tiny little hands and feet! I couldn't handle them enough. I took such care in bathing each baby. Washing their little faces. Never put soap on their face but lots on the rest of the tiny body. My first nurse, Miss Hodgins, for Billy, my first baby, told me, 'Don't be afraid to handle the penis. Pull back the foreskin and be sure you clean the lint from diapers. It sticks and irritates.' Oh yes, each baby I had, I wanted to look after just by myself.

"I couldn't understand your grandmother—Charly's mom. She'd say, 'I never wanted to touch a new baby. In fact, I always had an older woman do that.' "

Listening to Mom talking with so much love about babies, I found it to be a sobering thought that Momo felt differently about babies. After all, this was how my father must have been handled—totally without mother love. Momo would often say to Mom, "Why are you so fussy? Have a nanny do that." Momo had nannies look after my dad and all her other children. Curious about this, I asked if Mom had ever discussed this with Momo.

"No," she said. "That was not in Momo's nature to discuss anything personal. In fact, once when Momo actually changed little Billy's diaper, the pin was on the inside. From that experience for sure I knew that Momo really couldn't even change a baby's diaper!

"After that I was careful not to let the babies alone with your grandmother. We made certain a nurse was on hand when I left the house. With me, babies were my love. I wanted to sleep with them at night. I nursed all my babies, except you and Mary Sue.

"But your dad couldn't stand a pregnant woman. At night, I'd tell him the baby was kicking and pushing, and where to put his hand to feel. He'd want no part of it. Even got angry with me. He'd push me outta his way, calling me disgusting. I would say, 'Charly, I'm your wife, not just any pregnant woman. It's not necessary to rub up against all pregnant women, just me with our child.' "

Never in a Lifetime

Dad broke his pledge of sobriety shortly after Mom's first pregnancy. That ended the year plus of the dry-and-sober period—the period he had maintained to convince Mom to marry him. "Your father drank heavy during that pregnancy." Mom had heard Dr. Garland in Boston talk about how necessary it was to abstain from alcohol during the pregnancy. And while pregnant with Billy and thinking of what Charly's blood alcohol level must be, Mom worried about the effect of alcohol in future pregnancies.

"Wham bam, thank you ma'am! That was Charly! No tender intimacy. He'd want his way when drinking. I even told him it wasn't necessary to call me dear, no extras, just put his arms around me. That's all I ever wanted."

However, that just was not to be. Dad had sex only when he was drinking; rather, only when he was drunk. But Mom consoled herself with the thought, "Charly will get sober again and he'll love having a family, and that will make him happy." She hoped he would change again, as he had seemed to for the year and a bit upon her return from Boston. He had sobered up for them to be married; surely he'd do this now for his own children.

"No," Mom said slowly, "never in a lifetime did I ever believe that Charly would continue to drink heavily and to stay away from home weeks on end.

"I was still in love with Charly. I was getting bigger, this being my first pregnancy. Everything was new for me and I so wanted to share how I felt. It being April, we still had large snowbanks, so Audrey, Charly's sister, and I would slide down the piggery roof and Momo would get so upset, thinking I'd have a miscarriage. It took me a long time to clue in to Momo's fears. Though I, in God's good fortune, never had a miscarriage in nine pregnancies. Momo had suffered five miscarriages, and three infant deaths, so I guess that was why she was always telling me what to do. But I knew that living with the Culligans would not be for a lifetime—I knew that for sure. I wanted our own home. Somehow, even at that early period of our marriage, I worked hard knowing I would get our home on my own should Charly stay drunk."

Billy, Mom's First Baby

Mom remembers her first pregnancy as a happy one.

"Charly's renewed drinking didn't rob me of the joy I longed for in having children. On Saturday, October 3, 1931, Momo and the crowd were driving up to Aunt Annie's to play cards. The Ulticans and Culligans were feverish about playing poker. All day long I had pains but said nothing. Rather than sitting home alone, I asked to go along. Now, I didn't play cards yet. That was to come in later days. On our way to Aunt Annie's house, they dropped me off at Audrey's. She and Adrien had taken over one of the Culligan homes that summer, just the other side of the tracks from Annie's. No sooner had I arrived than Audrey looked at me and said surely I was ready to drop the baby.

"We both walked over to the Ulticans'. I remembered being in pain, but I so enjoyed being out walking. Aunt Lizzy, Momo's other old-maid sister, was making the lunch break while all the others remained at the card table. Audrey told Charly, 'Get off your arse and take Margaret home, because the baby's only hours away!'

"Oh my, that all caused quite a stir. Aunt Josephine, your grandfather's sister, got real worried, saying, 'You can't go anywhere, get Dr. Ellis here!' Momo jumped up, picked up the cards, threw them over the sink counter, pulled on her lamb's-fur coat and said, 'We're off!'

"I got home fast. Seemed like Dr. Ellis came in minutes. Five hours later— two the Sunday morning, worsening pain, but all I could think of was for them to call Father Trudel and tell him I won't make it to play the organ for Sunday Mass. I kept grabbing at everybody yelling how it hurt."

Since this was 1931, I wondered what it was like at that time—having her first baby at home.

"Momo arranged the scalding of sutures, scissors, bandages and containers. By midnight, she sent a driver to fetch the midwife, Mrs. Dempsey, who had a wondrous calming effect on everyone. Dr. Ellis preferred her to a regular nurse for the delivery. Billy took a long time coming. At noon Sunday, I recall grabbing Dr. Ellis by the necktie, almost choking him, asking for a needle to lessen the pain.

"Dr. Ellis looked me close in the eye, and I'll never forget his telling me, 'Margaret, my dear, you're a brave and courageous woman. You don't need anything for pain. Besides, I need you to remain fully conscious to push the baby out.' "

"Were you able to accept Dr. Ellis's explanation easily?" I asked.

"No, and yes. I was just beside myself. But Dr. Ellis and Mrs. Dempsey comforted me by their physical presence. I knew that I'd be okay with them."

Mom delivered her first baby, Billy, weighing in at fourteen pounds, at 5:30 p.m., Sunday, October 4, 1931. And when I asked her if she was able to fall asleep afterwards, she replied, "You must be clear out of your wits! No, I suffered enormously. Torn so badly from the size of him and the pushing. Torn right to the rectum. Blood, blood and more blood everywhere. They had to stitch me—which didn't last—so stitch again. The pain grew so immense I couldn't even swallow water. Momo placed ice pieces on my lips and forehead."

Deeply touched, I have listened to this tape of Mom's ordeal several times, trying to better understand where my father was during the critical times in their lives. His behaviour during his first child's delivery was better than most in that he was at least present for the birth. He was in the house, but not actually with Mom. And during the next eight deliveries, he would choose not to be anywhere near. But later that very night, after the birth of his first child, Charly abruptly left with the guys for a week's hunting trip.

"Next morning," Mom said, "I looked out my bedroom window wondering where Charly was and thinking he should be here with me and our new baby. I was lonely and all alone, and knowing he had been drinking, it would probably get worse—and that scared me. Then I thought, 'But he loves me. After all, this is our baby—he'll come back and stay sober.' I prayed a lot that week. It took ten days before I could get out of bed."

Early Years in the Hapless Marriage

After two years of marriage, Margaret and Charly were still living at the Culligan homestead, sharing quarters with Charly's mother, a new baby and another on the way. Early on in their marriage, she realized that Charly was not ambitious. Nor smart. He slept in every morning. When she pulled him out of bed, he often had a hangover. During that early time in their hapless marriage, I asked her what he did for work at that time.

"Well, he promised Momo he'd work the Culligan farm. Specifically, Momo asked that he be in charge of the winter storage of vegetables, ice and meat. In those days, Charly had everything at his disposal to make a prosperous and grand living. Momo handed him everything. The man had not a silver platter but a golden one with chance after chance to prove himself. But he failed miserably to prosper in anything."

It was when Mom was pregnant with her third child, Eugene, that the building for the new Quinn home and farm buildings began. This was a property, several hundred acres of farmland, purchased by my grandparents a few years earlier as an investment. Momo had decided to give Margaret and Charly their own place on that farmland. She even organized and paid for everything. One morning Momo handed Mom a book of house designs, saying, "Here, you look them over and decide which type of house design you want. I'm going to give you and Charly a special wedding gift of your own home and farm."

Momo not only had the home and farm buildings built, she also supplied a complete farm inventory of milking cows, teams of horses, pigs, chickens and geese, a car and truck, ploughing and cultivating equipment, and even seeds for planting. Just before they moved in, Momo visited the former Quinn farm with Dad and Mom. Standing in front of the large barn doors, Momo said, "Now, Charly, you get cracking and do what a man's supposed to do!"

Like Momo, even Audrey, thought that now Charly would wise up with having a home, farm and a family of his own. As they say down home in New Brunswick, "Jesus almighty, you don't get better than that!"

Imagine—a house and food, to boot. Along with the farm handed over to Charly was near three hundred acres, which included cultivated fields and generous woodlots. Indeed, Mom and Dad had plenty at that time, though there was a hitch. Like everything else back in those days, the whole kit and caboodle was in Charly's name. Under normal circumstances that wouldn't be a problem. However, as became evident over the next few years, Charly never did behave in a normal fashion, and scarcely deserved to be the owner of such property.

Life Overwhelmed Me

The little family, Charly and a pregnant Margaret, with the babies Billy and Ann (born April 9, 1933) moved into the Quinn farm in December 1933. Eugene, who we called Gene, was born in February. Ten months later, Paul was born.

"Glory be to God!" said Mom. " There was nothing left in me for Paul. I was worn out, handling four small children, an increasingly violent and drunken Charly, and the cows, pigs, chickens, haying, and with home and barns that needed maintenance. Even the geese were looking ragged."

One night, after preparing the children for bed, Mom's cousin Deany came by and she saw right off Margaret's exhausted condition. Deany insisted on walking miles down the road to where they knew Charly hung out drinking and playing poker. Her mission was to play on Charly's love for his children to get him to come home to help with the farming chores.

Deany returned without Charly. He had refused to be moved by the plight of his family's condition, loudly proclaiming to all in sight, "I wasn't born to be a farmer!"

The time that followed the birth of the fourth child was devastating for Mom. "Life overwhelmed me. I just felt abandoned and exhausted and like my nerves had collapsed." That's when Dr. George Dumont hospitalized her for ten days. Dad's sister, Patricia, whom we called Aunt Pat, was a nurse, and she arrived from her Long Island home to care for the children while Mom recovered. Dr. George insisted that Mom leave the children for an additional two weeks to rest up, and he also suggested that she take a trip to Quebec to visit her sister Tookie for some loving and healing. Mom considered Dr. George divinely gifted. In fact, he rescued Mom from collapsing into complete nervous breakdown on three occasions.

The weeks leading to her hospitalization were what Mom called her "descent into hell." The next ten years delivered plenty of hardships and challenges, yet none ever came near to the darkest nights that she described as the circumstances after her fourth child. Mom was never quite sure what did her in. No question that after four babies she was drained. "However," she told me, "I believe the constant battle to survive Charly's violence is what near killed me. It took every ounce of strength and faith to keep going day in, day out. For a while fear set in, leaving me mentally and physically paralyzed. At times I would think, should Charly kill me, the children would be left to die.

"This was the only time," Mom said, "when I thought, this is it, I'm losing my mind. Night after night I had no restful sleep, only maybe only three or four hours. Still I'd wake up on the dot to nurse my baby. Thank God for that. During those three months, for some reason, God was good to me. I loved the morning because that's when the blackness lifted. Until noon, that is, when the heavy feeling would set in again. It was like a motor in my head. The wracking of nerves would start up building louder, over and over, *tada, tada, tada*, to a ricocheting pitch. It kept playing and wouldn't stop. I prayed. Tried wearing a kerchief tied over my head and ears, hoping to wall out the noises.

"It was the last night that frightened me into getting my first cousin down to watch the children so I could hitchhike to Campbellton for help from Dr. George Dumont.

"The sound in my head had got so loud that I just ran out of the house, through the fields in pitch dark to the ocean and stopped at the cliff edge. The tide was running high that hour. Huge waves knocked against the cliffs jutting out below me. The swelling waves mesmerized me. The strangest sensation of being swept towards the water overwhelmed me. At that moment, I could have walked straight into the ocean and never stopped. But I couldn't move my legs. I was desperately pulling at my hair, heard myself screaming. Suddenly, something rose out of the ground all around me, flying every which way, screeching, screeching, until I was totally surrounded by hundreds of huge birds. I don't know to this day, geese, ducks, whatever.

"Those birds flew higher and higher in the sky even as I lifted my head to stare. In absolute amazement, I watched without moving as the birds slowly disappeared. I realized that my eyes had fixed on the North Star. I think even my heart stopped then. A calm rested over the ocean momentarily. My head turned to the East, where I saw the blinking lighthouse of the Culligan wharf. In a flash, each of my children's faces lit up in front of me. I felt myself slump softly to the damp grass, closed my eyes, and it was dawn when I woke up."

That day, Mom reached out for help, which resulted in her hospitalization and later, a family rest in Quebec. "Mostly, I got to eat and sleep in the hospital. Dr. George visited daily and encouraged me to talk. He insisted I take mild sleeping sedatives the first few nights." When Dr. George told her to make her way to Quebec for further resting, she said, "No, I can't afford such." But he answered calmly, "You better find a way."

As luck would have it, the Canadian National Railway introduced a one-time-only reduced fare of $10.00 return to Montreal, but Mom still had to get to where Tookie lived, in Sorel, Quebec. She couldn't remember anything about that fifty-mile trip from Montreal to Sorel. However, she sure remembers having no decent clothes to travel in, for after the train fare there was nothing left to spend on herself. 'Hard to believe," I said to her "how could you not have an overcoat? My God, with your bitter-cold winter!"

"Dear," she said, "believe me, I had used my overcoat to make coats for the little ones. So when I went out, I wore layers of anything to keep me warm. Even to church to play organ, I dressed in heavy winter underwear, old sweaters and a jacket. When walking the four miles to church, I'd wear three pairs of well darned-up socks inside an ol' pair of rubber boots."

But before boarding that Montreal-bound train, Mom had taken a little of several folks' clothing along. She borrowed a tan brown wool overcoat from Mrs. McClusky of Doylville, a dark brown, feathered hat from Aunt Honor, brown leather gloves from Aunt Alice and even a black purse from Frances Culligan. "Since I had no clothes," Mom laughed, "I managed to piece together an outfit feeling a bit of a bagwoman.

"The night before I left Sorel, a strange thing happened. After supper, I pushed away from the table and suddenly there in the middle of the kitchen I burst out crying. Torn apart every which way I was, still not feeling full well. The thoughts were racing around and around in my head. Could I stay right there? Not ever leave? But oh, my little children! And then I got to wondering who would let me park in their space with four little tykes?

"Up to that last evening, I had never spoken of anything that was bothering me. Finally, the walls crumbled. I cried and spilled tears through talking of all my worst fears. Tookie listened and talked. She joked a lot. I laughed, sobbed and laughed. In the midst of my confused emotions, I realized that I had neither cried nor laughed in many months.

"Finally, I'd stop crying for a while and Tookie said, 'We're going out tonight to have a good time!' I had no excuses then, for Tookie had bought me a real trousseau, three new dresses, foundation garments and real stylish heels with nylons. Dear Tookie had dressed me from the inside out!"

The dam broke for Mom. But all hell didn't break loose. Just maybe, the gods were not punishing her after all. Because, even to the end, she somehow believed that it was her fault that Charly drank. In her motherly way, she had always understood that living was for suffering. That had always been her mama's message. That was to be her lot too. Accept what was being dished out, that was the Catholic Sunday message repeated again and again that had embedded itself as her own echo.

I asked Mom if she had considered separating from Dad at that critical time of feeling so alone and abandoned.

"No way! Dear God, I knew I was trapped. But I also knew that I was married for life. That's the way it was. Not a notion entered my mind that I could be rid of this drunken man. My head would only deal with how I could provide for my dear little children. Because of these small babies, I figured my earning money would have to depend on some babysitting arrangement. I never considered the possibility of my not finding some way to look after and provide for my dear little ones.

"The worst time I ever had was just before Dr. George hospitalized me, and that was having to be near Charly when he landed home drunk and demanding. For a time I was terrified of his violence. He'd slap, hit and drag me across the floor in fits of rage.

"Then after a time, with him being so drunk, he'd just fall asleep anywhere, spread out over the living-room carpet or leaning overtop the kitchen table. In those pitiful conditions, I thought, 'If only I had a cabin in the woods where I could run to and just be alone and safe. God help me disappear.' "

After Paul's birth, there was a four-year gap until Gail came along. I asked Mom how she'd managed four years without getting pregnant. She hesitantly told me that Dr. George had inserted something in her body and asked to see her every six weeks.

"He only told me that my uterus was prolapsed and he'd inserted something to support it. Had Dr. George told me I was practising birth control, I'd certainly be punished, that I knew. Honest to God, later when I talked with him about my feelings and my fears, he told me that early on he had studied to be a priest, but left days before ordination because he wanted a woman. And then he said something I never forgot.

"Dr. George said, 'I well understand the kind of mother you were brought up with. Let me tell you something, God's not punishing you or me. Instead, he's helping and guiding us to do the right thing for you and for your family.' "

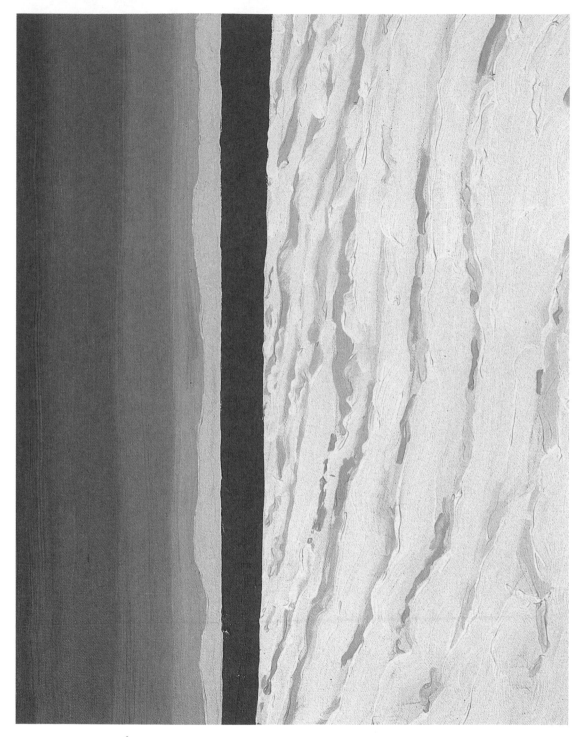

A kitchen view of blue winter and
blue waters

Four

Some Good Times

Time passed at the Quinn farm, and by Christmas 1935, Mom had recovered from being near knocked into the ground. Then, mainly because of Dr. George, there were no additional babies for four years. Mom laughingly admitted, "Paul at least had time to get out of his diapers, walk and talk before Gail came along in April 1939." But nothing changed for Dad except more and more alcoholic raging and absenteeism.

In the next six-year stretch, Mom produced three new babies: Gordon in 1940, Henry in 1942 and me, Tommy, in 1945. And that also turned out to be our last year of living on the Quinn farm.

The Quinn farm was a lonely, isolated property located far from any neighbours. At night there were no lights to be seen twinkling from any near-by windows. Mom recalled it as nights of total darkness that really got her down quite often. The farm was also too far for folks to make spur-of-the moment visits. And when the unrelenting winter storms swept in and dumped snow up to the rafters, any neighbour activity simply halted for several months, except for the necessities of living.

The Little Radio

"Like everything," Mom said, "you gotta find the silver lining. Mine was the little radio your Uncle Adrien built. He was an engineer and could build machinery as well as any woman could cook. I kept his little radio in the den, just off the kitchen. The radio was really only this piece of machinery sitting on a cedar board. It had no case. We'd get overseas stations and sometimes even long- and short-wave stations."

This was northern New Brunswick in the 1930s. The roads were gravel. Horses and wagons well outnumbered cars. Farms were not blocks apart— they were miles apart separated by fields and forests. The bridges across the Jacquet River, Benjamin River and Belledune River were rickety wooden con- traptions that shook and went bumpitty-bump when anything crossed over them—you wondered how they'd held up. We sure knew better not to forget making the sign of the cross when we got on them. Wire poles brought electricity to the lucky richer few. There were no pubs, restaurants, bars and the like. Really, the closest watering holes were those dug out of the ground where cows and horses waited their turn to drink. One thing though, there was no short- age of land for anybody looking for a patch to grow potatoes and vegetables.

Mom had the only radio in her area, so when the weather permitted, her women friends came to tune in.

"The radio made living worthwhile," Mom said. "Uncle Adrien and Audrey made this possible for me soon after my return from Quebec. I remembered the winter before—not having a radio—not hearing a new voice for weeks at a time. A craving would set in for company, faces, sounds or anything that let me know somebody else was around.

"With the radio, each day I had something to look forward to. I'd get the kids to bed. Pull the blinds in all the lower windows so it'd be nice and cozy. There was a high window over the radio in the den, but I never bothered with that window. Should anyone try to climb up they'd make way too much noise."

I found Mom's last comment interesting. Back in those days, I asked, would any person actually be out on the prowl in such isolated country? Believe it or not, the fears among local people were of travelling Gypsies, but Mom never saw one. Yet rumours circulated of Gypsies having stolen young children out of potato fields under the noses of locals. Finding this quite unbelievable, I wondered if these claims were true or not.

"Well," she answered, "in our day, the ol' folks around here could muster up any tale they thought would get their point across, and one thing those ol' farmers didn't want was their children leaving before they got every bit of work out of them!"

With kids tucked in bed, Mom boiled water to steep a pot of tea just for herself. "Occasionally," she remembered, "I'd prepare a hot bath. Soak in suds with a drop of an extract, maybe lemon. And in June I'd even crush lilacs from our trees or yellow and white daisies. When I sat in the den for radio listening, I readied myself as in a concert hall. Even the chair made a difference. I found the high wingback chair interfered with the listening, so I always sat in the antique oak rocking chair. I fashioned a seat cushion from flour bags and filled it with cotton-batting. At night, I kept a slow-burning wood fire in the kitchen stove. To change the air, I placed clove spices on the stovetop. But my favourite scent was—when I managed to get oranges—orange peelings, slow burning. I'd never set eyes on any Caribbean or far-off exotic lands, but the fired orange spice scents did the trick for me. To this day, I fancy the radio over TV."

"How could that be, I asked her, "when TV offers so much variety?"

"Yes, it does have variety, but the violence and just downright crazy opinions from any host of television galloots just leaves me high and dry. Not near the satisfaction and comfort I got from listening and fantasizing to stories and music on radio nights. One night I cried my eyes out while listening to a mother talk of her children. Hers was a bad situation of looking after a bunch of little ones, just like myself. She even read her own poetry. It all rhymed in her doing the children's washing, taking all the things out of their pockets—a piece of twine, a fish hook, and there was something she wouldn't name and wondered what he was saving it for. I loved to listen to those shows."

Even at that time, with eight children, she never lost hope that somehow Charly'd come to his senses. Well, everybody tried talking sense to him. Father Cerois would tell him, "Be at the rectory of an appointed time," and would have him swear on a Bible with yet another new pledge to give up alcohol.

"It was pitifully useless. Charly'd forget his promise and be drunk before he even returned home. Yet despite all the dirty drinking bouts and nasty hits, I still always hoped he would at least sometimes say lovely things to me. Maybe rub

my shoulders or just put his arms around me with not even having to say anything romantic to me. But your father hated all that. Despised my gesture of love
and romance.

"Charly would say to me, 'You and your foolishness. It's that goddamned
radio putting those crazy notions in your head. Who needs that? If you spent
more time doing a woman's work around here, you'd not have time to listen to
such foolishness.' "

Spurts of Happy Times

Women Friends

In the huge expanse of the New Brunswick sky, the deep gold of the harvest
moon had power. Its size and brilliance in the dark night sky couldn't help but
move people. "Even the most cynical," Mom would say.

"One night, even the wooden rail fences all the way down past Shannon's
Turn could be seen as clear as on a bright sunny day. The leftover oat stubs
through our fields down to the beach looked like painted stripes of shimmering gold. The barn's bright-white glow from the moon resembled a fresh
snowfall, and the ocean looked for all the world like a carpet that fell from the
sky. And under that moon's glow, the air itself seemed chain-linked by sparkling
currents of warm air rising off the freshly cut fields.

"Drawn by the evening spell, I'd sit out on the open porch, half expecting
and half hoping for company. A perfect night, with a radiant full moon."

Folks around home looked to the moon to tell them what to do in so many
areas of their life, especially for fortune-telling and teacup readings. I knew
that Mom had long ago always associated nature and emotions with the moon.
This included its effects on the tides, the weather, and above all, its powerful tug
on people's actions and feelings. It was always on such occasions that neighbours
and friends from all around would come to her and ask to have their tea leaves
read. Of course, this would always be along with a visit and a bite to eat. But
many people actually arrived at important life decisions through listening with
their hearts and their minds during those private quiet reflective interpreta-
tions with Mom.

But on this particular evening, Mom was remembering with a slow smile
lighting up her face, "I was just sitting there on the porch, when way off in
the light-pierced darkness, I heard the voices of Aunt Alice Culligan and Frances

Culligan. You had to know that we were the sisters of the moon. Somehow we always had felt the pull of the moon on such nights and the wanting to be together."

She laughed out loud then, recalling that half pint of gin that Frances carried in with her. "That was it for all three to drink?" I asked.

"Believe you me, it didn't take much for us girls to have a time. Aunt Alice opened the four living-room windows for the radio to come through. I remember the music that night like yesterday. Aunt Alice began waltzing to her own voice, raising her gin glass and toasting like it was champagne! We three pranced down the stairs and out on the lawn, holding each other's arms over our shoulders, circling in slow-dance fashion, singing 'Moonlight Bay' along to the music on the radio wafting out the windows just for us.

"We had a lot in common. All married to men with drinking problems— all lonely in our own ways. Our men drank and left us alone. On nights of the full moon in summer and fall, Alice, Frances and I chatted until the sun came up. Alice's quick wit entertained us. She could get under Charly's and Theo's skin with her sharp tongue. Nights like that saved my sanity and perked me up for days. And Frances would always be saying that her hubby Theo's a hell of a lot better than my useless Charly, 'cause Theo at least works some of the time!"

And There Was Music

Truth was, despite the few bright times that Mom clung to, our family situation was worsening. Because of Dad with all the drinking and not working, we were financially ruined.

No wonder Mom was so very worried and felt so terribly lonely at Quinn's farm, and sometimes took her frustrations out on us kids. My older sister Ann remembered sadly how Mom sometimes took a birch branch switch against their bare bottoms during those "bad" early days—her way to regain control after the kids' shenanigans. In my lifetime, I cannot recall so much as a slap. But then there were happy times for her, especially when she entertained musician friends, like the Cannon Orchestra. I couldn't say what Mom loved most—the moon or music.

The Cannon family, like Mom's family, all seemed to be natural-born musicians. Tookie dated Ted Cannon before he decided on studying for the priesthood, but Ted left ten days before being ordained. Our families always remained close, and in time, Ted, the saxophonist, conducted his own orchestra filled with brass and strings. And that's where Emile Breau—later to become Mom's special friend—played the bass violin. Tookie would sing, Mom would play the piano. Brass, strings, ivories and voice all made their way into the fabric of our hearts and souls as young kids. These were the sounds that even to this day make me feel the sights and sounds of those nights as if I was right there again.

Our home gradually evolved into the orchestra's "resting place." Mostly it was the Walter Murray Orchestra from Bathurst, with Pete, the trumpet player from the Dalhousie Cannon Orchestra, joining them. In the heyday summer of the 1950s, the orchestra swelled with Mom's visiting relatives. Her sister Camilla joined in with her electric organ, along with her husband, Uncle Art Foster, and his flute and trumpet playing. For these occasions, the kitchen wasn't near big enough and the musicians spread out in the two living rooms, and even out to the wraparound veranda. There, folks drank quarts of Moosehead beer, Gordon's Dry Gin with water and lemon and danced all night. Glenn Miller tunes waltzed the crowd, and in between, Uncle Art would mimic Louis Armstrong's "Blueberry Hill" on the trumpet with song and kerchief swipes.

Over the years, the players changed, but Emile Breau, one of the musicians, remained Mom's good friend, and he stayed with his bass fiddle to the end. He even joined in another small group, delivering up many a dance night. That other group was local relatives, Charles and Rose Marie Devereaux. (Seems most of us were related one way or another.) Charles would be on the guitar and Rose on the electric organ. Both of them sang near every number played, and my favourite was "I've Got My Angel on My Mind." But everybody's special highlight was Mom's chicken bouillon that got served up at the end of music evenings.   No matter the reason for folks gathering in the country, food was always at the center.

Besides enjoying her women friends and the music evenings, Mom did get out of the house occasionally. Dad's first cousin, Mary (Ultican) McCarron, told me of their earlier fun times.

"Margo (many of the locals called Mom 'Margo' or 'Margaret') and I attended a bridge club in the 1930s. From the Quinns' farm, Margo'd hitch the horse to the sleigh, cross over the high snowbanks to Papa's, and pick me up for the ride to Durham Centre where Jeanne Doyle McClusky lived. Remember, it was Jeanne who loaned your mom the coat for her Quebec getaway. Well, quite the lively gathering it'd be. Like any local event, the highlight was in just getting together for chatting, laughter and especially enjoying the table full with homemade squares, cookies, sandwiches and pots of steeped tea. Nobody let the night go by without Margo reading a teacup or two. And being the good sport she was, she always obliged us."

The Old Chevy Car and the Culligan Home

It was around 1940 too that they were paving our road that travelled along the Bay de Chaleur. Alton Roherty remembered that my dad had a gravel truck working on that job, though Dad never drove the truck himself. But it was some time before the gravel road became a paved one.

"Charly didn't work himself," Alton remembered, "because he hired me to cut his hay on the Quinn farm along with a few men to haul the hay into the huge barn. During that period, Margaret had an old Chevy car she learned to drive and used it to run errands. It had almost no brakes and doors that banged and didn't stay shut.

"Well, one afternoon when all us men were haying at the bottom of the field, we're hearing this noise along the gravel road, and when we looked up, we saw this car coming in a cloud of dust. It was Margaret come flying over the school hill way too fast for any car, and especially a car with no brakes. On turning into the house lane, I could see Margaret wouldn't make the complete turn, but without brakes she steered back down the road, on two wheels only, the doors flying open, leaving behind her bags of Robin Hood flour scattered all over the gravel road. Not many folks had a white road."

Of course, Mom herself never really talked to me about driving that car because the car didn't hold up for long and then she never had the money to replace it.

It was also about this time, when our grandmother, Momo Culligan, decided to settle her estate with Dad and the rest of their children. Mom and Dad were offered first choice of the remaining three Culligan houses. Without hesitation, Mom chose the grand old Culligan homestead. By fall 1945, we moved into our new home two miles down from the Quinn farm to the Culligan village. To this day that Culligan homestead remains in our family. With this move, Mom was only a few minutes' walk away from Aunt Alice and Frances, her confidantes.

And what a historic home it was—known for miles around as the Culligan homestead. As the saying down home goes, "Anything can happen." Just as it did when my great-grandfather John Culligan got the maid pregnant. That being no small matter for their Irish-Catholic community, the bishop insisted that John Culligan "do the right thing." The maid was Pelagie Hache, a half Micmac Indian, a strong and wise woman, widely known and admired for her generosity and kindness to others. Her response to those Depression times was to always keep the door to her back kitchen open to passing strangers, wayfarers and the needy. She had some kindly reputation. They knew that there would always be a hot bowl of soup and a pot of tea brewing for them.

Grandfather Culligan had died in 1933. After his death, Momo lived alone in the homestead for ten years. Now the Culligan homestead had been empty for a year. Still, this was one spectacular home and property. Hundreds of acres came along with Momo's new gift. The huge barns remained standing. Everything existed for Dad to become the gentleman farmer. Momo made it clear that "this settlement was the final family estate disposition." Momo had been hoping for only the best for the son she loved, believing now that with this gift a miracle of sorts would happen when Charly returned to his childhood home. Perhaps return to his senses. Or even perhaps take pride in the Culligan tradition from his dad to his great-grandfather, who had worked these wondrous farmlands and built this fine home.

Many folks had said that there wasn't a finer home and property along the entire New Brunswick north shore coast. The farm included prime agricultural land and was bordered by the Atlantic Ocean waters on one side and by virgin woodlots on the other. No question, Dad had the makings of his own gold mine.

Unhappily, as in the earlier case of his behaviour during the twelve years at the Quinn farm, everything only grew worse. By 1951, not keen to work the land, he, having title to all the property, finally sold off the last acre of farm and wooded lots across the street from the Culligan house. And again, Mom and us kids never got the use of one penny of the proceeds. The last thirty acres of land left was where the house and barns stood. But having the signature authority to our property, Dad could do as he pleased without any thought to anyone else, least of all his own family. In all previous years, he had wasted away the money on drinking and gambling. Nothing was different now.

After three years' living on the Culligan homestead, Mom got pregnant for her ninth and last time. Her baby, Mary Sue (Susan), was born August 2, 1948. Mom will forever remember leaving the hospital with her wrapped-up little baby and—no husband in sight to help—getting a bus ride up from Bathurst.

"I didn't have the money for a taxi, so I walked from the hospital, about a mile and a half, to catch the bus. And when the bus came through Belledune and entered Culligan, I could see your father sitting in the bleachers stand at the baseball field through my bus window. Then and there, I knew I'd never again let that man sexually touch me."

The Night of Fear

My memory of Dad is of him smelling of the sour stench of whisky. Never sober. Then again, not always drunk. I remember that last evening he lived with us. I was six. We heard him yelling as he barged in through the kitchen door, crazy mad and staggering drunk. Because of experiences with his raging, I hurried out of the way, scurried up top the kitchen stairs where, sitting in the dark, I poked my head and hands out through the staircase banisters to await the outcome.

Fearful feelings still surface when I remember this last night. If I hadn't shared and repeated the events of this night so many times with my brothers and sisters, what happened would seem unbelievable, even to me.

That night Dad looked worse than I had ever seen him. Because his clothes were so torn and dirty with blood from cuts everywhere on his face, neck and arms, I saw only a bloody raging animal in the kitchen. I saw no person in that body. My father stomped over to the corner pantry and picked up the wooden-cased radio and crashed it into the back kitchen door. The radio smashed to smithereens. The door was gouged, split and fell apart in the middle.

He shuffled into the pantry, where he flung every single plate, cup and dish every which way, crashing them into pieces and throwing with such force that they stuck into the walls, the curtains and even the floor. I held my ears, and held my breath, but couldn't shut my eyes.

As much as I would like to forget what happened next, I cannot. Until then, he had never threatened me with violence. However, that night he was totally out-of-his mind drunk. He suddenly spotted me hunkered down at the top of the stairs. To that point only slivers of broken china had hit me. He began cursing and bellowing at me to tell him where my mother was. He yelled for me to tell him "Right now!" so he could "Kill the bitch!" that night.

Dad grabbed the butcher knife from the pantry, ran up the stairs and grabbed me, yelling and cursing at the top of his lungs, "Where is she? You can't hide her from me. I'll kill her."

Seeing that butcher knife in front of my face changed me forever. *Terrified, horrified, scared* are words that do not even come close to describing what happened to me that night. I was petrified with terror.

Just then, my older brother, Bill, entered the house. Earlier, Bill had got wind that Dad was on his way home and in bad shape, and minutes before had managed to lead Mom and a bundled-up Mary Sue out the back door, through the hay fields, and off to our relatives by the beach. Bill grabbed Dad and wrestled him to the floor. But even drunk, Dad was like a bull. Somehow then, Bill, Gail and Henry piled on and together they subdued him.

Grateful to be in bed that night, I recall curling up in a tight ball to try to stop my shaking. I bled from so much vomiting. My body—every muscle—ached with pain. Plenty of years passed before I got over the nightmares from that night. Terror just got stuck inside my guts. After experiencing Dad's violence on that staircase when I was only six years old, I don't think I ever trusted another person until my mid-thirties. During all the previous years when Mom and the others were battling the effects of his alcoholism, I never had any inkling, never really realized, what had actually happened, or ever really felt that it affected me.

That night changed everything.

After that one night, none of us were kids again. Mom decided "Never again!" would such violence occur in our home. Her mind was made up. But her decision—as I learned so many years later—was based on much more than that one night.

Calculated Violent Rage, Drunk or Sober

It was only over many years of conversations between Mom and me that I was able to learn what she had endured the times when Dad was around. There was never any apparent reason for his abusing her. Physical or mental abuse, it seemed to just come out of the blue. He could be cold sober or staggering drunk when he'd punch, slap, kick, shake or knock Mom off her feet.

Often Dad would go from real quiet to a sudden violent rage, just like it happened one evening that I recall. After feeding us and cleaning up the kitchen, Mom went upstairs to take a bath. I was sitting on the stairs when she walked down and I remember that she smelled good. It was a sweet powder-and-lipstick perfume I always remember. Her hair was shiny and tied back with a yellow printed kerchief and her lips were glossy with red lipstick. And she wore button-size mauve earrings. To me, she looked like she must have looked as Miss Jacquet River all over again.

No sooner did she walk across the kitchen floor than Dad leaped overtop the kitchen table and grabbed her by the neck with his two big hands. At times like that he seemed possessed. Anything in his way got broken or knocked down.

For me, not even the most horrific fall storms were as terrifying as the fear I had of my own dad. As sickening and chilling as his choking Mom was, his grotesque language was even worse. He pulled her close and yelled at her, "You're a fucking French slut, a lazy no-good-for-nothing bitch! A fucking praying whore!"

He was berserk. Still with his chokehold, he dragged her across the floor to the stove. It was still sizzling hot from the evening cooking. With one hand he grabbed the oven door, hauled it down and kicked it off the hinges. Then with the full force of his arms, he yanked her down to the floor and shoved her head into the piping-hot oven. Thank God that he had to let go the chokehold to push her into the oven, because at that moment she flung her arms out behind to grab hold outside the oven, kicking Dad behind her. While he pushed her head and shoulders against the oven wall, he fell back and she broke loose, racing upstairs, with him in close pursuit.

I'd been sitting transfixed on those steps, and as he leaped past me, I grabbed his legs, yelling for him to please stop hurting Mom. He stopped only momentarily when my older siblings rushed him, tumbling on the steps and managing to subdue him once again. Even to this day, if I hear any sudden similar sound, the sound of the thudding, pounding fists smashing into Mom's head, arms, stomach and face returns to me. It still leaves me with a sickening sense of apprehension from head to toe.

As unbelievable as this is true, Dad at that time was dead sober. That attack just seemed to be a matter of simmering and calculated rage—an insane act from a very sick man. When us kids managed to talk about this and other similar episodes of savage assaults on Mom, all we could figure was that he just couldn't handle the fact that she was so pretty. We figured he must have really hated something, but at that time we didn't understand that what he probably hated most was himself. In later years, when she was able to talk to us about his seeming unfounded rage, she felt he just hated women.

From that night's violence, Mom's face, arms, shoulders and hands were badly burned, and from the choking, her neck remained bruised and swollen for weeks. As often with the case of Dad's violence, my sisters slept with Mom to protect her from him. For otherwise, he'd come in the middle of the night when she slept, pull her out of bed and beat her. Gail and Ann mostly slept on either side, making sure that Mom stayed in the middle. Dad never put a hand on my sisters. Thank God for small mercies.

Early one Sunday morning, Mom was just buttoning up the warm muskrat fur coat that Momo had given her, and she was still humming the music from her early-morning practice at the piano. There was to be a special Gregorian music concert in honour of a visiting bishop that morning. She was standing by the kitchen-pantry door humming her Latin chant as she waited for Father Damure to pick her up. Suddenly Dad smashed through the back kitchen door—he'd been out all night—and threw himself on top of her. He literally exploded into the kitchen and punched her out cold. In seconds, he had torn the muskrat coat off her limp body, grabbed the poker from behind the stove, pulled the lid off the firebox and stuffed the fur coat into the fire. Is there any reason for what Dad did?

It simply did not matter what Mom cooked or baked, Dad complained, criticized and bullied her about the food in front of us all. Always, he lamented, it was bad, poor, not enough or late. And yet she was known to be the best cook for miles around. He showed up at home for two things: to eat and to torture Mom—or to demand money.

Her door-to-door selling of Avon beauty products and her on-the-road hairdressing had earned a small income that provided us with the basics. It didn't really matter what she ever answered him, Dad battered, brutalized, hounded and raged until she handed over the demanded money, which he'd promptly turn into alcohol and gambling. He played poker day and night—

sober or drunk. In later years, when he had left us and gone off to Toronto, my brother Bill bailed him out many a time because of his drinking, horse betting and poker playing.

When I try to find some good in the man, I just cannot recall a single act that he performed to support us kids or to help Mom. God love this morbid man, all he could do was torment her, which, in turn, vilified him for us.

With the Help of the Law

The Catholic Church ruled our community in those times. Ninety-nine per cent of all the people in the area were Catholic. Back then, we knew the opinions that were held concerning Protestants and fallen-away Catholics. There was only one ticket to heaven and that was through the pews and confessionals of the Catholic Church. Any other passage led you either to hell or limbo. I remember no ifs, buts or in-betweens within the preached doctrine.

Despite this harsh reality, Mom decided to legally separate from Dad. Let me tell you, that decision was "no small potatoes," as they say around home. In doing such, she knew that she was ostracizing herself from the entire community by not living up to the "forever married until death do us part" promise. Divorce was out of the question. Lots of religion and no money made that kind of decision impossible. New Brunswick civil law, however, permitted legal separation. Mom chose that route. But you have to grasp how deep our family pain was.

It was only many years later that Mom was able to confide some of her feelings to me. "Thank God," she said, "for the brave soul who vowed support. That was Frances telling me, 'You did right in separating from Charly.'

"I never had to explain myself to Frances. As soulmates, we understood our place, as women and mothers, who accepted the full responsibilities of caring for families. The men did as they pleased while we did what was necessary. And that often meant doing both the man's and woman's jobs, like so many of us did."

But then the tears flowed freely, and it was as though Mom had forgotten that I was sitting there with her. These memories shook her deeply.

"Sure there were many others like me, who had no happy young life and thought that when you get married, you'd be your own boss, be happy and have a life to look forward to. Like many women from here, all we got was an absentee for a husband. But no sense in trying to get mad or punish Charly. That only made me miserable. Living this way made it difficult to laugh or even joke about anything. I never had hate for Charly, or any desire for revenge.

"There really was no other choice for me but separation in order to survive with dignity for myself and you children. Listen, it's a tough old world going it alone. Even with his drunkenness, I only ever wanted to love him and be his wife. Letting go completely was the only way I could help myself. For sure, I discovered the value of family and friends."

Because Dad did not contribute any financial support, through the court ruling, Mom was able to charge him with abandonment. He left New Brunswick immediately. Were he to remain, the sheriff's outstanding arrest warrant would have put him in jail for failure to support. News travels fast in small towns. We all knew that the local sheriff, Guy Leblanc, had warned Dad he'd do his job if he had to, so he ordered Dad to leave the province. "That," Guy said, "made it easier on everybody."

But the talk of our community was not about Dad's drunken behaviour, his violence or even his obvious financial irresponsibility. Instead, they chastised Mom for not sticking by her man.

"After all," people said, "doesn't every real man drink a little too much?" They were only partly correct. Most men drank too much. They were also dead wrong in believing we should live one more hour in the insane dread of active alcoholic violence or unreasoning rages. Most Culligan men were especially double-fisted drinkers. In our community, they exacted their cruel ways on wives and children alike. To this day, most of my cousins still do not know what hit them as children—not the foggiest notion that alcoholism had affected their own thinking and action.

When Mom made the difficult decision to separate from Dad, no support existed to understand and to encourage families as ravaged by the terrors of alcoholism as ours. The opposite to support was the general attitude. Our family was tagged as defective. As a result, we became the victims. And we certainly hadn't volunteered for the job. Mom's decision to save and protect herself from additional physical and emotional violence ought to have received community support. Instead, she was criticized and judged as being unfaithful and unworthy. No priest came to her saying we understand and support your courageous, righteous decision to look after your family.

For Dad, it seemed that being born in New Brunswick turned out to be ticket for living in Ontario. Eventually, all the drunks worth their salt made their way to Toronto, seeking fame and fortune. Instead, many found the Don Jail registry. Dad made it to Toronto. He got to see the Don Jail opened for room service. Seems he sold off hundreds of acres of land at home so he could end up sleeping in jail or on Toronto's acreage of park benches.

Months skipped by after he left before I could allow myself the thought that maybe he really wasn't coming back. Whatever the reality of our home life in the early 1950s, I half expected we'd have a drunken dad show up anytime, intent on setting the house on fire and getting rid of us kids once and for all. Somehow his leaving felt open-ended. Fear still trembled just under the surface of my feelings. He had, in fact, returned to our area twice that year after he left, and I never felt safe from what I knew he was capable of doing.

On those two visits, he had turned into the lane of our house, stopped his car and just stared. One time, seeing him, I jumped off the veranda with a broom, figuring to fight him off, and I got as close as his car window where I could smell the same sour whisky smells that always sickened and scared me. Even at seven years old, I hated him with a willingness to use force if need be. Strong feelings for just a mere child.

You've Got to Think About Saving Your Soul

Within a year of Mom's separation from Dad, she found a little diversion with her women friends, and even with attending the odd club dance off in the nearest town with Emile Breau and her other old friends from her world of music. They were the folks that played in the nearest town's symphony and even had a band of their own. Great brass and string sound.

"It bothered me sometimes," Mom said, "thinking maybe I should behave as people thought I should and told me so."

Of course, that meant that she should stay home and out of sight. She recalled saying to some of the local people that one day she'd reach the end of her rope were she not able to go out once in a while—definitely go clear out of her mind. One lady challenged her with "Margo, you know what our religion says—you've got to think about saving your soul!"

At that time, Mom recalled clearly how terribly sad this woman's own life was, and told her, "I know all about that. No matter my own circumstances, I still feel the same way about my religion. Yes, I've got to save my soul, but first I need to look after my head. I understand well what happens with a miserable existence. I cannot let myself go crazy. My God, I've a large family to bring up. They need me healthy and preferably not as a sad and miserable mother."

She says, "That afternoon, there were four women talking. Not all religious or pious. I told this one in particular, 'I know what I'm supposed to do in my religion.' Even though it was long over with Charly—his sleeping around for years—the church saw it only one way, and believe me, it was never in light or favour of the woman. The church meant for me not to enjoy myself, nor ever to make a new life, but just to wear black and carry the rosary.

"I knew what the neighbours thought—stay with Charly no matter what. In spite of my knowledge and understanding, I said that I had to save me—me by myself! And you can rest assured that I am going to look after me. 'Cause it will be me who'll have to live and to suffer the consequences. And what of my children if I can't care for them and love them?"

It didn't take long before Mom's day of Catholic reckoning. Late one October afternoon, Father Parker knocked on our kitchen door, arriving for his annual parish visit. Mom was in the kitchen making peach marmalade. I was studying upstairs in my bedroom just above the kitchen. Shortly into his stay, Father Parker said, "Margaret, even though you're separated from your husband, as a married Catholic, your seeing this other man (Emile) places you in mortal sin, and I could refuse you Holy Communion." I heard Mom quietly respond, "Dear Father Parker, I understand full well what you're saying, and from this day forward, you need not worry, for I'll never again place you in a situation where you have to make that decision."

From that day forward, to when Dad died years later, Mom never approached the communion rail, yet she faithfully attended Catholic Mass. Within our community, that judgement of her as sinner and not worthy of receiving her God, was only some of the public attitude Mom quietly accepted as her fate.

So from my upstairs bedroom, I listened thoughtfully as Mom graciously went on serving Father Parker tea and pie, even though I knew how shocked and heartbroken she must be feeling.

She paid our annual church dues, then gave him her usual contribution for his personal use. That was the kind of response Mom gave under all circumstances: charity and kindness in the face of rejection and abuse. Neither she nor I spoke afterwards about that sad afternoon. For both of us, being Catholic and breathing were one and the same.

I knew that day Mom's heart was crushed, as was mine.

Our grove of birch trees; George and
Florence's farm across the road

Five

Times as Tough as Nails

For Mom the late 1940s and early 1950s delivered times as tough as nails. There was no money from regular wages, but there were lots of mouths to feed and feet to cover. I remember those tough years of us all existing with just the bare essentials. Until I was about eight, we lived through the coldest, skimpiest worst times. Those years were certainly not abundant in meat, potatoes and rubber boots. As Mom repeated later to us so many times, "Lots of folks were in similar situations, some better off than us—though plenty were worse off." Sure, we experienced going off to school with nothing but buttered bread in our lunch pail, too embarrassed to open the pail in front of others in fear we'd be made fun of.

Mom's Briefcase of Avon Samples

My sister Ann recalled, "I can still see Mom on those bitter cold wintry days and evenings, making her way down the unploughed laneway, hip deep in snowdrifts, lugging her briefcase of Avon samples, order sheets, hair scissors and curlers, making her way to the highway where she'd either walk or manage to hitch a ride to her prospective customers. She never shied away from any chance of making a few dollars to support us. As demanding and determined as she was herself, she also expected that of all of us."

Deany, Mom's first cousin, explained this sad time to me: "Margaret survived those years through selling Avon products and doing hairdressing. Remember, she'd been cutting hair even in her dad's barbershop, and later she got her beauty certificate during her stay in Boston. Besides, she was talented. In the 1930s she did finger waves with an old-fashioned curling iron that got heated in the coals of the wood stove. I loved watching her test how hot it was by poking it through an ol' rag, giving smoke signals when ready.

"On the road and at home, Margaret just never rested. I remember her house had hardwood floors throughout. Well, she hand-scrubbed, waxed and polished every bit on her hands and knees. The children followed suit. Margaret wore her skin to the bare knuckles washing clothes (there were no washing machines then), using glass-ribbed scrubbing boards and strong yellow soap bars. I think sometimes when she was doing heads, she forgot they weren't the washboard!"

Clara Flanagan, a neighbour up the road a bit, remembered those times too. "I first met your mother not long after Andrew and I married in 1949. She hitchhiked up the road and came in to do my mother-in-law's hair, so then and there she became my hairdresser too. Faithfully, Margaret called at the house once a month. She would bring the Avon catalogue just in case we needed something. Saved us ever fussing about running out.

"Margaret had a charming personality and I instantly thought of her as a good friend. Being young at the time, I looked forward to her visits and her pleasant way of making me feel at ease. If I was lonesome or feeling bad, she'd cheer me up with an Irish joke, a song or a two-step across the floor."

We knew that hairdressing and selling Avon products was Mom's primary financial source in the 1940s right through to the late 1950s, but when she set out on her money-making route loaded up with Avon products, catalogues and hair-styling equipment, us kids would never know how long she'd be gone. By the mid-1940s, the older of us did the babysitting. And I remember Mom telling me how tight money was, especially around the time that our youngest sibling, baby number nine—Mary Sue—was born in 1948. The following four years were the worst.

Mom had told me many times the story of her leaving the hospital with the baby that was to be her last one, when the Sister in charge stopped her in the corridor and told her bluntly that she couldn't leave without payment.

"Well, Sister, that wouldn't make much sense. How can you keep my little baby and me here, feeding us when we can't pay for what's already gone by?"

"That's policy. You can't leave until paid up!"

Looking the woman straight in the eye, Mom told her, "Dear Sister, I have no money, and my husband is a boozer and he's got no money. I've got to leave and hitchhike home with my small baby where my other eight children need me. Rest assured, Sister, as always, I'll be working immediately, selling Avon and doing hair door-to-door. You'll get paid. Every cent. I'll send you a little each week as I earn." Then Mom made weekly payments until the bill was paid off. This was her way—handling bills a little at a time.

As kids, we took on adult responsibilities real early. Of course, this enabled Mom to hit the road to earn a living for all of us. And we knew that.

Ann was the principal teen looking after us all for a bunch of years. And then after she joined the Air Force in 1951, Gail took over the main job until 1957, when I took over at age twelve.

Mostly, Mom stood at the roadside until a free ride came along. Her business route took her to Campbellton, fifty-two miles west, up along the Bay de Chaleur. She prepared for her "business trips" by scheduling dozens of women to have their hair done. Her very kind and good friend, Irene Firlotte (not a relative), always let Mom bunk in with their family. Campbellton sure provided Mom with a portion of the dollars to feed and clothe us those years. After a couple of days at Irene's, Mom would walk to different houses where there were regular customers year after year. Often, each house would invite along another head or two for her to do. It was kind of a social thing too.

"In the 1950s," Mom recalled, "my biggest-dollar customers came from Campbellton and Dalhousie. Once finished with my Campbellton regulars, I'd hitch a ride from the street and the highway road that intersected at Campbellton's entrance, down to the Dalhousie junction. From there I walked into Dalhousie, visiting my regulars on the way. I sold more Avon cosmetics, creams and lipsticks along that highway than in Campbellton and elsewhere.

"Of course, those country folks didn't have the easy access to the drug-stores and department stores of the larger towns. Sometimes I'd leave my hairstyling bag behind because of being loaded down with delivering Avon products. That would be an occasion for when I had the highest number of orders. With folks seeing the actual products purchased by others, I sold from the packaging. Then other times I worked it so that I just did the heads so I only needed to carry my hairdressing stuff."

"How much money could you earn doing hair from house to house on the road?" I asked.

"Remember," she said, "many of these ladies were the wives of the executives and bosses at the large newsprint mill, the Canadian National Railway headquarters and even hospital doctors and staff. A few were big tippers. Working hard as I did, for hours on my feet, nothing made me happier than a large tip. Sometimes I even received a $5 bill for a tip. At the end of my road days doing hair, I'd get $10 for the top-of-the line perm or tint. That included a wash and set, but not a cut. For that I charged a dollar extra. A wash, cut and set was $2.50. Aside from selling Avon, I did a nice little business selling my hairdressing products, like hairnets and hairspray."

Listening to Mom go on about the individual items she sold to earn money, I inquired about what kind of living that provided.

"We weren't driving a Rolls-Royce for sure. There were no extras or anything. My main concern for that period, before I was able to open my own shop, was money for wood to feed the furnace and the kitchen stove and to buy the essentials for our meals.

"One of my favourite road stops was at the Doyles' on Dalhousie Hill. I looked forward to a hot meal there, knowing they'd want me to read their teacups afterwards. And because that often was my last selling stop before heading back home, I could relax. They were educated people and talked well. No matter where conflict existed worldwide, I'd hear them discussing the latest. Especially after World War II ended, with problems starting up in Korea and the fear of communism, they expressed judgements on all of those concerns."

Waiting for Mom to Come Home

I guess what I remember most about Mom's road trips is our waiting for her to come back home. Sometimes she'd be away a full week. We never knew. However, by the fourth night, we all went into high-vigilant stance waiting. We took turns on this—one time included Gail because she was the oldest, then

Henry next, and then me, and Mary Sue took a turn too when she was big enough to watch out the window.

I especially recall when Gail was in high school and I was nine years old. Gail was fifteen and in charge. She was the chief cook, bottle washer and disciplinarian during these years, always helping, but especially when Mom was on the road selling Avon products and doing hair. And when Henry was twelve he worked at our relatives' neighbouring farm—George and Florence Culligan's place. At nine I was already helping with the clothes washing, the housecleaning and wood piling. Mary Sue got to be just the kid at six years old.

If we climbed up the stairs to the west-end bedroom, we could see a half-mile up the road to Culligan's Hill. That's where I kept watch for the Smith Maritime Transport (SMT) bus, heading east to Bathurst and Moncton. That bus would be coming down the highway from Campbellton, and stop anywhere along the route to pick up passengers. Towards the end of Mom's business selling days, she was able to afford the fifty-cent bus ride home.

It was easy to identify that bus. For openers, it had three level sets of lights. A car only had one level. Most large trucks had two or four. Across the very top of the bus, rising overtop Culligan Hill, I first would see the yellow and green row of small lights, followed quickly by the two large oval headlights and then the bottom row of small red and white lights beaming through the dark country night. Already dressed in my coat and shoes, I went lickety-split real fast down the kitchen stairs, out the door and out of breath, reached the highway at the end of our laneway just before I could hear the squealing brakes that meant Mom was home.

And that sickening diesel-fuel smell of the SMT! No matter where I am today, if I get the scent of diesel fuel up my nostrils, I land right back at our laneway awaiting Mom's exit from the bus, arms full of bags. Soon as I spotted her, I'd run across the road to grab bags and help her make it into the house.

Mom's treats from her road days were tailored special to each of us. Any book with illustrated stories entertained me for the next week. Second to books, she knew I enjoyed and used colouring pencils, scribblers, sketch pads, moulding clay and coloured paper. Henry couldn't wait for "funny books"—the latest Dick Tracy, Lone Ranger and Tonto, Superman and Donald Duck. With Susan, it could be marbles, bubble gum, a Hula Hoop, skipping rope or a ball. For Gail, any new piece of clothing did the trick. Not every sales trip brought such joyous rewards. Guess it depended on how well Mom did. Yet there would always be a little something, like a bag of peppermints. Opening the bags gave us all the most excitement.

A job I always did for Mom was unraveling the perm rollers. When Mom reached the end of her heads, the perm curlers from those last few heads remained full of the crinkled perm solution-soaked papers. The papers would still be in knots, mostly hanging on to the attached rubber-band clamps plug that held the hair curls tight. Boy, that was another puckish smell that'll never leave me!

When Mom returned home, the last thing was the money counting. Strange, how she often waited for days to add up her new wealth. She just left it on the kitchen table, the piles of quarters, dimes, nickels, one-dollar bills, two-dollar bills and five-dollar bills sitting there to be counted. When she'd have a big sales trip of Avon products and hairdos, the booty sometimes totalled near three hundred dollars. That put a dent in the grocery bill.

Of course, she couldn't be the travelling saleswoman every day because there still remained the day-to-day baking, maintenance and her keeping a close eye on us kids. After all, we *were* just kids. Though we dug in to do just about anything, Mom remained fully in charge.

That reminds me also of how I learned that cleanliness was next to godliness. The nights Mom returned home by bus from selling also meant that Gail and I scurried about every room and corner of the house, making certain everything was tidy and super-whistle clean. As a kid I had a broom, mop or rag in my hand far more than a ball and bat. All I had to hear from Mom on her return was "Oh dear God," to place me on full alert. I knew prevention served me far better than her scorn and disappointment on finding disorder and dirt. Her demands left no room for discussion or for who was right or wrong. For there was only one way to do anything: Mom's way. And that was order, spic-and-span cleanliness and all tasks completed.

A lot of Mom's habits and her disciplined ways stuck out for me, even as a child. Very early I saw how she only stopped in anything she did when the task was completely finished. She never left anything undone.

Even to this day, when I feel the exhilarating rush from achieving what seems impossible at the time, I always feel real close to Mom. In my life now for sure, I understand deeply the many times she would tell us how she'd be wondering, "How can I keep going?" And instantly her answer would always be "Just do it!" That sure got to the point for her then. It gets to the point for me even now.

Mom never called it "marketing," but I often heard her saying, "Spread yourself around like manure on a field and plenty will grow!" Making money—and not incidentally, holding the family together—came as a result of her determination and energy.

Mrs. Mallaly

Mrs. Mallaly lived a bit away in the Lorne settlement, three miles in the backwoods off the main highway, but that didn't matter, because Mom hired her to come sew our hand-me-down dresses, coats and pants, and to knit up mitts and stocking caps at least once a year. Nothing fancy and nothing new or store-bought. With Mrs. Mallaly's help, Mom even collected used clothing and fixed some of it up a bit to sell for extra dollars or sometimes to barter for other necessities. It all added up to provide the essentials to keep us fed and warm. Through all the tough times for Mom and for us kids, there was always Mrs. Mallaly.

To me, Mrs. Mallaly always seemed like an old lady. By that I don't mean weak. Quite the opposite, for I remember her being as strong as a team of horses. She could do anything that needed fixing, and I figured she also knew just about everything there was to know. No matter how fierce the storms, this woman ploughed through mountains of snow even a horse couldn't get through.

I don't ever recall her being without "that bag." It seemed every bit the size of her. Almost. Full to the brim of darning, sewing and knitting needles, torn pieces of cloth and balls of yarn, blades and measuring tapes, scissors and glue. She was always ready at the drop of a hat to mend, sew, darn, alter or tailor anything, and remake and "fix" whatever was thrown her way. And that could be the horse's saddle stoops for boots, burlap bags, mittens or socks worn full of holes, hand-me-down dresses and pants, broken handles of cracked teapots, or even peeling wallpaper.

Mrs. Mallaly was what the doctor ordered to treat whatever ailed us. And although she had her routes and her "regulars," if you needed her, she'd be there.

The knock would come, and there the woman herself would be with a crackling wide smile full across her face. And with that devilish twinkle in her eyes, everyone knew that she was famous for being a prankster and quick with a story. She was always up for fun, and she was the only soul I knew who shook all over laughing with all her heart, soul and body.

As kids, most every piece of clothing we wore got mended, sewed, darned, altered or tailored by Mrs. Mallaly. Each piece was reconfigured to suit our individual needs. I remember when my older brother's black winter coat, mailed home from Niagara Falls, got cut down to size with a sewed-in, spanking-new, shiny red lining for me to wear when I was in grade three. Wearing my new coat with the high-peaked hood that Mrs. Mallaly had added, I was some proud sliding down our snowbanks. I felt like Batman on a snowboard.

Like everyone else who came to our house, Mrs. Mallaly couldn't get enough of Mom's teacup readings, the food and the sticky buns. I can hear her smacking and gulping now.

"Surely a good ting, there'll be no wastin' me spot o' tea that's got leaves floatin' all da way to da top. For sure, 'tis the sign of happiness forever I'll not be missin'."

Mom's down payment to Mrs. Mallaly—a full-treatment hairdo! This included a wash, special creme rinse, cut, perm, dye job and set. That quickly totalled up to put a decent dent in Mrs. Mallaly's charge. Along the road, on her other jobs, she might be receiving a side of beef, live chickens, freshly churned butter, a sack of potatoes and even boxes of home-tinned canned meats. Sometimes folks gave her fabric. They'd all be hand-me-downs from some faraway relative's special mailed box of goodies. This was a Maritime way of folks just plain looking after each other, even when thousands of miles apart. But only with Mom did she get to leave looking and feeling some special. Mom often paid the balance of Mrs. Mallaly's charge with hair and cosmetic supplies, homemade breads, sticky buns, gumdrop cakes and a little cash.

I always loved to be nearby when Mrs. Mallaly was sewing. Bent over the sewing machine, peddling and sewing, I'd hear her say, "Golly gosh dash it— me eyes are leavin' meself!" While sewing, her tongue stayed hanging out always so as to be at the ready to catch a fallen thread.

Unlike the shoemaker's kids who went without shoes, Mrs. Mallaly always dressed becomingly even when hanging sticky wallpaper. Mom would say, "How lovely your dress, the pattern so colourful!" And Mrs. Mallaly would answer, "'Tis nothing but outta old curtains sent from the Culligan girls in New York." Just so you know, Mrs. Mallaly, as did many older folks around home, always spoke like that. "Oh, let me tell you dear, 'tis nothing for me to do for you. Ah, 'tis a bountiful garden you've got here!"

She fashioned anything out of nothing, be it worn curtains, faded bedspreads or bleached flour sacks. Fall or winter didn't matter; she wore the thickest heavy cardigan sweater of anyone I knew. Of course, she had knitted it herself, too. Around home, folks would plain exclaim, "Mrs. Mallaly's just the most delightfully charming handsome woman." Only my Grand-Aunt Aupal (Grandfather John Culligan's sister) had that same laughing magic as Mrs. Mallaly. I remember their simply walking into our house lightened the mood and put smiles on all our faces. They had the same effect on me as a pan of homemade divinity fudge. Some others, like Frances and Marion Culligan come close to that grand-entrance manner of just putting everybody at ease.

No! Not Even One of My Children!

Remembering those tough times when she had to be on the road for days at a time, leaving her children alone at home, Mom told me, "I knew I could never give away not even one of my children from the day I was approached by Mary Buckley, a relative from the Culligan side, asking me to give up Gail to her care. Mary told me that she and Aunt Josephine were talking about my hard financial situation and Mary told her she'd like to adopt our Gail. Apparently, Aunt Josephine agreed that might be a good thing 'cause she knew what a hard time we were having.

"It didn't take long for me to say, 'My goodness, Mary, the answer is no for sure, and further, my children wouldn't want to leave me.'"

As young as I was at the time, I do recollect the discussions of Aunt Josephine and Mary Buckley's attempt to adopt us. And there were other requests by two other locals to take Mary Sue, our youngest. Nobody asked for me. Even that young, I remember how relieved and somehow safe I felt that I had not been singled out for adoption. That perhaps nobody else loved me never entered by mind. Living elsewhere was unthinkable. We couldn't have had a darker, sobering experience than those realities. We were in deep financial trouble.

Our family despair had even been reported to the provincial Social Welfare Office. There are so many incidents from childhood that will never leave me.

Just like the day Mrs. Burns, the social welfare representative, came knocking at our door.

Mom, too, remembered the misery caused all of us by the neighbours' attempted solution to our crisis. "With them coming right into our home and speaking so openly of breaking my family up as a way to help me financially, something just happened inside of me."

Listening to Mom reminded me of my own feelings at that dark time. I was afraid to leave for school, fearful that nobody would be left at home upon my return. Seven years old, I sat in the back of Sister Delice's classroom, trying to figure out a way to work so I could earn my own keep. Billy, Ann, Gene and Paul were on their own working, and I thought then, "It's time to do so." Gail, then thirteen, cooked and cleaned. Henry, age ten, started to work at the neighbour's farm and handed his earned wages over to Mom. No matter what, even with Billy's and Ann's generous monthly mailed cheques home, the piling-up debts and bills crushed us.

Coming out of my own reverie, I heard Mom talking softly, "I was desperate now to find a way to get out of my predicament. Right then I never thought I'd have to give up. Or give anybody up. I'd fight to the end. Somehow I felt there would never be a time to go down that road of giving up my children. I'd find a way. Each night on my knees in prayer with you children, I'd repeat: 'We'll find a way. We're being looked after.' " And we did."

Whether she was out on the road or at home, the whole lot of us knelt around Mom's bed every single night, saying our prayers out loud, blessing ourselves before and after with Holy Water from Mom's St. Ann shrine.

Somehow, the word got around of our desperate financial situation. For it wasn't long after that offer to adopt one of us, there was a knock on our door. It was Mrs. Burns from the provincial Social Welfare Office. Now you couldn't ask for a sweeter lady. She calmly told us of the neighbours reporting my Mom's recent separation from Dad and her probable inability to support her family. But Mrs. Burns could see for herself how well cared for the home and children were. No better testimony for Mom was needed.

Who could believe groundless rumours from prying neighbours when there you are, as was Mrs. Burns, surrounded by Mom's freshly baked loaves of homemade bread, and enjoying some with Mom's magic, refreshing cup of tea.

In fact, later on, Mrs. Burns helped Mom apply for the so-called Widow's Allowance to help provide financial assistance, and she assured her that there would be no more threats about breaking up our family. Yet we couldn't help feeling the indignity and shame of it all, just the fact of being visited by the welfare office. And a threat of others, in this case from our own neighbours, was made real by the presence of provincial officials. Because just the everyday chore of surviving these hardships was so devastatingly challenging, this outside threat stirred even greater unease and fear that we could ever be able to survive together as a family.

The County Tax Notice and More

To add to this insanity, not all that long after Mrs. Burns's visit, Sheriff Leblanc appeared on the scene with a public notice, a hammer and two shingles. Inside the veranda, under the porch roof, right next to the kitchen door, he nailed the "County Tax Notice Bankrupt Sale" sign to the clapboard. Mom and us kids just stood staring in speechless shocked disbelief as he banged in the nails.

Sheriff Leblanc put his hands on Mom's shoulders and said, "Margo, I have no choice but to do my job, but as soon as I drive out the laneway, tear the sign off and find a way to save your home. You've got at least a couple of months before final judgements." On top of being unable to pay the taxes, Great-Aunt Annie Ultican (she and Grand-Aunt Liz owned the grocery store) had registered a lien against our property for several months of unpaid grocery supplies. Time had run out for any further excuses.

Mom acted quickly. Our house was still in Dad's name. "Your brother Bill, working for Ontario Hydro in Niagara Falls at the time, approached Charly with a notary. Somehow he got Charly to reluctantly sign over the property to me."

But that didn't pay the back taxes or outstanding grocery bill. Mom knew she had to find a way for a loan. And that would be only part of her long-term solution. Our cousins Marion and Leslie Culligan came through. They took a mortgage on our home against the loan.

"For sure, that was temporary. I could hardly live with an outstanding loan and no long-term solution to pay off the mortgage to Leslie. Really, I was left with only one choice, to ask my parents for a loan to wipe out the mortgage. Tommy, you can't imagine how hard that was to do. I'd've preferred to work day and night than to have asked Mama and Papa to do that. But much too much was at stake for my pride to get in the way of saving our home."

Mom's siblings helped by urging their parents to come through. They did—but not without a condition. Though at the time their condition of coming to live at our home seemed hard for Mom to swallow, in the long term, their coming from Ontario to live with us proved to be the solution to our financial problems. Granny and Grandpa Boudreau came to look after us—and their new investment. They were hesitant in putting up the money. Living directly on the property gave them control over any future financial crisis. But taking on a bunch of young kids at their age was not appealing.

The next step came when Mom asked her sister-in-law, Aunt Trudy Boudreau, and Mom's brother, my Uncle Stan, if she could come live with them in Val d'Or, Quebec. Living with them would give her a chance to acquire the apprenticeship necessary for her to be able to open her own hairdressing shop in New Brunswick. That was a lot of planning! Aunt Trudy's hairdressing salon boasted chairs with four separate chair-sink stations just for shampooing. Uncle Stan was a big "galloot" (Mom's reference for a big shot) for Champion Savings in Montreal. Between Stan and Trudy, big-time money jetted them off to Paris and London. And since in those days, with Mom and us having to hitchhike rides to see a dentist or doctor, their lifestyle was a bit like the outer space dancing Northern Lights to us.

Talk about a mixed blessing. Mom being able to live with the Boudreaus in Quebec to apprentice for a year and receive her shop licence also meant that she'd have to be separated from all of us in order to do it. Having her own hair salon so that we could eventually become financially independent was a solution that came with a heavy price.

At that time, I was only seven years old, Mary Sue only four, Henry ten, and Gail thirteen. It had been only a year earlier that Dad left, never to live with us again. I can't aptly describe my feelings during those years, but for sure, I figured my mom would never return home again, and that these grandparents, who we barely knew, would sell us off to pay their loan.

Too suddenly the day came when Mom left, even as the taxi arrived to take her to the train station. I know now that she held back a lot so as to not add fear to an already dangerous situation. She blew kisses at us while tears flooded her face as she held a hand over her mouth, covering over her "I love you all" screams. Mom knelt on the back seat of the taxi looking through the window, waving her last goodbyes, while I desperately—still disbelieving—ran behind the car, up the road all the way as far as I could. But the taxi was too fast, or my legs weren't long enough. Mom and the car disappeared beyond the next hill. Nothing anyone said that day or the next—or even the next—really penetrated enough for me to hear, let alone understand. I was sure now that Dad had left forever, just as I knew now that Mom would never return. I felt utterly abandoned, and my child-heart froze in despair.

One Car I Was Happy to See Leaving

Christmas without Mom hit the bottom of my scale that measured emptiness. That Christmas, we received the most games, clothes and candy than any Christmas before or after. From Val d'Or, where she was still apprenticing for her licence, Mom mailed parcels filled with even the cooking essentials for our grandparents. But none of the bright wrappings could ever replace having her home for Christmas.

It seemed like longer, but only after near a year away, Mom earned her hairdresser's licence and returned home to us. No matter how bleak our future times were from then on, I never complained. I guess deep inside I was just in fear of losing her all over again.

While she was away, her parents had sold off ten acres on the west side to pay themselves back for their $500 loan to her. The mortgage was now wiped out.

"Selling that ten acres with me away really hurt," Mom said. "I told Mama and Papa not to sell another inch of our land and to sign that property back over to me. The whole painful reason for my leaving the kids was to earn enough money to pay off the mortgage and start a business. Were it about selling land, I could have stayed home and done that myself!"

My grandparents also sold off the huge barn for the lumber. They repaid themselves their expenses in looking after us. Because of what Granny and Grandpa did, Mom returned earlier than planned. It wasn't long after she came back home, my grandparents left. That was one car I was happy to see leaving. Crazy or not, when they were here, not a day passed I didn't think they'd be selling me off to cover their expenses. Granny sure complained lots. Never stopped nattering after Grandpa about the money and the work on the farm. I felt a stranger in my own home.

Margo's Beauty Bar

Within months of Mom's return, she opened her very own hairdressing shop, turning our back parlour into a business place. While apprenticing in Aunt Trudy's shop, she had managed to save a few hundred dollars. These dollars paid Don Culligan to install the plumbing and sink for her—"a brand-new black neck-fitted sink with spray hose and all," and additional electrical for the two new standing hair dryers on wheels, shelving for products, a working station, and even a big mirror and fancy green leather chairs.

Outside, on the veranda porch column, Don screwed on the white and blue- lettered Formica sign—Margo's Beauty Bar. Wow, talk about excitement! The closest shop competition was twenty-six miles away. Mom made a first in our entire area with opening her own hairdressing shop, and with that, living changed for the whole family. Many financial hard days still came and went, but never did we return to the days of the sheriff coming to our house with a For Sale sign. Nor did Mrs. Burns from the welfare office have to come back because of neighbours' spreading rumours about Mom's inability to care for us kids.

Theresa McDonnell, a neighbour and dear friend recounted those early times of Margo's Beauty Bar. "It was early in the 1950s when Margo started her business at home. I went to her when I needed a perm. Like other times making my way there, it was not easy getting a ride in those days. So few of us had cars. And once Margo finished my hair, I'd often have a long wait for someone to pick me up. So, besides the hairdressing part, I would have supper with Margo along with whoever else was getting their hair done. Margo's collection of the long-playing 33 record albums introduced the whole community to music never heard before, my favourite being Lena Horn's 'Whispering Pines,' and Chet Atney's jazz guitar-playing."

Recalling Mom's business, my cousin Bobby Culligan remarked, "When your mother started her business in the 1950s, she displayed real courage and strength. No woman around here did such things. I think if she had been born a generation later, there would not have been nine of you. She probably would have been a woman executive—and also managed her family. She could handle that."

Folks kept coming back mainly because of Mom's hair-tinting reputation. Though I believe her pots of tea, teacup readings and sticky buns counted every bit as much. Because I was always curious, she let me in on her mixing secrets. She never let me treat heads, of course. "Mixing colours is an art," Mom said.

"Of utmost importance," she emphasized, "keep all blended colours natural." Her supplies were delivered in short squat bottles labelled dye. In black, brown, red, yellow and blue. In time, L'Oréal de Paris offered premixed ash blonde, bright auburn and dark brunette. Even then, Mom kept right on mixing. She derived her own colour chart directly from Mother Earth.

"Colour needs to show texture," she told me. "And you'll find your best colours when you can touch and feel what's real."

Ever so true, because her sought-after tinted colours became synonymous with our local women's heads. Aunt Audrey's red hair evolved out of Mom matching our orchard's rust-red winter apples. Helen Devereaux's blue hair captured the tint of the Bay de Chaleur in early June—a translucent light wavy blue. For Lorraine's sunny disposition, Mom mixed a tint of blonde just like a wild-oats field. Liddia, the down-home wife of Maritime-famous Charlie Chamberlain, got her tint from our Queen Anne mahogany-brown settee. Mom demonstrated to me how yellow and blue would produce green, then that got added to brown and red to create her "sassy brown auburn." A touch of beet juice with lemon in a mixture of red and black yielded a shiny silver-black stallion dye. That was a special hair colour for Shirley, our next-door cousin and one of Mom's favourite people.

Any sweltering July week in the 1950s was much the same as any other. I remember this scene of women's bodies all over our house, but the 1954 Firlotte summer wedding was one scene I'll never forget. Literally, some of the heads were so fully covered, I could only recognize who was who from the neck down. I was nine that summer, but already I was an experienced helper and trained in brewing tea and grilling cheese sandwiches. In the springtime, we all picked the field of dandelion greens to be boiled for table greens and served up too. They're called lamb's quarters and taste great with fried bologna and mashed potatoes.

For days that busy summer, Mom washed, cut, permed, tinted and styled near fifty heads a week or more. But a really big rush came just before our cousin Sherman Firlotte tied the knot with beautiful Lou Dione. Well, to be fair, near every man, woman and child within a few miles was a cousin on one side or the other, be it Culligan, Firlotte, Ultican or Doyle, so for the upcoming wedding, Mom did all those heads too.

In addition to all the local cousins getting done up for the wedding, we also had all the "Irish Mafia" ladies from Boston, with Aunt Alice sitting on the outside veranda, smelling strongly of perm solution and looking like an alien with huge rolled-up curlers sticking way past her ears and forehead. Alongside her, Aunt Lena with foil-wrapped hair that got pulled through dozens of holes in this red plastic shower-looking cap for "streaking," and seated nearby, might be four other Firlotte cousins in one stage or another of their hairdo transformation.

Meanwhile, Mom would be racing from the kitchen stove, where she monitored scalloped potatoes baking, down to our basement preserves cellar, fetching bottles of pickles, beets and jam preserves, then back to her black sink where she soaped a new head while instructing me to cut some bread, set the table for all the waiting ladies and brew the tea. For that day, this was the second meal eaten by the wedding party, for I had earlier put together a bunch of grilled cheese sandwiches alongside Mom's dish of pan-fried potatoes. That's where and when I also learned to serve up lunches on a tray, piled high.

No assistants prepped the heads for Mom. She did everything. She even had to leave a group of wet and curled women sitting on our couches while she fulfilled yet another of her duties—getting to the church on time for the wedding rehearsal! Mom was still the church organist. Fortunately for that wedding weekend, nobody died, because Mom would have been required to play their last organ piece as well.

But I have to tell you about how we made tea for many. We never brewed the usual "pot of tea" because we never had a teapot as such! We boiled fresh water in the big kettle on the stove—which meant the stove had to be stoked with wood for a hot fire—and all that was usually my job. Then I'd put a handful of tea leaves into our big old, white granite mug, pour in the freshly boiling water and let it all steep 'till the brew was really dark. Then I'd stir up the tea leaves and pour some of the steeped tea into cups, adding more hot water if that's how the ladies liked it. With the big kettle on the stovetop for hot water—ensuring plenty of tea—all I needed to do was keep topping up the granite mug after throwing in handfuls of tea leaves.

But I also had another important job helping Mom, and boy, did I learn a lot! It was always my job to keep an eye on the containers of shampoo and creme rinse that she used when shampooing. Those gallon jugs under the

Margo's Beauty Bar sink looked good enough to drink. The concentrated shiny honeyed liquid poured like molasses when I turned the heavy jug upside down to fill Mom's measuring container. I wanted to drink the gulping, bubbling gobs as they funnelled out. I tried once. Not a good idea!

Depending on the thickness or thinness of the customer's hair, the amount of creme rinse used and the length of time setting varied. Too heavy a concentration of the rinse on thin hair rendered the texture flat and unmanageable for styling. Even worse, should the creme rinse remain on longer than two minutes, the hair would be left with no body, thus not able to maintain a wave or curl for any decent time. Not enough creme rinse concentration and length of time on thick, heavy hair would leave the hair tangled and dull. Overbrushing then leads to electrified hair—real bad for hair setting and styling.

Once the proper amounts and correct timing were calculated, Mom was always absolutely certain to thoroughly rinse all of the creme rinse out of the hair. She taught me that leaving any of it in for a long time attacked the hair roots. She always said that hair requires a natural air environment to remain healthy. I never touched anyone's hair, but I never forgot all I picked up from listening to and watching her.

Along with wearing all the hats of a hairdressing shop owner and church organist, Mom had to take time out to play Dad too. We had no red and green signal lights in our house directing where to be or which way to go, but she truly could chew gum and run at the same time. From when I was knee high to a grasshopper, I learned to follow behind her. I got to figure out real early that you just couldn't wait for anybody else to do small chores, otherwise you'd be left far behind.

Guess I learned early that if each of us didn't get in there and do stuff, it might not get done at all and we'd all be out of luck.

One of my favourites of Mom's good paying customers was Josie. Actually, she was Aunt Josie, the second wife of my Grand-Uncle Herman Ultican. I always prepared myself as Mom asked Josie, "Can I get you something to eat, Josie?" Of course, the reply always came, "No, Margaret dear, that's kind of you to ask, but I ate just before I left, not hungry one tiny bit." That being one heck of a mouthful, because before Josie's hair got rolled, she'd be sitting at the table having already eaten the potato scallop and bread and pie and saying, "I've always said, Margaret makes the best pies in Jacquet River. That apple pie was so good, I'll take just another wee taste."

And that's how Josie got to weigh in at near three hundred pounds. Her heart was just as big. Besides, Josie was a good tipper. And too, she was always interested in me, inquiring about school and what I liked doing.

Birch Bark and an Inner Tube

Once upon a winter's night, Jack Frost came to our home in New Brunswick and left behind a minus-forty-degree chill factor. That winter was a tough one for us at home; we were on our own without Dad (though he sure was never much help for anything), and Mom was making every earned penny count—not easy with a bunch of kids.

There was not even enough wood to keep the furnace burning through that bitter-cold night. As a matter of fact, the sunlight was what we pretty much depended upon to break the afternoon chill. So, there'd been, unfortunately, never a hint that Jack Frost would actually take a bite out of our pipes. Sad to say, he did that night, leaving one huge cracked hole in our main sewer-line pipe. Which, by the way, went straight up from the basement, through our kitchen to the upstairs bathroom. Aside from the mess all over the kitchen table, we were now plumb out of our you-know-what, which meant we no longer could use the bathroom. In summer, we might have had some choices.

With no money to spare, and just like all situations those days, Mom figured the solution through how and what she created. And this crisis led her to act in the same manner of gusto and immediacy. She dressed in her warmest layers, waded into the huge old barn way in back of our house and returned some time later with a much-patched inner tube from a rubber tire. Dropping it off onto the kitchen floor, she then went back out again and ploughed her body through many feet of freshly dumped snow to the birch tree grove up the hill from the house.

When she came back, she had her arms filled with strips of birch bark peeled off the trees. Then, she produced a roll of black sticky tape. I especially remember that tape because she never failed to keep a roll in the closet. Long ago she had learned the essentials of living with little money: flour, oatmeal, potatoes and black sticky tape. But never in a month of Sundays did I guess what she'd do next. I just figured we'd be out of luck in the toilet category for a long time.

Mom cut the birch bark, held one end against the pipe where the open gap was, then turned the bark until every inch of the hole and crack got covered; holding it in place at the end, she stuck sticky black tape to fasten. Then she split the rubber tube down the middle and proceeded to wrap and stretch it all around the bark-covered sewer pipe until several layers tightly held everything. Ensuring that nothing could come loose, she completely black-taped the rubber and bark.

To this day, more than fifty years later, all remains intact. Nothing got changed and never a drop of anything ever came out. The only difference was in Mom drywalling over the visible sewer pipe when she later renovated the kitchen.

She accomplished what few others could do, even with money at their disposal. In this case, no plumber, man or money factored into the solution. Mom got the toilet working.

Teacup readings

Six

The Moon, Teacups, Crows and Vigil Lights

The Telling Moon

Maybe it all started that wonderful winter-chilled night at the Benjamin River Logging Camp that Mom had described as a "Cinderella moment" when, out on the shimmering frozen pond, she'd stood transfixed as "that moon enveloped me into its white-silver and yellow arms, and seemed to pull me inside as it hovered overtop a cathedral of silhouetted dark evergreens—like giants in white snowy coats."

From that time, it seemed that the moon never hovered far from her, or at least that's the way she always felt. Long before she got so known for her mystical ability to read the drained tea leaves in a teacup, Mom had always believed there was something special about the moon.

Thinking about her incredible ability to "see" things, and her ways of communing with nature, it occurred to me that I'd never asked her what early experience had made her realize these special sensitivities. So finally I did ask her. She sat back in her big rocker and I knew a good story was coming.

"Tommy, I went through a long period with terrible headaches. So bad, I'd hold my head over the bed at night. Nothing I did stopped the throbbing hurt, until I was visited with a message as clear as the ring of a bell. After weeks of pounding pain, very late one night I had been walking the hallway for relief, when I found myself stopping and staring into the mirror, and in the background I could see the full moon shining brightly through the bathroom window reflected off that mirror right into my eyes.

"With that, I heard a voice tell me to open the cabinet door, and upon opening it, there sitting directly on the top shelf was the blessed holy oil Father Cerois gave me just days before. I took it out. And just as I saw Father Trudel bless my little brother Gregory on the forehead as he was dying, I did the same sign of the cross, anointing my forehead with the blessed oil. And as God is my witness, the headaches stopped. Near fifty years have passed now and I've never since had a headache."

Since that time, Mom never gave another thought to the fact that folks thought she had special sensitivities. These sensitivities were just a part of her and she used this insight always to help others. Probably this honest caring is what so many folks felt about her and why they trusted her.

Teacups, Twirled and Read

Right off, you have to know that in our Culligan village surroundings of the years gone by, not only were many of us related in one way or another, we also lived just a stone's throw from each other. And we all made a point to be together for whatever reason or occasion. Nothing much got passed around that didn't get handled, seen or heard by the generations of this thickly stewed blood.

Tea was our common thread, the bond that everything got passed through and it was a frequent and common remark to say, "A cup of tea now. You'll be wanting a wee drop of tea before moving on." Or one might hear, "The tea's just steeping, so don't leave us just yet." Or sometimes, to get more of a story, you'd hear, "We'll be putting a pot on, so don't be gettin' up yet till we've had some tea together!" Another time it might be "Glad you've come by, let me just throw in a new handful (tea leaves) so we can sit while you tell me what's new."

It never mattered the time of day. Teatime started first thing every morning and the kettle only got moved to the back of the stove before bed. Yes, the evening was fading when you damped the stove (slowed the draft for the nighttime wood burning) and sipped your last tea drop at the same time.

Day to day, Mom's "teapot" was that white granite tea mug along with the ever-boiling kettle always on the ready. What changed was the food. Depending on the time of day and the season, it could be sticky buns, mocha balls or tea biscuits that got offered up. Though even Mom's tea offerings were often worth every bit as a meal, especially when a bowl of steaming chicken bouillon, meat pies and sour cream chocolate cake just as often got served up.

I remember a typical summer's evening after a rip-roaring bonfire, when the whole singing bunch of us paraded through the hayfield (crops changed every summer—potatoes, oats, barley, clover or hay) and we ended up gathered round the kitchen table for a cup of tea and, of course, a piece of pie. Visiting cousins galore! Their eyes popped at seeing Mom's spread of flaky crust lemon-meringue pies, apple pies with cinnamon and nutmeg, raisin and even strawberry rhubarb.

You'd think we'd would run out of tea leaves, with them all clamouring for extra leaves in their cups. You didn't pour with much restraint when teacup readings were in the air. "Please, no strainer!" The special celestial vibes were irresistible those nights when the late summer's new moon illuminated the sky with a soft haze. "A perfect predilection interval for private pining," as Aunt Alice would say, "when folks got amorous." So notions of poetic romance and whimsical desire also got thrown around.

Most folks wanting their teacups read usually had some personal concern or problem, so Mom would ask them to consider possible solutions while twirling their cup. In silence, of course. The readings might be just with one person, or as was more usual, it might be the family bunch or the ladies come for their hair being done—most thrilling when there was an audience!

All watched—with awe—at how Mom both separated herself from everybody at the table as well as enveloped them all. It truly was her scene. Under that spell, she was the writer, creator, designer and producer. No one dared utter a sound. A trancelike state seemed to bond Mom and her subject. All on the sidelines fell into a hush, respecting the invisible boundaries. It was always like that.

Charly's Story

As regular as Mom permitted anyone to be, Charly Frenette was a regular at having his tea leaves read. I must say, I heard many insights articulated through Mom's readings that became reality. This was going to be one of them.

Early on a full moon summer's night, Charly drove in for a visit. Though the moon was just birthing for its night, Mom agreed to read Charly's teacup. That night he seemed agitated, and Mom even asked him if he was okay.

"Just a little matter between me and Gus" was Charly's reply. Gus was Charly's boyfriend. Though everybody knew such, nobody dared speak in those terms in the 1950s, because there could be nothing worse than a homosexual. So, while Charly and Gus did their thing, it was always well hidden under the cover of night.

I'd seen that absorbed, intense look on Mom's face only occasionally when she was studying the formation of tea leaves at the cup's bottom and sides. And as clear as the bright moon's light, the cross and wheels on its side was evident as could be in the piles of tea leaves. Not a good sign. Especially when such sights are at the end of a long trail of tea leaves, as at the end of a road. Under such circumstances, Mom would say— as I had observed over the years—"The conditions are not quite right for me to continue your reading tonight."

But on that night, Charly insisted that she tell him what she saw. So she did. "Charly, tonight go home and get some rest, because what I see is unfavourable. There is an accident and someone dies."

Charly left. He drove back up the road and picked up Gus. They partied. Before the night was over, they ended up in a ditch, the car turned over. And Gus, Charly's boyfriend, was killed.

Earl's Story

Another astonishing reading was for Mom's long and dear friend, Earl Divine. She and Earl enjoyed poker playing together as much as he loved having his teacup read. As the boss for the mines in Bathurst, Earl travelled a decent amount by train, air and car. To make a long story short, Mom, on making out Earl's heap of tea leaves, saw a large set of wings, high up in the cup, not having drained down. When Earl twirled his cup, one wing was broken.

On seeing this formation of the tea leaves, she asked Earl if he had any scheduled air travel for the near future. Earl did—a trip to the West Coast with Air Canada. Mom suggested he change his plans. Now, Earl, a strong believer of Mom's forecasting, obliged her suggestion by taking the train. You may think what happened to that Air Canada flight was coincidence, but believe what you may, it crashed on landing at Toronto airport. That was in the early 1960s or 1970s, and it's apparently been the only Air Canada crash at Toronto airport that caused fatalities and injury. Mom earned a special place in Earl's life with that teacup reading.

Cousin Bobby's Story

My cousin Bobby told about the time after his graduation from high school when he had stopped by for a visit before setting off for Ontario to make his fortune.

"We had a cup of tea. Your mom then read my cup. She said I was going to travel far and wide. I said, 'That's because you know I'm going to Toronto!'

" 'Oh no,' she said. 'I mean, you're going to travel all over the world.' She showed me the ships in my tea leaves and added that she meant a life on ships. I knew in my mind that I wanted to join the navy, but I had never ever told anybody. Your mother certainly didn't know. Six months later, I joined the navy and saw much of the world. Surely enough you could say, I had a life on ships."

Mary's Story

No sooner did Mom's first cousin, Mary (Firlotte) Roy, from Montreal, come visiting home in Jacquet River than she'd be on our doorstep to see Mom. That particular evening, the kitchen seemed to be overflowing with relatives, and nothing brought a greater thrill for us than the visiting families from afar. When Mary arrived, the stove and the warming ovens were doing overtime, baking dozens of loaves of Mom's potato bread for the evening supper and sticky buns for tea, and casseroles keeping warm at the ready. But her evening baking shift didn't slow down demands from folks wanting their tea leaves read, and Mom's wonder-working, tea-steeping granite mug filled each cup several times over. That evening the warmth from the stove compared to the warmth of family in that room. It was a comfy presence I wanted to preserve forever.

As everyone drew nearer the kitchen table, clinking and clanking china cups and choruses of variations on "Lovely cup it 'tis!" were heard around the table. Sipping, swishing the tea leaves, mingled with the freshly baked smells of sizzling sweet sticky buns and fresh crusty bread cooling on the table as Mom made her way around to everyone, reading tea leaves, exchanging jokes, laughs and merrymaking. But she hadn't seen Mary in quite a time and wanted to make her feel special, so picking up Mary's teacup, she sang her a little song.

"Mary had a little lamb, and a cupful of tea leaves to read, and hopefully, with no Big Bad Wolf"

Then Mom decreed, "Mary, drink these last drops, then swirl your cup, hold on and make a wish!"

In an instant the kitchen mood abruptly switched to hushed expectancy. But when Mom picked up Mary's teacup, her face went ashen. This was so unlike her. All who were there knew the difference between Mom's playfulness and her seriousness. Finally she broke the silence by announcing, "Mary, let's you and I spend more time later and visit your tea leaves then." Not an easy shift to make. But Mary insisted on learning what this teacup held. It seemed, then, that no one breathed. Reluctantly, Mom began.

"Mary, we have a blackened formation, as you can see here, that totally blankets the cup up and down, side to side, down to the bottom. My dear, this indicates something's not all well with your health. Energy being drained from you."

It was all too evident that Mom was choosing her words carefully and spoke them slowly. Nothing could have prepared us for what Mary asked.

"Could that mean death, Margaret?"

With a pained face, Mom struggled to say, "Not necessarily so. Perhaps this is a warning of some future illness alerting you to quickly seek medical attention."

"No, Margaret," Mary blurted out while tears welled and spilled over, "it's true. Only last week I was told that I have inoperable lung cancer."

Glory be to God! A gasp went up and then tears. Just silent tears as everyone sat motionless—dumbstruck. Nobody had had any inkling of Mary's condition. Though Mom's reading of Mary's health was accurate, and a shock to us all, it didn't affect the pain and fear that Mary already was processing.

Mary died within the year. Mom mourned Mary for the rest of her own days. Mary had only been in her forties.

Patsy's Story

By now you can pretty much depend that there'll always be one teacup reading around the table not to be forgotten. While teacup reading down home was part of the sharing, "taking tea" was always akin to Holy Communion. It's a bit like a church ceremony, a blessed event of communal participation. We think of and approach teatime with more reverence than any serious clan of wine tasters. Wine tends to be of one purpose, whereas tea is an ordained part of our way of life. It's a time-honoured observance, an act that proclaims, "Nothing's more important than taking time to share right now!"

I've always felt that Mom elevated this sharing by the cherished mysterious intimacy of her teacup readings. This particular night with Cousin Patsy was no different, in her drawing us all in close to one another.

Mom understood how to conjure up the appropriate atmosphere, setting folks up for a memorable moonlit night. Patsy wasn't the only one enveloped in my mother's personal magic, so by the time Mom turned her eyes to Patsy, it seemed that Patsy was beside herself with excited anticipation when told to drain her last tea drops with a wish.

So hasty was Patsy that as she jerked her arms off the table, she spilled some tea drops. So tense and expectant was everyone by that time that a gasp arose from the group. Spilling your tea meant only one of two things: either it was a gravely ill omen, or the luck of the Irish. And looking around at everyone's faces, you'd think that Patsy had just dropped the Communion Host from the tip of her tongue. You have to know that in our day, letting fall the baby Jesus Host at the altar rail was likened to a mortal sin. It was only more sacrilegious than touching the baby Jesus Host with your teeth. We all knew that if you bit into it, you could go straight to hell should you not have had a chance to confess first.

You can imagine how severely shaken Patsy was. She managed to hand her cup to Mom, and in that instant, the tension in the room drained as Mom's face beamed in scrutinizing Patsy's cup.

"Well, well, well, just look at that! My, my, my, such a long time since I've seen the likes of it!"

Patsy couldn't contain herself hearing Mom's delighted enthusiasm, and she burst out, "What is it! For heaven's sake, Aunt Margaret, tell me!"

Mom cupped both hands around the fluted china teacup and drew closer in to the circle, pronouncing, "See, my dear, to the very top of the cup's rim, the lightly criss-crossed band of tea leaves are completely encircling the rim while all else remains at the bottom. And the bottom leaves have separated into densely packed formations with many different patterns, such as this herd of animals.

"All of which, my dear, tells of abundance and prosperity and life-giving symbols. This rim at the top surely speaks of an opportunity immediately at hand, one that offers a fortune to be made. The message, make hay while the sun shines!"

Needless to say, the questions flew left and right, probing Patsy about any imminent prospects. The only one she could think of was that time was running out for her to exercise stock options. Well, that's all anyone needed to hear and a unanimous shout went up, "There's your fortune at hand!"

"Well," Patsy mused aloud, "I could make a little off the offered option price, but who really knows? The share value could plunge the day I exercise the options."

Back at work, Patsy, as they say, bit into a fortune cookie and exercised her options. For near a year, she berated her quick decision. The share price was stuck. Then before the year rang out, the company got bid for and the shares sold for double their listed value. Patsy was not long in broadcasting that she'd made thousands and that, indeed, Mom's teacup reading had materialized.

Perhaps my nephew Brent, Mom's first-born grandson, described her special abilities and sensitivity best. (He, like the other grandchildren, always called my mom "Mamère, " a kind of loving condensation of the French, Grandmère.)

"Mamère, she is the Bay de Chaleur, the birds, the clouds and the wind. She is a child of the universe and can read the world. She knew of the future. Mamère, reading my teacups, told me years before I joined the military that she saw me in uniform over water. That was just after I'd graduated from engineering school and was working for General Motors. Six years later, I was an Air Force captain flying a jet and then a helicopter from a ship, over the ocean. She also saw my career in medicine, but there's one other thing seen by Mamère from my teacups still remaining to materialize."

John's Story

And then there was a testimony from a doubting John Partington, my sister Gail's husband, a psychology professor, who hesitantly told me his experiences.

"Every trip to New Brunswick, I enjoyed watching visitors come into your mom's kitchen to chat and most always enjoy a good lunch and get their tea leaves read. I viewed those sessions as great fun, but never felt that the messages passed on had any validity. That is, not until my turn.

"Late one night, Gail asked Mamère to read my cup. The wind suddenly changed. This happy little scene of witch-playing became real. Now it wasn't a joke. I went from an audience to a pot in the fire. I became uneasy. Felt totally transparent. My God, all I could think was—what would she see in there about me? All eyes turned on me. You see, I was only ever used to focusing on others, and I thought, 'Goddamit, I'm the psychologist!'

"And for what seemed like forever, Mamère studied the sediment as though she were gazing at jewels, turning the cup this way, that way, up and down, and saying, 'My, my, my, my, my, my.' Then with a straight back and in a confident tone, she told us what she saw: 'There was someone in a black robe who was holding something to be of help to me and bringing me good news, just in the offing.' "

John went on, "Well, she was dead on. Upon my immediate return to the university, I received a memo from the dean, who often wore a black robe, congratulating me on being granted tenure and promotion. A totally unexpected early appointment!"

But John wanted to know more, and he pressed Mom to share how she prepared herself and how she was able to interpret a shiny wet blob of tea leaves in a teacup. This is what she told him.

"I convert the symbols I see in the tea to my own language. I don't make it a practice of reading everybody's cup. I just do it sparingly. The moon's waxing and waning needs to meet people in their own particular circumstances. I get asked all the time for any inkling or hint on how to deal with a myriad of situations. Relationships, romance, finance, career and health frequently change in our lives. So many people I've known over the years, and plenty I've met only the once, come asking for some insight.

" 'Oh! We'll pay you,' they say. 'No dear, I don't do that for money,' I tell them. The folks just show up at my door. I have to say, 'Dear child, the time's not right, you watch for the full moon and only when you feel a connection, then you take a chance on that and come to see me.' "

John went on, "I wanted to know from her whether the landing of spaceships and men on the moon changed her thinking about the moon's relationship to her clairvoyance. She just looked at me thoughtfully and responded quietly.

" 'Have the tides on our Bay de Chaleur changed their shape or movement in relationship to a full moon since men walked it? I think not. Have wolves changed their howling with the full moon since men have landed on the moon? No dear, the moon's effect on the universe and all remains as strong and mysterious.' "

As I listened to John, I thought of when Mom had told me that a full moon even under the cover of heavy clouds affects all living matter here on earth. "The parts of human beings that decide moods are influenced by the moon's stance," she said. "It's not that the moon's just a romantic notion, but rather that it somehow controls our sexual drives. Over the years, I've evidenced this by reproduction in humans and animals alike."

Yes, Talking to the Crows!

Deany, Mom's first cousin and her beloved friend, came visiting with her daughter Faye, from Ontario. Faye, recounting the visit, told me what happened.

"The second evening of our stay, Margaret prepared fish cakes, and set them to panfry on the kitchen stove in the back kitchen. Anxious to chat with them while busy mixing and cutting biscuits in the front kitchen, she forgot the fish cakes. The smoke detector shocked us out of our conversation. With smoke swirling through the archway, Margaret grabbed the blackened burnt fish cakes, opened the porch door and flung them out, calling for the crows, 'Caw! Caw! Caw!' The black crows got to eat fish cakes that matched them, while Margaret cooked up a new batch, but this time with all of us standing around the stove watching."

Faye also told me an amazing story of Mom's clairvoyant sensitivity.

"In the mornings when I stayed with her, I found your mom to be much less communicative than in the evenings. But I soon came to realize this was Margaret's quiet time that she reserved for reading while nursing a cup of tea, or later, religiously feeding and talking to the crows. Yes, the crows!

"In your field off the back porch, facing the ocean, Margaret communed with three pairs of crows almost every morning. She'd invite them closer to her and each one would prance over to her. Occasionally she sang, and they responded in unison with their cawing. Before this experience, I had no idea a person could communicate so intimately with such creatures. And throughout the day on seeing the crows fly by, Margaret would sing out her special song about counting crows."

I knew about this too, but hadn't realized that anyone else had taken note of Mom's relationship with crows. Because seeing only one crow meant sorrow, she would always hurry us up in order for two people to see that one crow so then she could say, "Two crows for joy!" Other times, on seeing only one crow, Mom would be saying, "Come on now, send me another," and mostly, sure enough, a second crow would fly by, again bringing joy not sorrow. I remember the whole little ditty went something like this: One crow sorrow, two crows joy. Three crows'll bring us a letter and four crows a boy. (This would be aimed at anyone expecting a baby.) No question—for Mom, crows held a special fascination and meaning—as did most of nature.

Sanctuary Lamps and Vigil Lights

There was never a person who didn't think of Mom as a woman of faith. And over the years she expressed her faith in many different ways.

The common message in all her cards and letters that I've saved carried essentially the same thing: "Have faith in yourself, dear Tom. Though at times it dims, hang on to what little you have at those times, especially have faith that you'll always be looked after, no matter the circumstances."

The moon, stars, vigil lights, beach bonfires, northern lights and burning sanctuary light—all were external signs of her inner strength. Light was Mom's faith. Call them symbols, images or representations—these lights seemed to grow stronger with her prayers. The softly lit sanctuary lamps held the hope of life for whom or to whatever Mom's intentions were directed. The act of lighting was for her a holy instance that remembered the person or event that was prayed for. Not a thought was ever wasted. Only positive energy ever was released. Whomever she evoked those symbols of lights for seemed to know of her spiritual work and was able to draw positive power on their own, in just seeing the moon or the lights. Every good thought seemed to be multiplied.

Each sanctuary lamp cost $2.00 to burn. Surely she burned the cost of a good- sized car in just this one devotion. The burning light was a vigil for the person prayed for. No matter the ailment or cause, this person somehow knew he or she was being thought of. This act moved the desire for healing far beyond good intentions.

Mom oozed faith. In everything she'd play on the piano, you'd hear, "How this music carries me through life. It gives me joy every day!" Mom played daily on both her piano and the organ in the parlour. They stood like altars. Folks came by simply to soak up the music, and as they listened to her, their troubles seemed to fade away. Playing the piano was one of Mom's acts of faith. As was her picking wild strawberries. I knew, as others did, that receiving a bottle of those strawberry preserves, prepared so lovingly, was every bit as nurturing as receiving a bottle of holy water.

"Mamère is as close to being what I understand is Mother Nature," said her grandson Brent.

"Only a saint could do what Margaret accomplished throughout life," observed June Culligan, Mom's nurse.

"She truly lived in the presence of God," declared Mary Young, a distant relative and neighbour.

Aunt Yolanda remembered how Mom "was one of a kind, in touch with her surroundings. She brought life to who and whatever she touched."

I know different people who appreciate one thing or another; some, perhaps orchids or an ocean sunset, a painting, music arrangement or a certain time of the year. Mom's veins seemed rooted into earth. She breathed the elements. No matter how preoccupied with her business affairs, she tilled the soil. Trees and flowers were her passion. Teapots full were poured to her lilac bushes, cedar trees, honeysuckle trees, snowball bushes, tiger lilies, plum and apple trees and wandering beds of perennial flowers. Our house was always full of plants. And winter never changed that. I knew no one who could encourage plants to flourish the way that she did in below-zero weather for winter months at a time: African violets, geraniums and ferns. Gardening worked as prayer, feeding her faith. It was a faith that healed through each blossom and every delicate scent.

Faith also got wrapped up in icons for Mom. It's not that she was deadly serious over church doctrine, for church dogma came and went over the years. The only one that really stuck for life with her was the Catholic marriage vow. Though it did not stop her from doing the right thing—for her and for us. Yet it still left its sting to the end of her life. Mom's religious experience reached into designated blessed figures and events. She held a lifetime devotion to St. Ann, to the sacristy sanctuary light, to the power of holy water and to the Mass.

Each found a place at the heart of her life. Like blankets, ladders, tools and comforters, they provided the solutions for her daily life.

For Mom, faith was not just about believing in herself. It was much bigger than that. It was also about the power from outside oneself. The connections. It was the communion of relating to all the mysteries and wonders of the universe. Mom knew she "didn't ever have to understand exactly how it happened. Just that it did." The power was always available, whether from the moon, stars, earth, ocean, icons or from other people. Her wisdom flowed as a result of believing that all and everything is possible.

In the conversations with her that I taped in her later years, she spoke of the one time that she near lost all hope and faith—the dark time when Dr. Dumont, twice, helped to pull her through. She believed in her doctor. Listened to him. Through his wisdom, she healed over time and gradually emerged out of severe depression.

Only after recovery did she fully understand the cause of her depression. "Bang, bang, bang, bang, that's how it happened," she said. Her first four babies all within four years. The depression she suffered was caused directly from sheer exhaustion and loneliness. And because of her difficult life with an alcoholic and abusive husband, no companionship or core relationship existed. Her bleakest and lowest point ever was the two years following her fourth pregnancy. Mom recovered with the help of her doctor and the use of all her blessed icons. Prayer and faith returned her to sanity.

Feeding the crows, wishing upon the new moon, bending over to pick up a four-leaf clover, burning the sanctuary lamp, dropping to her knees in prayer and packaging a box of baking for others were Mom's acts of faith "that always removed me from feeling sorry for myself," she said. "A good turn gets better return than money in the bank."

Mom with one bake after another!

Seven

Memories Round the Kitchen Table

As long as I can remember, the kitchen was always at the centre of our life. The whole kitchen including front and back pantry was bigger then most neighbourhood homes. Laughter and talk was as much a part of the snack or meal as Mom's home cooking. And so often when the cooking and eating were done and cleaned away, that floor got cleared of anything not nailed down, and it served up good ol' fashioned square-dancing times. Seems there was almost always someone to play music and even to sing. There never was a body coming to our home who ever got missed being served a filling hot dish, then enjoying some time for step-square-and round dancing, or at the very least drinking a cup of tea with us, along with some good home baking in our kitchen. In fact, the kitchen was often the place where most everything happened. It became a memory storehouse for many of us.

Bobby Culligan went way back to early memories when he told me, "The first time I ever danced was in Margaret's kitchen. Shy, nervous, two left feet, but Margaret came by and told me how well I danced and how good I looked out on the floor. That felt some nice!"

Over a meal, it never took much to get Mom's grandsons talking about their times at our home. Bobby 's memory got some of the others started on their memories, and I enjoyed listening to them. Brent Culligan, Mom's grandson, mused over the many ways that being with Mom made him feel warm and secure, and how, over the years, he always knew that he could call her whenever he felt troubled, puzzled over his future, or just wanted to hear her voice. He said that a call to her felt like he was in the kitchen right next to her. Then he laughed and admitted that no matter where he'd be, thinking of my mom always brought memories of the taste of her wild-strawberry jam with fresh crusty bread and "her playing the piano and singing and just loving us all."

Mark Culligan, another grandson, was listening to us and shifted his chair closer, so I knew he had a story to tell. He said that listening to the others, he was fondly reminded of a special time with Mamère when he was only twelve years old.

"It was 1976 and it was my very first trip by myself. In Quebec City my mom put me on a train to Campbellton, where I was to meet Mamère for a three-week stay on the Bay de Chaleur. When I arrived, there was no one at the station to meet me. I got real scared, but I remembered to stay put. When I finally saw Mamère approaching, I was overcome with a feeling of relief. She was with a friend who I don't remember, but I do remember how proudly she hugged me and introduced me as her grandson. There was a huge paper mill in the town and I remember even now that awful rotten smell. Sulphur, Mamère explained, and then assured me that it would dissipate as we got closer to home.

"It was mid-July and the drive down home will stay with me forever. She knew everyone in each home along the way. I remember her telling me little bits of history and stories, like pointing out the significance of Heron Island (in the middle of the Bay de Chaleur) settled by pioneers in the 1700s. As the settlement grew, it wasn't long before the twinkling lights from the farmhouses served as a lighthouse just off what was a treacherously shallow shoreline. Then, as we approached Jacquet River, and crossed over the ol' iron bridge where the ocean comes in, I remember being overwhelmed by the most amazing mixture of smells: sea salt, sweet wheat and potato stalks, all wafting in the warm air through the open car windows. From that point, I remember Mamère's increased sense of pride as she told stories on every piece of property, with special animation for where her Firlotte grandparents and her parents, the Boudreaus, lived. And she even pointed to the huge church on the hill where she played the organ starting at the age of fourteen.

"As we neared her house, her tone changed when she laid down the law I was to follow during my stay. Especially, to take off my shoes on coming into the house, making my bed first thing on arising and not to go into the potato storage shed.

"I was a frightened twelve-year-old boy, who had very low self-esteem from living in my own violent, alcoholic home. But as the days passed, I became more comfortable with Mamère, knowing that I would not get yelled at or hit when I made a mistake. It was the best and most enlightening trip in my journey through life. From that visit, I began to develop some understanding for my father's drinking, and realized that everyone had a potential for being good. I left New Brunswick feeling loved and high on life. That feeling started changes in my way of seeing family.

"Probably my most vivid memories will always be of staying up late at night, listening to stories of Mamère's childhood in Jacquet River, beside her grandparents' farm. She reminisced about backfield skating rinks and the ski hill. And all the while that she's talking, we're sitting at the kitchen table beside Mamère's pantry filled with wonderful aromas of freshly baked breads, bottles and bottles of warm homemade jam, hot steamy pies and especially those sticky buns!"

Hearing loving memories of visits with us borders on the phenomenal for me. Nothing of the kind existed with grandparents in my childhood. My Grandmother Culligan (Momo) provided thousands of dollars in cash, properties and land to our family. She had a generous heart. However, I never really got to know her, maybe because I have no recollection of her touching me or even talking to me. For absolute certainty, Momo never danced with me, made cookies for me, let alone baked a pie or even served me even a glass of milk. No warm relationship existed. Yet, despite the distance I feel, she did provide our family such a spectacular home. As to my mother's mother, that relationship was a slight notch above Momo's.

It was all so wonderfully different in our home. Family and relatives with all their children shared their lives with us frequently—especially for summers when these children lived with us for weeks at a time. We truly each own a piece of that kitchen table for all the years that we shared Mom's cooking, good talk and laughter. Our place resembled a central train station. At any one time there would be aunts, uncles, brothers, sisters, grandchildren and first cousins checking out or unpacking. I simply couldn't tell who was walking upstairs. Bing, bang, cling, clang, yahee-de-dah, yelling, sniffling, pouting, panting, smacking, arguing, gulping or munching—these were a few of the familiar sounds heard throughout the summers.

Ah, The Food!

Experiences varied. Pizza made from scratch, piping-hot fresh corn boils, luscious chicken bouillon plump with dumplings, laughing fun with taffy pulls, finger-lickin' fudge making and oh! the smell and the taste of maple syrup-baked apples. Those were only a few of the goodies that our family and visitors shared. Even the odd Christmas, when my siblings and their children packed into their cars and chanced the rugged winter driving through snow and sleet and icy roads, was fun— just so we could all be together.

First cousin Susan Priddy told me she'd never forget the lobster feeds at Mom's kitchen table. Even though she was just a youngster in the early 1960s, she had no trouble recalling the sounds and smells of the time.

"When Aunt Margaret covered the table and chairs with newspapers and provided us with hammers to crack open the lobsters, we knew the feast was almost ready. Newspapers everywhere, beer and booze flowed and cousin Henry, Tom's brother, was up to his trick of making a hypnotized lobster walk on our heads, while we screamed and tried to jump away. No one ever knew how he did that. Aunt Margaret would be manning the steaming pots, and the lobster smell of the ocean mingled with the smell of cigar smoke from my dad."

Susan laughingly recalled how Mom managed to keep all the kids quiet with bottles of pop—a rare treat for us—and how we were sent to sit on the kitchen stairs and watch, while staying out of the way of the steaming pots of boiling lobsters. Susan even recalled the pantry full with loaf upon loaf of potato bread, and rows of pies ready to complete that great meal.

"In my mind's eye, I always picture your home and that kitchen when reading *Anne of Green Gables*. The smell of Aunt Margaret's home was a mix of fresh baking, cigarette and cigar smoke, hairspray, and oh yes, those boiling lobsters."

And the Turkey Not Even Yet Touched

The kitchen table was also witness to that tragic Easter weekend that my dad's double first cousin, Mary McCarron, remembered vividly. And when she talked about it, I recalled it too. Mom had invited Mary and her husband, Albert, to an Easter dinner along with Papa (Uncle Herman) and Aunt Josie, Aunt Annie, cousins Cully and Ada, as well as Walter and Yvonne, Tom's godparents, and their children. Mary sighed as she recalled that weekend.

"My God, what a crowd around the table, and the turkey not even yet touched. Suddenly, my husband Albert just up and dropped dead at the head of the table! A massive heart attack!

"Long after Albert's sudden death, your mom would often come to visit me, bringing the usual baking she always so generously shared. Her charming ways always gave me a lift."

I was fifteen on that shocking occasion when Albert died. As a matter of fact, it was me that Albert fell into, just as I was standing behind him holding two baskets full of Mom's homemade buns. As he went down, so did I. Poor Albert lay half slid under the table. And, oh my God, the commotion! Everybody, including Albert's sister, Aunt Josie, tried digging into Albert's throat, thinking maybe he'd choked. Finally I decided to bring some quiet dignity to Albert's situation by pulling him out from under the table, and with help, into another room where we could cover him with a blanket and close the door.

Our local undertaker, Lloyd McMillan, arrived two hours later, followed shortly thereafter by Father Miller and Dr. Desjardins.

Meanwhile, we all stood, sat and moved in a kind of shocked daze. The cooked turkey remained in the blue granite roasting pan on top of the opened oven door, and the just served-up plates remained untouched on the table.

I can't recall how long, but it took me a heck of a long time before I could ever even think of eating turkey again.

Tire Ruts and Bruised Apples

By now the storytelling was in full swing. Seemed those were the evenings when everyone had a story to tell. Bobby Culligan told me another one.

"Margaret was always nice. But when something didn't please her, you would hear about it. One summer evening, a bunch of us home on vacation arrived to do a little partying in the kitchen with some of your family, also home on vacation. Your mother arrived home later in the evening, not too impressed with the lot of us. And, I guess, for good reason

"I think just maybe too many quarts of Moosehead beer went down a little too easy. Everybody was in a hell of a hurry gathering up stuff to reach Roharty's Point first to start a bonfire. Stan Culligan, a cousin, thought he'd be the first. So we sped out the laneway, past Stan who, in his haste, had backed his car onto the lawn and smack into your mom's apple tree. Left heavy tire ruts in the lawn and a heap of bruised apples on the ground. Caused one mean dent in his fender. You probably remember the song we composed that night, to the tune of, ' In the Shade of the Old Apple Tree.' The first line went 'You could tell by the tint of her hair, that Margo was cross as a bear…' "

Braving The "Bay de Froid"

The Partington family—my sister Gail, her husband, John, and their sons and daughter—made it "down East" faithfully too. John recalled a visit when it seemed the really warm summer days would never arrive.

"One summer day after several days of not yet having had our first swim in the 'Bay de Froid' (that year anyway), the boys Sean and Eric were getting mopey. So Mamère put on her faded blue bathing suit and marched us all down through the potato fields to the beach. We still couldn't get into the water past our tootsies. There I was, yelping with my boys, when we saw Mamère wading out past her knees, the icy water quickly covering up those wicked blue varicose veins. Then, after dipping her hand into the water and blessing herself, she just plunged in. I swear, the shock could have killed her, because the water temperature hovered near the high fifties.

"But it worked. That's all it took for Sean and Eric to follow suit. I finally got in and—quickly—out too. I tell you, there's nothing speaks louder than action.

"After Mamère was swimming with the boys, we gathered driftwood and lit up a roaring fire to thaw out. The goose bumps never quite disappeared. Soon we built a wind shelter using logs and an ol' piece of heavy canvas. The boys were happy. Me, I was thrilled that our family vacation had finally kicked in, all thanks to Mamère.

"On another visit when the boys were getting rangy after a couple of rainy days, in the late afternoon, your mom noted the wind shifting back from the east and predicted that the weather would clear by suppertime. Instead of our usual gathering at the kitchen table, she proposed supper on the beach. And just as sure as daylight appears, the sun broke out of the clouds, exposing the tops of the mountains across the bay.

"Talk about excitement! We each carried something down to the beach, walking through the still-soaked fields. We were lucky to have (neighbour and cousin) George Culligan's newly dug potatoes, for they were famous in New Brunswick—a feast in themselves. We boiled a huge pot of them, then steamed cod on a salted rock in the big blue granite roasting pan—and did all this cooking on an open beach fire.

"Sitting cross-legged around the fire, we couldn't have felt more native. With the fire, salty ocean spray, freshly dug potato field and our cooking feast, it was hard to tell what smelled stronger!

"That was Mamère again—showing us how to celebrate being fully alive with only the simplest things."

By now, John was in full swing again with memories, as he helped himself to another serving of scalloped potatoes. Nobody loves to eat more than John. At the table while eating a meal, John's already talking of the next meal's menu. Still talking about the food that he loved, John laughed as he told me this one.

"My first visit home with Gail was to meet the family and, of course, to be judged as to my worthiness to be Gail's boyfriend. The second night, Mamère baked and served fresh homemade bread, new potatoes and crocked beans in molasses and onion.

"Later that evening, Gail and I went to a bonfire at Roharty's Point. Every time I tried to embrace Gail and steal a kiss, I would fart uncontrollably. Later, when Gail told Mamère, she just hooted with laughter. In that moment, I could see how open she was. And later, in a quiet time, she also let me know that she would be happy with Gail's choice of a man, just as she had been with daughter Ann choosing Art. His being a Protestant like me was not an issue.

"A few days into that visit, the house became bedlam when Mamère hosted an open house after Theo Culligan's funeral. I remember that he was another neighbour and your dad's first cousin. In retrospect, I can conjure up a blur of music, with piano, electric organ and guitar, animated conversations, shrieking laughter, food and more food, and booze. And I'll never forget the heaps of dirty dishes that I had—in a weak moment—volunteered to keep washing. Amidst all this, and literally in the centre of it, was Mamère welcoming, chatting, singing, playing piano, dancing and consoling. Mamère's energy and hostessing seemed to go on forever. She never got tired. Never went to bed. She was always the last one working. Talk about energy!

"That last day of that first visit left me with wonderful memories of Mamère. I was driving back to London, Ontario alone. Gail remained home for another week before returning to London to pack, and then leave for a year to nurse in California. Her mom had made a huge lunch of homemade-bread sandwiches with cold roast beef, bits of green onion and mustard for the trip. Then she asked me to take her up to Campbellton on my way. To this day I don't know whether she had truly legitimate reasons for going there or whether she knew I needed support. It sure was a great help to me. Every time I'd get engulfed by a wave of sadness at leaving Gail, she'd say, 'I know, dear, it's hard leaving.' I felt that she was my friend and ally from that day.

"On visits in later years with Gail and our family, sometimes I'd awaken before anyone else—I thought—and steal quickly down the back stairs. Halfway down, I'd see Mamère sitting alone at the kitchen table playing solitaire with a half full 'water' glass beside her, surrounded by bursting shiny loaves of potato bread, pastry-covered pies and trays of the sticky buns that we all loved.

"The telltale purple spot in the middle of her forehead explained the situation. She'd stayed up all night baking for us and drinking gin to keep going. Soon after, my children would come giggling and tumbling down the stairs and rushing to the kitchen table, to be welcomed by Mamère with the offer of anything they wanted for breakfast.

"They'd end up eating thickly cut slices of fresh bread, cold roast beef and those sticky buns. Sights, smells and tastes that went beyond even dreams. Could there ever be a better grandmother, despite the gin? Don't think I haven't thought, just maybe, I should have burned vigil lights too.

"Think of the times your mom did all this summer after summer. Her house invaded by uncles, aunts, cousins, Gene's, Billy's, Henry's and our kids. It wasn't enough that she was doing hair, hurrying back and forth to play the church organ for every parish event and out on the road selling Avon products. In the mid-sixties, she also took on a job with the Dominion Bureau of Statistics doing house-to-house survey work. She also had to patiently watch the house getting abused by our sometimes-unruly children and even their irresponsible parents. When did she ever have a summer vacation? Is it any wonder, in her final years, she hadn't learned much about downtime?

"The way in which she welcomed us home, and later said goodbye and watched us leave, always left a lasting impression. We'd arrive very early in the morning, after driving all through the night and day with kids asleep in the back of the station wagon. Mamère seemed always to know our arrival time.

"There she'd be on the back stoop crying out, 'Mercy me, look at those big fellas, my, my, my, hello dear (big hug for Gail). Now come on in for some breakfast. I just made some fresh (always a table full). Incredibly, each one of us felt special, genuinely welcomed and excited to be there. We also felt the fresh coolness of the morning air, the dewy-wet grass, the smell of saltwater and the sharp, clear edges of everything in sight. The air itself seemed cleaner and sharper than anywhere else.

"How could she create such an at-ease atmosphere, when in her mind, surely she knew, the floors were going to get dirty daily for weeks, and there would be spills on furniture for sure. After all, she'd already once done all this with nine kids of her own. With bunches of kids and parents there would be friction if not outright fighting, leaving her big kitchen in an uproar until nine every night.

"Mamère was either a great actor or a saint who truly loved her kids and grandchildren. Just before we'd leave on our scheduled departure morning, we'd hear the piano playing from the front parlour. Off by herself when she felt lonely for us going. It made me feel sad, as I would picture her alone at the piano long after we had left.

"Then as the bags got dragged through the house and out to the car, she'd always get Gail to try on some skirt, sweater or slacks that she said didn't fit her anymore. She just had to send you off with a part of her…then the long wave from the front door and then through the window.

"But we could barely see her by then for our flooding tears. Those goodbyes were tough on us. How must *she* have felt?

"God, I'm crying right now!"

Crisp waters of our backyard

Eight

The Bay de Chaleur—
Icy Water and a
Roaring Fire

I'll always remember those early summer mornings when I lay half-awake listening to the sounds wafting through my bedroom window. There was the steady *putt, putt, putt* of the local fishermen's boats as they headed out for their daily catch on Bay de Chaleur, while high above them the squealing, squawking seagulls rallied behind. Then visions of that cold water with me floating and bobbing on top of the waves would almost lull me back to sleep.

But then I'd spring out of bed and drop to my knees in Morning Prayer, with my eyes shut tight and my head bowed towards the small wooden crucifix above my bed. I always prayed three Hail Mary's, then Our Father and the Glory to be…asking protection for Mom, for me and for our family all this day long. Once satisfied that I'd been heard, I'd make the sign of the cross with one hand while making up my bed with the other, so as not to waste any time.

Back then, we never lingered in our bedroom. There was always lots to do on a summer day. Usually Mom would be well into her day by the time each of us slid out of bed. Often, on looking out my window, I'd see a bent-over body moving slowly back and forth in the middle of the small field on the edge of the shore. She'd be clutching her pail, full to the brim of those sweet, tiny berries for eating and preserving.

That was Mom picking wild strawberries.

Before returning back up the field to the house, she'd disappear down the steep bank, strip down to her panties and bra, and then march directly into the ocean, pausing only to scoop up a handful of saltwater to make the sign of the cross. Didn't matter whether the water was frigid, jelly-fished, frosted, waves over your head or seaweed thick, she did her thing.

Growing up in our Culligan village in New Brunswick, overlooking the Bay de Chaleur, only rarely did I ever see any other neighbour's mom or dad on the beach, let alone swimming in the ocean. Seems like we spent our childhood with Mom on the beach. Her time with us on the ocean's edge was most always evenings and into the dark night. This was for obvious reasons, because she worked on her feet all day, whether it was fixing up heads of hair in her own Beauty Bar, cooking and baking in the kitchen, hitting the road as a travelling Avon saleswoman, or playing the church organ for weddings, funerals or whatever.

It was good that we had six bedrooms because especially in summer, we needed to find sleeping space for all the relatives and their kids. Some of those sweltering nights, we—that is, our American cousins and us—slept on our covered veranda, which wrapped round three-quarters of the house, with the south-facing veranda being the favourite. Underneath the hanging, stuffed moose head, there was a very long wooden-back bench. Two could cozily sleep there. Rolled-up mattresses accommodated the rest.

No summer passed without Aunt Camilla, Uncle Art, Patsy and Veronica motoring up from New Jersey, and Aunt Tookie, Uncle Leon, Ann Marie and Junior coming from Berthierville, Quebec. They were regulars. Mixed in over the years was Uncle Paul, Aunt Ruth and their eight kids driving all the way from Terrace Bay, northern Ontario. Uncle Hubert, Aunt Yoland and their three kids also came from Terrace Bay, as well as Uncle Stan, Aunt Trudy and Glen. In the earlier summers we'd get Uncle Adrien, Aunt Audrey, Ann Marie and Patsy and a "whale" of others like Grand-Aunt Aupal, Effie Audit and children, Irene Firlotte, Grand-Uncle John and Aunt Amanda Robichaud.

I loved meeting and getting to know aunts, uncles and cousins who lived in what I thought were faraway exotic places. Mom always agreed. "I loved the company. Having my family around gave me support and encouragement. And in the earliest of years when times were tough and you kids were small—the early 1950s—their visits provided much-needed help. They would fill the kitchen cupboards with grocery supplies. I didn't mind the cooking. That made me happy. And I know my brothers and sisters loved the opportunity to vacation on the ocean. After all, they came from here."

Mom worked hard in her own beauty salon located at the side of the house—Margo's Beauty Bar. The end of a day arrived only when she had brushed out the last head. Being way north meant longer summer-lit days. Mom took advantage of this daylight frequently. I knew the telltale signs when we'd all be off to the beach for a night out. She'd line up the large empty gallon vinegar bottles by the kitchen sink where she mixed crystal Kool-Aid packages by the gallon. I smashed the ice cubes to fit through the skinny bottlenecks. Everything else was made ready to go with all hands helping.

Looking like a ragged army column with no height restrictions, we all marched in between the ploughed drills of the fields down to the beach. Even the littlest one got to carry a share of the night's requirement—usually something soft, like towels, blankets or empty pots. Mom was wise as to who not to load up, because the untrained city kids were a bit like the ol' grey mare that was in sight of the barn door. At the approach to the bank where you first got a peek of rolling waves, some cousins just plain forgot they'd be holding anything. That meant even the butter might hit the ground before we got to use it on our corn.

Depending on how the wind blew, even before sighting any beach, the visiting cousins could barely contain their elation on hearing the roar of the smashing ocean waves. Oftentimes, four- to five-foot crashing waves could drown out the sounds of screaming, yelping kids half a field away. I often thought our relatives never worried about their little ones because they knew that Mom somehow always knew where everyone was.

"It's not necessary to lose track of anything. Devise a way that satisfies your needs," Mom said to me more than once. And years later, she would tell me how she'd always be counting heads in the water—even under the bright moonlight during those late-night swims. She never lost any of us.

The first order of business in landing at the shoreline was gathering driftwood for the night's bonfire. Each previous winter had its own delivery system supplying the shoreline with abundant pulp logs that had cut loose from floating lumber booms. Washed up on shore by the shifting tides were saltwater-bleached trees of every size, and loose branches in thousands of twisted configurations. The middle of the bonfire got built first by stacking three- to five-foot logs on top of one another, teepee style. With a good five-foot diameter wood tent constructed, we then formed the outer rim with gigantic logs leaning into each other, finishing off the "teepee." The outside logs could sometimes stand twelve to fifteen feet tall.

Mom served as the chief architect for the evening's construction, making darn sure that the about-to-be raging fire got built plenty distant from the very dry bank grasses and the coming night tide line. She certainly didn't want a grass fire blowing its way up to our home. Then again, she had to be sure the upcoming tide would not float out the newly constructed teepee before it got to burn. In the past, we had in fact experienced all those things, being just lucky enough the wind was blowing west, away from the house towards the beach, and not the other way. And yes, more than once, the logs floated away before we got to light them.

We all got scattered up and down the beach. What a sight! Especially when we were mostly in the six- to ten-year range. The American cousins beamed at being able to lift, drag and pile on their driftwood for the night's bonfire. Legends got passed on through this ritual. Like how someone's mom or dad wrestled a whole drifted tree onto the fire in a contest, the winners, of course, getting to sleep outside under the stars.

Don't know that any town or city could design or create a playground anything near our Bay de Chaleur beach. Every day delivered new goodies to our shore, coming from the ocean bottom or floating on top. Bottles, tree stumps, broken lobster traps, fishing nets, buoys and "stuff" simply turned up every day. Every bit was fascinating. And with every changing tide the ocean's bottom swooshed up seashells and seaweed of every possible size, colour and texture. At the top of any beach visit had to be digging in the sand. My God, there's just no bottom to this stuff! All of us kids just dug bucketfuls by the hour, building mountains, castles, towns, wells and just plain ol' holes to bury each other.

Sea Kelp, Moss and Mussels

When the tide receded low enough, Mom led us to the newly exposed point of gleaming ash purple rocks, covered in rubbery sea kelp and silky moss, to pick mussels. She made certain we picked only the mussels still buried under the water, taking no chances that either the air or seagulls had contaminated a single one. But if we were not immediately on site picking as soon as the water receded, those hungry squawking gulls would get there first.

It was what the gulls dropped in the area that Mom feared most, not what they grabbed in their beaks. Mostly, the night's pickings would last only a few minutes with all our cousins helping out. Some of them were squeamish about dipping their hands in the slimy, slippery green sea moss to pluck out a mussel. But heck, they're easy to detach with a quick pull of the wrist. In a plentiful mussel harvest, I could fetch six or more in one scoop because they'd formed into a tight ball. Our special pot for cooking the mussels and its eighteen-inch height could hold enough for all of us. Once that ol' blackened aluminum pot filled up, I covered over the top few inches with handfuls of thick kelp and seaweed. Then I mixed it all through the pot with salty ocean water, making it ready for the night's boil.

Now we were ready to swim, rock and roll. Mom's siblings were of the same stock. We all crossed ourselves and directly ducked into the water with never a hesitation. Then, as now in my life, I've never witnessed any other folks arriving at the beach to swim and jump into the ocean no matter the condition, without even so much as a pause.

Let me tell you, I learned early to follow through with what's intended, and to do it with gusto and purpose. So, should any faint-hearted soul follow me to the water's edge, you'll have to expect to keep on plunging through the water until we're in over our heads.

Mom's "Tricks"

More fun was had when we had Mom's sisters pumping alongside. When my back was turned to them, I could never recognize who was issuing the orders. Joking or not, my first cousins called them the "control sisters." Whatever their method, Mom and her sisters preferred having us kids shaking and moving our bodies to stuffing them.

Though their voices were darn near the same, there was a huge gap of fifteen years between Mom and her youngest sister, Aunt Camilla. Aunt Tookie (Clara) being only three years younger than Mom, could have passed as her identical twin. In this era of the mid-fifties, Mom was forty-six, Aunt Tookie forty-three, and Aunt Camilla thirty-one. Yet each one had that same five-foot-five-inch firm, strong body.

Mom's beach routines were famous to all who knew her. We'd have made great competition as the most colourful, acrobatic family television show next to the old "Beverly Hillbillies." It was Billy Russell, a local lobster fisherman, who coined Mom's beach exercising as "tricks," telling Urban Devereaux, a neighbouring cousin up the beach one day, "You'd not believe da sight of de old girl today! Just passed Margaret down the beach shakin' and vibratin' her tricks and scarin' the hell outta the mussels and gulls right off the beach!"

Even during Mom's last visit with us to the beach in her ninetieth year, she worked her routine. She started by standing completely upright; then, with her feet spread about twelve inches apart, she'd wiggle her body to ensure that all knots were loosened. Then, with a loud sigh, she'd slowly raise her arms to better touch the sky, while lifting her body onto her toes so that they dug down into the sand. With extended arms, straight at the elbow and wrist, she'd lower them down over her head, past her chest, thighs and knees while carefully holding her head, neck and shoulders in between her two extended arms. She'd reach her toes with her fingers, never once breaking at the knees, and hold that pose for a count of eight. Then she'd slowly return to standing erect.

Next, with scarcely a breath, she'd start all over again with the wiggle to loosen up some more. These tricks were repeated at least six times. After this, she went on to her second set of exercises. Standing with hands on the waist, she slowly twisted her body all the way turning left, then to the right, starting over again by bending at the waist to the left and then to the right, never forgetting to wiggle the body in between each new set, while continuing to let out deep sighs and take in deep fresh salt-air gulps. Ending the body tricks, we'd all kick into the sand for a jog up to George's beach and back, three or four times. That sure served to open the lungs and pump up the heart.

Afterwards we'd all plunge back into the saltwater for a quick dip, usually just in time for the slow sinking of the red fiery ball of sun setting behind the Gaspé Mountains. We could still count on at least another hour of daylight after the sun dropped below those mountains. That served up a glowing candle-light setting for us to dine. It was a brilliant light show of the vast expanse of ocean and sky. I guess we all have our own favourite sunsets. I remembered mine in how I can taste the salt from my nostrils, feel sand between my toes and the sensation of my skin tightening over with goosebumps, all inducing me into a wondrous trance. Just recalling those familiar, happy routines on the beach with Mom returns those warm feelings and goosebumps to me all over again—summer nights too awesome for words.

Did you ever try lighting a fire in thirty-mile-an-hour winds blowing directly off the Atlantic Ocean? Easterly winds at that! Though we had many a sunset with a calm ocean, there were just as many stormy sunsets with turbulent waves and winds to hurricane level. During our years of living on the Atlantic shore, I bet we got to see and feel everything an ocean delivers.

But nothing, except an all-out drenching downpour or full-blown hurricane, stopped us from the night's highlight treat of a roaring bonfire! Our American cousins were always given the honour of firing up the stacked, dried straw under the teepee of logs. The strong winds swirled those first smoke fumes right up our nostrils and into our eyes, giving us our first happy tears of the evening's fun. Those first flickering flames and pungent smoke smells always gave us shivers of excitement. As a kid, not even the "Lone Ranger" movies surpassed the sensation derived from a night around the roaring bonfire.

Funny Thing About Food and Music

The mussels could be eaten when the water boiled over the pot, and hissed as it hit the fire in the burning logs. We watched the mussels on top opening up, the meat inside the shells now ochre yellow, and changed from slimy jelly to firm meat. With care and anticipation, we gingerly hooked the pot out of the fire by its red-hot handle, always mindful to use thick crooked-cane driftwood so it wouldn't get burned right through.

Funny thing about food, didn't matter how fancy the spread Mom prepared—like maybe ham sandwiches—the best by far were the hot dogs we got to stick onto long, whittled spears of driftwood branches, and then poke them in the fire to sizzle and blacken. On our beach, no hot dog or bun was ever wasted by falling into the hot coals. Those were the tastiest. This was probably because they were coated with more than a little sand and ashes along with the mustard and ketchup.

Aunt Camilla had been a volunteer Girls' Scout leader in New Jersey. She was a natural for campfires. With high cheekbones and a wide mouth like her two sisters (Mom and Aunt Tookie), Aunt Camilla sure was a beauty! Her clear, olive skin and twinkling green eyes, tall dancing agility and sweet melodic voice set her apart from all others. But our oceanside perch made a far different setting than their country camps, and she loved the beach. She played the pot drums and spoons as well as Mom. As a kid, I was sure that Aunt Camilla and Mom knew every song written and could play every instrument.

After the wonderful food, it was time for music. And that's about when the bonfire would be at its raging peak, sparking high into the dark night, sending smoke signals out of sight. Adding dry seaweed covered us with an umbrella of thick white smoke that spurted out red burning cinders. When the salty driftwood smoke stuck to my skin, I felt as if I was wearing the ocean's overcoat and a part of the seashore too, probably much like my ancestors, who lived and participated in these bonfires rituals three hundred years earlier.

Aunt Camilla choreographed the Indian Wahoo Dance for us to circle the fire with her pot drumming. One dance we never missed, all singing through bursting lungs, was "When the Saints Go Marching In." Uncle Stan, Mom's youngest brother, and Uncle Paul, her eldest brother, were the best and loudest playing the spoons, giving us the Acadian square-dancing version for the evening.

The song to end all songs, even more so than our own "On Moonlight Bay" and "Goodnight Irene," was our harmonized "frog" composition:

> *"There's a frog on the log,*
> *on the hole,*
> *in the bottom of the sea, (repeat)*
> *There's a hole,*
> *there's a hole,*
> *there's a hole in the bottom of the sea…"*

Well, you get the idea.

"Oh my Margaret dear, can you believe this Bay de Chaleur! Kids, this is something you'll never forget in all your lifetime, lying here under what has to be God's paradise, for there's nothing anywhere in the world like what we have this night."

That was Aunt Camilla. She adored the spell of these summer bonfire nights. As young as eight, it always seemed to me that everyone—even Mom— left troubles at the end of the field where we landed on the beach for a night's fun. I could have slept all night on the beach. And we did too—a bunch of times. Though mostly we all tramped and stumbled back sometime after midnight to our beds. Every one of us breathed and smelled of roasted, smoked driftwood, and tasted of salt. Going through the fields to home, under the cover of stars and dancing northern lights and moonlight, were times when Mom created—out loud—some of her best poetry. Here's one that I especially liked.

GET GOING, MAGGIE

So cheer up, Maggie
Winter's here, but spring's on the way
Our life should be part of
Some work and some play
Everyone knows we must keep nature in mind
We toil to relax and we rest to unwind
Let's share it for all to heed
I know that it worked
For it helped me
Each day to get through.
1995

· I learned how infinite and limitless my possibilities were from those enchanting, spirited bonfires and midnight walks through the fields. As a child and teenager, I lived a big part of my life on this fantastic oceanside beach. Closing my eyes today, I can see and feel it all still. Early spring mornings, at low tide, I'd run to the beach so I could wade out to swim where I knew the water would later rise to three or four times higher than me. When I stared beyond the farthest waves, I figured the rest of the world started right there, and that there were no limits to where the waves or I could go. Because the sand beaches and forested shoreline stretched to where I no longer could see, it seemed to me that there were no limits or definition to what was available to me. Just as everything at the ocean went on forever, even as a child, I felt that my possibilities would be limitless. It truly amazes me that I've felt this all my life.

I know now that the late-summer afternoons and nights lived on the beach determined how I experienced my entire existence. I see, I hear and I feel life from that vast phenomenon created through Mom's relationship and communication with nature that she shared with us. As a kid, I remember how my eyes widened with wonder at Mom's animated gulping salt air as "the cure-all for any-thing that ails you." Or as she'd say, "The saltwater heals the inside as well as the outside." She was unlike any of the neighbouring adults. Even when she stood on the beach, energy emanated from her.

Mom never treated kids differently than adults. To her, a person was always a person, regardless of age. We were never dismissed from any event or con-versation. Even the beach sand became a classroom when Mom was with us. She picked up driftwood, rocks, dried seaweed and moss to demonstrate the ocean's artworks. And to show that there was beauty everywhere.

One late moonless summer night, when all had quieted down, except for some hoarse whispers and fading crackles from the fire, we witnessed an aston-ishing sight. Near autumn, you can expect brilliantly lit skies that would have strangers thinking the world is at an end. Instead of streaking fireballs lighting the night sky every other minute, this night they appeared streaming, and within seconds of each other. They were followed by the dancing northern lights spewing sheets of colour across the entire sky, shifting up and down, bouncing off the ocean and reaching back up into outer space. All the while flash-ing white and yellow lightning as though in sync with a full orchestra. Eyes popping out of our sockets, we uttered sounds of disbelief.

Then to our startled amazement, the ocean water at shore's edge broke into a huge wave. Knowing there was no wind, we all stood in shocked surprise. Just then, there was another break in the water and a massive dark, shiny form surfaced. Never before had we seen such a sight. Curious, but with some cau-tion, we edged towards shore, when suddenly the massive form leaped out of the water. It was a whale! Fortunately the large mammal was able to work itself back into the deep Atlantic waters. I believe that night the whale heard us singing and laughing, so came on by to join the fun and watch with us the incredible skies.

Intermission

Intermission

Take a Break and Bake

Well, you've done a heap of reading and you're due for a break, so let's go to the kitchen together, get the kettle boiling, have the tea leaves ready and brew a cup. And just so you don't go hungry, here's the original recipe for Mom's Sticky Buns. Don't be shy. Pull out a bowl, turn on your oven, and let's get started.

I confess to waking in the middle of the night after one of Mom's baking marathons to gingerly tiptoe down the creaky kitchen stairs with just one craving thought—to sneak a chunk of cooled, crusty, sugar-coated sticky bun. In the dark pantry, I'd grope to find a knife to slice round the glaze-smothered bun and lift it carefully, not losing a morsel of the stringy sugary gobs on the way to my mouth.

Because Mom mixed piano playing while baking sticky buns, I still seem to hear Chopin when a pan of bubbling hot sticky buns comes out of the oven. Classic notes ringing with sizzling sugary aromas. Mmm, what could be better?

Mom's Sticky Buns

Yield: 18 to 20 buns

This recipe fills two 8 x 8 x 2 inch (20 x 20 x 5 cm) buttered baking pans. Preheat oven to 220°C /425°F/Gas 7. Buns can be baked ahead, cooled and frozen, then rewarmed to serve.

The Dough
4 rounded cups (1 Litre) of unsifted all-purpose flour
8 teaspoons (40 mL) baking powder
1 teaspoon (5 mL) salt
2 cups (500 mL) shortening or soft margarine
2 cups (500 mL)skim milk

Soft margarine or softened butter
Brown sugar

The Syrup
2 cups (500 mL) water
1 cup (250 mL) maple syrup
3 cups (750 mL) brown sugar

Measure flour, baking powder and salt into a mixing bowl and gradually cut in shortening and/or margarine. Add skim milk while stirring with a fork to make a round ball of dough. Turn dough out to a floured surface and knead gently until a soft ball of dough is formed.

Using just a sprinkle of flour, roll dough to a large rectangle, about one-inch thick. Spread lightly with the soft margarine or softened butter, sprinkle with brown sugar, and roll dough into a log. Cut into one-inch slices.

Prepare syrup in a deep-rimmed pot by bringing water, maple syrup and brown sugar to a boil. Drop the cut buns into the boiling syrup, a few at a time and boil on each side for about one minute before turning over to cook other side for one minute. Flip the syrup-coated buns into the prepared pans. Pour remaining syrup slowly over the buns.

Set pans of buns on middle rack of preheated oven and bake 20-25 minutes. Turn out on rimmed plate to catch the syrup and serve while warm. If you plan to freeze and re-heat the sticky buns, cool in baking pan, then wrap for freezer. Warm the buns before serving.

Our home; our Bay de Chaleur

Nine

Slab Wood,
Round-the-Clock-Poker
and Stories

That Truckload of Slab Wood

When Bert Winton drove up the laneway with the heaped, falling-over truckload of slab wood, I knew summer days were over, and a sign of things to come! As the enormous truck turned around to back up, all the kids ran out to untie the clotheslines that stretched from the corner of our house to the old shingled shed out back, so Bert could back all the way in close to the cellar steps. Mom made sure Bert squeezed in real tight to make the piling and throwing of the wood somewhat easier.

Up and down our village road, a cow's moo or an approaching blowing east-wind storm were familiar sounds. So when the crashing wood slid off the truck's steel cab and exploded onto the ground, it stopped folks dead in their fields, a couple miles up and down. They knew either something got delivered or an old barn collapsed.

In Grandfather Culligan's day, horsepower delivered the slab wood right from the three sawmills they owned, where plenty of lumber got milled. However, in

Mom's time, Grandpa and his sawmills had long since shut down, though slab wood still got made the same. In producing two-by-fours, the spruce and pine-rounded logs get squared off as they move along the conveyor belt through the saw. The rounded parts of bark would then be sawed off in four lengths of slab. Then these two-inch-thick slabs would be cut further into two-foot lengths. Called "kindling" then, it was used to kick-start furnace fires all winter long.

Balsam, that fragrant sap from some trees, dripped over many of the cut pieces, sticking a black gum to our hands. It looked real different from bark, appeared much like honeycomb, only blacker. And it made the best chewing gum you'll ever taste—raw spruce ball gum. So we knew we'd be chewing as we worked.

We'd get two loads of slab wood delivered each fall. Except, of course, those two winters we near lost our house for back taxes. Instead, that winter, with not a penny to buy wood, we burned old torn-down pieces of barn wood and freshly cut green poplar from way back in the woods.

Unlike the neighbours who dumped their slab wood down the cellar steps upon delivery, Mom had us pile the wood outside first. This was to "air-dry it properly for clean burning." Aside from the kindling slab wood, several other loads of three-foot hardwood logs would be delivered. These piles of assorted wood stretched clear across the back of the house.

As an eight-year-old, I thought that woodpile seemed to grow every bit as high as the mountains I could see across the ocean. But I could never be grateful enough, knowing that I'd not again have to wear my overcoat inside the house to keep warm, or to bed for that matter. Even then, work to me never meant "hard" —I could only think of comfort. So, no complaints when we had to first pile all that wood outside. Then after a month's drying, it got thrown down the cellar steps, to be piled all over again.

Our five-foot-high brick furnace ate up this wood all winter long. It had a heavy black cast-iron door that looked as big as a Volkswagen door. What better place for a kid on a cold winter's day? The rows of piled wood in the cellar became the neighbourhood kiddies' hide-and-seek place. Somehow we all knew the dangers, so nobody ever played with the fire. The log piles created a bumpy highway for the mice scampering back and forth—that is, until we posted our "no vacancy" traps.

There was nothing quite like those raging red and yellow bursting flames that licked the blackened, ribbed sides of the old furnace. There was no window in the furnace, but we often opened the small door on the big black door just to watch the flames and feel the heat. That little door was really just for checking the burning logs for refilling time, or for emptying the filled-up drum of ashes. As soon as we got a mild day, I'd shovel out the red-hot coals and empty them sizzling in the snow.

Old habits die slowly, if at all. It doesn't matter what I set out to do, shortcuts have no part of me doing it. Like Mom's method of drying out the wood first before storing it, she'd always warn us, "When you get it right first time around, you'll never need to go back the second time to see if you've got it right." Mom was talking about the fact that disorganized wood piling results in crooked, falling-down piles. And when that happened, we just had to start all over again and do it right.

Mom sure had a knack to getting things done. She had the "carrot-stick" reward theory working in our backyard long before the Harvard crowd wrote about it. We knew that at the end of long days carrying and stacking wood, she would treat us with her famous "Kick Cola" homemade ice cream floats. Occasionally, neighbouring cousins showed up to fling down a few logs, but they never stayed long enough to get the treat, because it was really hard work. To be sure, Mom's ice cream float tasted nothing like a carrot.

Storm Windows and Logs

The dozens of huge windows all the way around the Culligan house were a beautiful sight, as opposed to the neighbouring Quebec stone homes that had only small dormer windows. In the late 1800s, insulated windowpanes didn't exist, which meant that winter storm windows had to be put up. Our window casements stood five feet high and were cut over one foot deep into the walls. Each wooden frame was carved like a doily in intricate patterned curves. Like the other chores for winter of storing the winter's wood and window cleaning, we knew that installing the storm windows was another big deal involving all hands.

We all learned real early that when it came to those windows, Mom hadn't any intentions of looking through cobwebs, fingerprints, dirt or even the slightest hint of a smudge for the whole winter long. Before we ever got to think of starting the "hot vinegar and water production," she led us in unison singing all around the house as every one of us scrubbed and brushed the window frames, inside and out.

That's when I discovered that putty knives weren't only for fixing windowpanes, more likely they were intended especially for digging out the ground-in dirt in the corners of each pane. Mullions divided our winter storms into four separate panes. That meant sixteen corners in just one storm window. I know—I counted them over and over again as we ended up scraping for days while Mom directed her spit-and-shine army. Believe me, we left no dirt trace for the "enemy," taking no chances because of you-know-who.

Picking up logs and heavy storm windows got done in only one way. That was Mom's way. Her mantra to her army was "Children, dear children, don't lean over to pick up a log, instead, slowly drop your bum to the back of your knees, until your arms can reach the log to pick it up…. And when you stand in front of the window, drop your bum until you're square in the middle, and reach around to the sides to grab by the middle.

"Then you pull straight up, no bending, carefully carrying while stepping one foot in front of the other, and always look straight ahead, never up or down. It's the same as riding a horse. The steering's to be done by the legs. Always looking straight ahead. The window or the log—like the reins—stays balanced in the middle.

"You always got to pay the piper, " Mom told us, "or the rooster will land on your doorstep and stay home to roost." So, be it paying taxes or slab wood bills, Mom always found a way to pay the piper. And often, it was barter that paid the wood bills.

We had a special barter system for wood. First we scavenged the beach hunting pulp, then we dragged and rolled pieces and washed-up logs up and down the shoreline; neighbours used tractors and trailers to pick and haul. Mom commandeered our brute force brigade by demonstrating how lifting logs, ends over to tumble and roll, while all the time holding our feet flat, worked a lot faster than trying to carry the logs. After many spurts of combined sibling energy, our stacked cords were then traded for truckloads of slab and hardwood.

Mostly, though, it was Rhoda Winton and Margarite Firlotte, the wives of the wood suppliers who traded in their heads for hairdos, that paid for the delivered truckloads of wood. From one September to the next, Mom washed, cut, permed, dyed, set and styled Rhoda and Margarite until the bill for the wood got wiped out. Mom started the calendar over again when all the wood finally went up in smoke over the winter.

After we'd stacked one hell of a pile of pulp on the bank one day, along came one of our neighbours from down the beach, Billy Russell, a local lobster fisherman. Billy's earthy Bay de Chaleur accent was thicker than the low-tide kelp floating inshore. Lobster was Billy's main stake in "a man's got to earn a livin'," but he took, as he said, "whatever the Lord lovin' Jesus" put in his net.

"Don't talk to me about the feds, those yella bastards," he said when told one time that the inspectors were on the prowl checking each man's catch. When Billy noticed all the pulp Mom's brigade had gathered, he said, "Lord liftin' old Jesus, Margaret, don't you know this is Sunday, the Lord's day? The whole lot 'a you'll burn in hell!"

We sure got a kick out of that. Aside from the fact that Billy liked to be first on the beach to pick pulp pieces and logs before anybody else, we also knew the only time we ever saw Billy sitting in church was maybe once a year, just before lobster season opened, to drop fifty cents in the plate as his offering to God for help.

"You won't find a more genuine fisherman than Billy Russell," said Mom. "And if you were thinking of making a movie, 'The Fishermen at Sea,' just think of old Billy steering the rudder!"

Once Billy was asked if he sailed the sea for fun. "Now, why in good Christ would I do that? Were I meant to do that, I'd have fins, or walk on top the waves like Himself."

The Coming Frost and New Scents of Autumn

The early frost signaling the end of summer delivered more than a chill. It brought new scents, sights and sounds. The scent of the slab wood's balsam would soon be followed by the first snow flurries, bringing the squeaky-clean smell of frozen air. Yet, no sign of autumn yelled bigger and louder than that harvest moon.

"That moon shifts everyone's thoughts," Mom said. "Get going, it said. Fall is the season of scents that tells you what's cooking and what's being harvested. Scents are even stronger than our will. Over time, ne'er a thing will ever stop our memorized smells. So, in a sense, everything starts with our nose. Follow your sense of smell and it'll tell you where to go."

Up and down our village road, the syrupy-sweet smell of threshed oats honeyed the air and lingered throughout fall. As did decaying potato stalks. Though nothing surpassed the sharp salt air that stuck to our faces, clothes and hair. Even in wintertime, our nostrils froze from the wet salt air. Yet against all these natural fresh country odours, nothing quite equalled each particular house smell. Dr. Smith, a professor of philosophy who moved from Montreal to Jacquet River to retire, once told us, "You'll better understand your own selves when you understand why a dog sniffs."

Just a bit up and across the road from our house, George and Florence Culligan's place was built in the late 1800s just like ours, and built by the same Culligan lumber mills. George's father, Arthur, was my Grandfather John's brother. John and Arthur owned and operated the lumber business together. They inherited and successfully grew their family business from their father who was, of course, my great-grandfather, John Culligan. And Great-Grandfather John Culligan was a chip off the old block of Great-Great-Grandfather John Culligan, who arrived on the shores of northern New Brunswick in 1824 from Longford, Ireland.

Even though both our homes were Culligan homes, each gave off different scents for good reason. George and Florence worked their big farm, and the porches got walked through before people reached the kitchen. My memorized smells of cow shit and separated milk kicks in just thinking about that kitchen entrance. In the porch nearest the kitchen were hung all the men's overalls, and their stacked black rubber boots reeked of stale cow shit. Not like fresh cow shit, because I know the difference. Stepping into a fresh cow pile round the barns and pasture fields sets off a pungent stinging scent. No, on their porch this was a cow smell that hung in the barn air and got layered and penetrated into overalls and coats over time.

Our Brooklyn cousin, Paddy, reacted to our calling shit "shit." She corrected us country kids, calling it "manure" instead. I remember telling Mom of this sophisticated New York encounter. She responded, "Well, dear, they do put labels to cover things up in the city, but no matter what you call it, it only becomes manure when it's spread onto the fields, until then, it's shit. Just like milk, dear, it only becomes butter when you can spread it on bread."

On George's other porch, huge round steel bowls and three-feet-high covered shiny milk cans crowded the table. Drying strainers used to separate floating cream off the top of the milk still dripped after Sadie, George's step-aunt and Aunt Katie's half sister, cleaned them. Everyone passing through George's porches got a strong whiff of the fresh-milk smell mixed in with bits of soured milk, and inhaled the blended air of cow and barn smells.

Due to the daily lobster catches that were cooking all day long to sell as ready-to-eat lobster, some neighbourhood homes had strong seaweed and fishy smells. Cod fishing left your hands, arms and face stuck full with scales so that you stunk. No ordinary washing could get that smell off. Only a bucket and a hard scrub brush would do. On the school bus, with my eyes closed, I figured who'd be sitting around me just from all the familiar smells, like who smelled of wet sheep's wool or who smelled of boiled lobsters.

Dissolving perm solutions and evaporating sticky-sweet mist of hairspray saturated our air. Times like Christmas, weddings and church events, Mom's dryers worked day and night, leaving us smelling of burned hair. Thank God, for in between we picked up the scent of lilac creme rinse. Other days, you detected a pharmacy of lipstick, rouge, powder, perfume and deodorant sticks from Mom's waiting hairdo ladies.

Floating over all the hairdo scents were the cooking and preserving smells of autumn. During weeks of Mom's chow-chow pickle-making, green tomatoes stewed in chopped white onions, slowly extracting flavours from her tied cheesecloth filled with ginger, cloves, pepper, rosemary and nutmeg spices. No airspace remained neutral, because the spiced steam even filtered outside, where it mixed in our nostrils already sticky with spruce gobs. Growing up, chow-chow pickles and potatoes was for us a meal, like meat and potatoes was for other families.

And the Storms

Spring, summer, fall and winter—each season flies with its own winds. "Good St. Ann and Mary, Mother of God" meant one hell of a north windstorm was brewing in over the bay. The easterly winds could also wallop one heck of a storm, but none delivered the blow like an October northerly storm.

"You can depend on it once each year. No more. On or about October 10," Mom said. Strange, for you'd think, wouldn't it be December or March packing the highest winds? For sure, the winter blizzards, driving all the way in from the Gulf of St. Lawrence, blankets wicked wet snow over everything in sight. What makes the difference in the October 10 storm is that the high winds hit directly square to the shore, with tides that rise up to six feet high— all delivered along with the brand-new moon. Mom always could feel it approaching. She'd know whether we'd get an extra three- or six-foot tide.

I remember only one year in which the tide came in that extra six feet. Over the banks it came. The pelting winds flung wet red clay from our beach banks to well all over the back of the house. Seaweed got flung onto our roof. The ocean waters rushed deep up into the middle of the potato field, nearing the back of the house, making me think for the first time ever that we'd end up, all of us, sinking into the ocean. That was a day when Mom invoked every saint that could be prayed to. For certain, this incident turned into a recurring nightmare. As close to Noah's ark I'll ever get. I hope.

Winter—Round-the-Clock Poker

Threshing the oats means to beat the small beady oats off the top of the oat shoots, and when an old-geezer farmer announces beamingly, "I've threshed the whole field of oats today," you know a big job's been done. Once all the oats got threshed, crab apples picked, turnips stored and pickles preserved, the decks of cards got dealt. Time for poker! And I don't mean the kind that stirred the fire. With all the wily and different characters at play, thank God it wasn't strip poker. This poker got played around the dining-room table with money thrown into the middle. Winter meant cards every bit as much as winter meant snow.

On Friday, I knew a marathon was on when the Smith Maritime Transport bus stopped out front of our house, delivering Yvonne, Angus and old Mr. Savage. The poker game was on. Talk about excitement! Got to keep in mind, back in those days—mid-1950s to mid-1960s—there were few cars in our community, so folks visiting from a bit of a distance was near as good as delivered parcels.

These folks arrived with loud greetings and lots of news. You just never knew whose cow just had a calf or how many bags of potatoes got picked until you heard directly. Even the slightest hints of local romance spread fast through word of mouth. No newspapers ever carried that kind of news.

Yvonne is my godmother. Her large round roving eyes were always laughing heartily. Yvonne's husband, Walter, my godfather, was never let in on the fact that the trip down was really to play poker. Instead, Yvonne came to Mom's to have her hair done. That's the story she gave Walter even after Mom closed up shop. Getting away on the bus took strategic planning for Yvonne.

Now, I have to tell you about Angus, because he was no relation to Yvonne. He was an old sea captain. Looked like one till the day he passed on, with a full shaggy, white beard and a full head of hair even in his nineties. He always wore a dark blue captain's blazer and tie. From what I knew, him having lived such a seafaring life, the fact that old Angus was the most gentle and mild-mannered man sure puzzled the heck outta me. He always had a pipe clenched between his teeth. I don't ever remember it being lit.

Yvonne and Angus always caught the bus separately, even though Angus lived directly across the road from her. Yvonne made Angus walk a half-mile up the road to catch the bus, lest Walter catch on. That was no small task for Angus, because he managed with two canes. Keep in mind, this wasn't an affair, they were just partners in crime.

Following on the brakes of the bus, Parnell, our resident (and only) taxi driver, delivered more gamblers. Parnell offloaded my Grand-Aunt Annie and Grand Uncle Herman. Both were nearing ninety and severely deaf. So they talked real loud, thinking perhaps we were as hard of hearing. Tough as old goats they were, with sparse white hair, but they had no canes or walkers to manoeuvre. Even snowdrifts never came between them and cards. Keen and anxious, they wasted no time lollygagging over our recently constructed snowmen.

Aunt Annie's smoky-black, tightly curled, lamb's-fur coat hung straight as a poker on her back. Uncle Herman, Aunt Annie's brother (both were my Grandmother Momo's siblings), likened himself to a sophisticated businessman, having managed the local government liquor store from its inception.

The third group of arrivals was the next-closest generation. Ralph Flanagan from four miles up the road worked for Uncle Herman. Ralph took over as manager when Uncle Herman died in 1971. George Guitard waltzed in loaded down with Pepsi bottles, which nobody dared touch! He'd suck on them like a baby while he figured out his poker plays. Near bald-headed, with a perennial squinting eye, he sat for the whole time without ever removing his black felt-rimmed hat. My sister Mary Sue and I called him "Mumbles." We could never quite get the drift of anything he said—though it seemed no problem for the gambling gang.

When Edmund MacDonald and Cully made their entrance, that added up to a table of ten, including Mom. As we say in New Brunswick, you just don't get more Irish than the MacDonalds—and that couldn't be truer than of Edmund himself. Edmund's bushy straw-red hair, dangling over his ears and forehead looked somewhat of a moving red cloud under his ever-present Canadian National Railway's white and blue-striped conductor's cap. That's way before it was the fashion to wear peaked caps. He always looked like a train conductor from the westerns we'd see in the local cinema.

In the hustle and bustle of the gang's getting settled, conversation filled the space until the first deck of cards was shuffled. Of course, that couldn't happen until Mom had waved off her final hairdo customer.

Edmund, like Ralph and Uncle Herman, was a real talker. They all read the daily *St. John Telegraph* as well as the monthly *Readers Digest* and the *National Geographic*. Their conversations about Prime Minister Pearson and the Arab-Israeli conflict were played right alongside their "double you and I'll pass" card bids. Interesting and intriguing debates from round the poker table helped me win several high school debates.

Our formal dining room served as casino hall. I wrapped a thick grey wool blanket over the long dining table and pulled all corners inside the legs with huge safety pins. Then, fast as the door closed behind Mom's last customer, the cut was on to decide who dealt first. This was important because of dealer's choice. Should Ralph win, you could depend on his call of five-card stud. Ralph liked a fast game, and sat tapping his knuckles on the table in sync with his foot. Yvonne's eyes rolled when she got her turn for Chicago. Uncle Herman liked Twenty-One, as did Aunt Annie, because at the end, that was the simplest game to keep track of. Towards their final card days, both required plenty reminders of who was in or out, or if they had even placed their bets. Oftentimes, because of all the banging of fists that went down with the bids, poor Uncle Herman and Aunt Annie and old Mr. Savage would think the game was over.

Yet, as the stakes got higher, with bids doubling and tripling, the gang became quieter and quieter. Some didn't have the stomach to bluff their way along to keep raising the bids, so they'd fold and throw in their cards. No matter who won each round, it was played over and over until the new deal started them again.

Back in those days, you'd think they were sitting in the midst of a pulp-and-paper mill. Everybody smoked. Past midnight, you'd need to get close to the table to figure out who sat at the other end. Sooner than later, with every one of them rubbing their teary, burning eyes, old Angus would politely request, "Margaret, how's the possibility we kin open the door so's all of us can start breathing again?"

At that checkpoint, Mom would open up the kitchen and living room doors to create a draft to clear the smoke. That is, until the card players all complained of the cold.

Whether they were hungry or not, lunch was always served one hour after midnight. Starting real young, I helped Mom fix lunch. Plates heaped with sandwiches—eggs with tuna and onion, and each with a slab of old cheddar cheese. Oatmeal cookies sandwiched with fudge or dates. Gumdrop cake gobbled by the handfuls. Cups of tea filled and refilled till they all had their fill. They stood around, grabbing, chomping and discussing, always with an eye to their chairs at the card table. But the gang wasted little time around the kitchen table. Anxious to deal the next round, they'd get in line to relieve themselves, then return to the game again.

Back then, games started on Friday nights and lasted through to early Sunday-morning Mass. With just bare minutes to swallow lunches, there would be no rest periods. Two straight nights without sleep. Occasionally, one or two left for errands but then returned.

Old Angus usually grew real tired and wanted to go home early Saturday night. Of course, he'd ask his busmate, Yvonne, to call Parnell to taxi him home. Little needs to be said about why Yvonne didn't want to go home. So Yvonne would go to the telephone and pick up the receiver. Then, while holding the button down with her finger, she'd talk real loud, "Yes, Clara, would you please ask Parnell to come to Margaret's right as he gets back from his emergency trip to Bathurst?" Then she'd hang up and say to Angus, "We'll have to wait a little longer—you heard me talking to Clara." In this way, Yvonne kept up her prank telephone calls until early Sunday morning. Every now and then Angus would chime in, "Didn't you say Parnell would be here in just minutes?"

Just as God made little green apples, the card gang managed to leave our house in the knick of time for Sunday Mass. My God almighty, mice didn't scatter as quickly. You'd think there was a fire, mind you, with the smoke and all, it could've been there in the house. I tell you, around home when God calls, even gamblers throw in the cards— well, most of them anyways.

Card playing also supplemented earned income on the New Brunswick farm. Late fall, farmers and folks gathered round tables to gamble off chickens, geese, ducks, eggs, churned butter, knitted socks, sweaters and blankets. For these stakes, they played Auction Forty-Five instead of poker. To this day, as it was back then for my cityfolk cousins, Auction Forty-Five was near impossible to play. It's the game of exceptions. Just when you think you understand, you learn a five-card will beat a king card. Again, the game rolls on, and a red nine beats a red eight. Then it happens again, where the Ace of Hearts will beat near everything. Bridge looks easy once you've seen Auction Forty-Five.

No matter what, that's what folks used to empty their chicken coop. The local families did not want chickens in the barn or chicken coop during winter. Too cold. No extra food. With the ground frozen, chickens can't scratch into it. Thus, the fall card games to empty the chicken coops. Money, through card games, was exchanged for live chickens to kill for meat. So all the chickens got thrown into burlap bags and sent home with the winners. Mom won her bags. Since they came home live, we learned to do the ugly deed.

All these devoted players were called card sharks. It was a way to pass the long haul of winters. Mom never made money playing cards. All the odds evened out over the years.

"Yes, early on, I kept count after each game, and would write down the amounts," recalled Mom on my question about eventually winning or losing. "However, after keeping count for a couple of years, I remained even, so then I decided there was no need to keep counting."

Then she added quietly, "Playing cards took my mind off the daily struggles and any sore bones I had to contend with. I got lost in the night's game."

And the Stories

The Tale of Stephen John

"Tell me another one!" everyone repeated at once, to Mom's Chaleur "lore." Grandchildren and cousins, we all pleaded to hear the stories of the past generations' life on the "good old Bay de Chaleur." Mom could really tell them. And story time would be whenever there was an audience, and whenever she had some relaxation time.

"Did I tell you of Stephen John? Tall as a pine he was, and every bit as spindly. Yet he had a voice like rolling thunder. His pant legs hung high above the ankles. Hands like shovels they were. I guess because Stephen John always bent down looking to see us, he had shoulders rounded like a barrel, stooped to the ground.

"Now, for a man so tall—twice most men—you'd think with the size of him, we'd hear him coming. Not a chance, for Stephen John slinked in his own shadow, quiet as a passing cloud. Strange though, for no matter how often I saw him, each and every time he approached, the sight of him always shocked me.

"Automobiles were few in our time. Getting rides by hitchhiking or asking was routine. But not so for Stephen John. Far too large to fit in car seats, he took rides on tractor-trailers, or in a cart drawn by a horse or in the back of trucks. But he never asked anyone for a ride, just hopped on. Even with the regular passing bus that stopped out front of McMillan's wholesale store, Stephen John just marched through the ticket stall, stretched himself out in the back-row seat, paying, but saying nothing. Everybody just knew where to stop to let him off.

"Now, there was this one late morning on a brutal cold November day. We'd all been up to a funeral to Jacquet River Church, top of the hill where the wind howls across the cemetery near knocking stones against each other. Nobody lingered after Lloyd McMillan let the coffin down the hole for burial. As was the custom, we threw a handful of dirt to dust the coffin that now lay six feet down, and hurried away for cover.

"Soon after Lloyd and the gravedigger filled in the grave, Lloyd drove down the road and stopped his long black hearse in front of Herman Roy's store, dashing in to buy a quick bite before heading on to the hospital to pick up old Mr. Lapointe, who had died. Lloyd stayed on a bit in the store to thaw his cold body, having felt half-frozen from the funeral service.

"After chatting up Herman, Lloyd hurried out of the store back to the hearse. Heading eastward, Lloyd busied himself negotiating the miserable wet and blinding snowstorm that had just blown up. Just as Lloyd's hearse approached Armstrong Brook, he felt a tapping on his shoulder and heard a voice telling him, 'I'll get out here.'

"With no time to think, Lloyd slammed both feet to the brakes, stopped the hearse, pushed open the door and flung himself out into the storm. Frightened out of his skull, shaking to the teeth, Lloyd jumped to the road. He couldn't believe what he was seeing—watching the rear door slide open, knowing full well he had just emptied the coffin minutes earlier. From behind the black curtain that separated the coffin-bed area from the cab, a figure rose up and jumped out the rear door. Stephen John! He said not a word, nor gave even one backward glance. He just lumbered up the laneway to his house.

"To this day, Lloyd uses no black curtain in his hearse. Unknown to anyone at the gravesite, Stephen John had silently got himself into the hearse for a lift close to home. Never suspecting live passengers, Lloyd had no reason to glance at his rear."

The Devil's Hoof

Heaven and hell was a serious matter with folks down home. "The devil as he may" wound through generations steeped in old-time religion. But nobody much took the idea of limbo seriously. That was a place where only babies that had not been baptized hovered for eternity. Hell seemed the more popular resting place. Most folks generally found themselves in a state of cardinal, mortal or venial sins, and felt that heaven was out of reach. Conversations and stories about the devil were every bit as popular as death, wakes and funeral epics. The following related event topped the scale for the "best" the Bay de Chaleur offered up. Mom settled in her chair to tell us about it.

"Grandmother Rubber could size anybody up. She didn't necessarily need to chat you up any. She could see right through you, and her look gave you a chill. Right up to the very end, to when she died at a hundred fourteen years, nobody could miss seeing her. It didn't matter the time of the year—on her daily gallop to fetch her mail, she always wore those ol' black rubber boots way up past her knees. From the hips up, she remained stiff as an ironing board and always stared right through you during her hellos.

"Now, danger's a thing we're all familiar with, though few can warn of its coming as Grandmother Rubber did. Even those most doubtful of the special senses in seeing into the future didn't fool about when Grandmother Rubber warned of things to come. Nobody who played with a full deck passed up listening to her.

"The Cedar Lodge will forever be remembered with heaven and hell.

Indeed, for some long time, there was talk over whether there had been outright flouting of God's law at the Cedar Lodge Dance Hall.

" 'Not a matter to take lightly, how they mock the gods, dear child,' Grandmother Rubber said of the folks who kept on dancing, drinking and carrying on past midnight, into the Lord's day.

"That was the crux of the matter," Mom said. "Past midnight Saturday, frolicking and partying. Way back in my day, when the clock struck midnight Saturday night, everything was to stop. Not a second past. Only fools dared trespass on God's time, the Lord's day. We Catholics were expected to receive Holy Communion at Sunday Mass. That meant strict observance in fasting from all food, drink and entertainment from midnight sharp. To act otherwise was under the pain of mortal sin. And mortal sin's grave circumstances meant hell. Oh, dare say, we thought about that. A Sunday didn't go by that Father Trudel didn't bark about the imminent danger of the devil taking us to hell.

"Oh, but that was life. Folks worked hard. And there were few pleasures. So when the Cedar Lodge opened to Saturday-night dances, the younger crowds flocked over there, attracted by live-music groups that travelled from as far away as New Orleans.

"Not at all liking the changes drifting in among the church obligation and sainted days, Grandmother Rubber lamented to anyone who would listen, 'Child alive, don't go testing the devil in what is only a fool's paradise, because my dear, that dance hall is his den, so you can rest assured the time is coming when the devil himself will make you pay in the fires of hell.' Even though most folks had plenty good reason to heed Grandmother Rubber's warning, they joked and danced instead.

"No buildings were near the Cedar Lodge. It stood alone on the shore's edge, just where the cliff leaped high above the incoming tide. What a sight it was. On a clear summer's night, you could hear music straight across the bay to the Quebec side. A spell hung over the place. You couldn't help falling under its charm. After the little red school house dances at Jacquet River that we were used to, where folks had nipped on their own homemade brew, this set-up, with whisky and beer sold by the glassful, felt like we were in the movies.

"As a rule, we showed no ankles or even a peek at one shoulder. We used to say, 'Skin was akin to sin.' Heavens! All the saints couldn't help you were you to show yourself. My mama would say, 'Hang your dress square off your shoulders so as not to touch any part of the body.'

"Going to the Cedar Lodge was definitely not a church service. Dresses covering up to the neck still got worn, even to our local fiddling dances. That's what gave the Cedar Lodge dances even more of a thrill. Women and men enjoying themselves with skin exposed in fashions that wouldn't appear at any other occasion. It was surely that 'The devil will get you for seeking pleasure.' Mind you, the Protestants among us—and they were scarce—feared the devil even more. They'd not so much as skate on Sunday, let alone play a sport.

"This night like no other, just before the hand struck midnight, a strikingly imposing-featured gentleman appeared on the dance floor. He stood tall in a white silken suit. Not a soul missed his entrance, for his deep, intense eyes seemed to draw everyone's notice. Gracefully he moved, catching the attention of every man and woman on the dance floor. With a tap on a man's shoulder and a nod, he took the partner swooning into his arms. Later, it was said, he looked more beautiful than any woman, handsomer than any man known, and akin to a figure chiselled of marble, perhaps even like 'David.'

"Both air and music became one and the same, like a current had just electrified everything, as if his presence touched off this intensity. The clock struck twelve bells. Not a single soul left the dance floor. Suspense, wonderment and emotion gripped everyone. Pleasure, fun, playfulness, dancing and drinking was in the air. You could say every single person got caught up in the heat of the moment, now well passed into the Lord's time. It was hard to know what happened first because it seemed all to occur at once.

"The beautiful young girl dancing in the arms of this gentleman looked at the floor and could not believe what she next saw. Instead of his fine leather shoes, she was dancing in the arms of a man with two hooves instead of two feet! In an instant, all around witnessed his hooves burn through the dance floor, creating a widening gap. The floor erupted with flames as it separated into half. Suddenly appearing on the forehead of the finely exquisite gentleman were two horns. Excitement and pleasure turned to panic and horror. People ran for their lives. Within minutes, the dance hall blazed like the fires of hell.

"In the days that followed, no one ever could account for who everyone now knew was surely the devil. 'In disguise,' Grandmother Rubber had warned. To this day, nothing was ever rebuilt on the devil's site."

Mr. Lapointe's Wake

Stories abound of wakes and funerals. For one thing, while the funeral was short and usually to the point, the wake—a time for remembering, drinking and sharing food—often lasted longer than any party, even a wedding, which might run through the weekend. Wakes wore on three days to a week. They were occasions, 'specially for down-home folks who lived off in cities elsewhere. They'd get home for a loved one's funeral and stay awhile. Somehow, religion didn't frown on drunken wakes. Could take up to several days to make it home.

Since there were no funeral parlours in our day, the body just got washed and laid out on the floor or on a large table in our homes, and sometimes laid in a plain pine box.

Mom now settled herself in her favourite rocker. Any chatter that erupted after the telling of the previous story now fell into a hushed silence. Everyone settled once again into chairs as she started to tell the story of old Mr. Lapointe, at whose home she'd frequently enjoyed a game of poker.

"Old Mr. Lapointe had been very ill and he was a long time dying. Plenty early wrong calls went out that he'd died. On two occasions, too late to tell the family way yonder that he still walked, they made it all the way home, but they were not long in claiming some happiness that their father was alive and kicking.

"Of course, the real day came when the call went out that indeed, old Mr. Lapointe had finally died. Now, this would probably be the fifth or sixth night of his wake, with the whole family playing poker. And I'd say that some were every bit double-fisted whisky drinkers as well. If they were up to a game, they agreed.

"By the wee hours of morning, what with card playing, the late-night waking and whisky drinking, they seemed to all talk at once. They began to reminisce of their father's love of the game and the drink. This being the last night before his being buried, they all decided that they wanted one last game and drink with their father.

"Cross my heart, so help me God, they lifted old Mr. Lapointe out of the coffin, sat him up to the table, poured him a good drink of whisky, then dealt him a poker hand and put on his old winter stocking cap. And they say, for the rest of the late-morning hours, old Mr. Lapointe quietly sat, passing on each poker hand called."

Heraldine and Captain MacCoran

Enjoying her attentive audience, Mom continued with her storytelling. "I'll not tell you his real name, for we'll keep that part sacred. We'll call him ol' Captain MacCoran.

"Getting to the end of his life, he died. Of old age, in his early hundreds. He was treated no different than all kinfolk round here, and got waked his due time. There was the usual hearty food and drink, with the priest's regular prayer time to deliver up the old man's soul. That's important, so as to get any dead sinner some lead time out of purgatory.

"There's no telling the 'dirty' or 'sensational' pranks folks will perform for the dead. Call it an 'evening up.' Sometimes it was against the attending mourners who did 'something towards the living dead.' In this case, the caper planned for Heraldine did the trick.

"Heraldine, above and beyond anything, 'shiver-feared' attending wakes. She absolutely hated dead bodies in coffins, not wanting to even be in the same room. Mind you, growing up in the country as we folks, knowing every single soul for miles around meant frequenting hundreds of wakes in a lifetime. Feeling no different this 'waking' night for ol' MacCoran, Heraldine came calling to do her religious duty.

"Our coffins had full-length kneelers so as to face the dead one in personal prayer. I'd say we considered it a prerequisite for at least saying a few Hail Marys and Glory be to the Father in a kneeling position. And precisely at Heraldine's moment of personal prayer, with a roomful looking on, one finger of ol' MacCoran's dead stiff hand slowly lifted, then a second, and then a third, by which time Heraldine popped straight up, screeched and promptly collapsed. Fainted cold. Certainly a stunt that overreached its intent.

"The conspiracy was accomplished by tying transparent fishin' line to each of ol' MacCoran's fingers and pulled on up through the ceiling's open-air register above. It was just like playing with puppets on strings. I'd say that ruse was over the top."

That Hot Dry Summer

Now on a roll, Mom continued. "Did I ever tell you of the summer we had that was so hot, even long after sunset, you dared take only baby steps? Oh, it was a barnburner of a summer! So hot, even cows, the most serene of any beast, crashed through the barn doors using their hooves for blows. The trains travelled nights in fear of meltdown. Codfish, salmon, smelt and even some lobster made it up the rivers seeking shade. The likes of all unheard of before.

"Time passed, most wells dried up. The worst came after the rivers shrivelled to dribs and drabs. In a matter of time, the only washing that got to be done was at the scrub board on the Bay de Chaleur.

"Folks began twittering in irritable ways. Not used to such extreme severity, the heat took its toll on everyone, especially the elderly.

"Though I'd say ol' Mr. Meltier, having been so stricken with bowel restriction, would've popped off sooner or later. Word got passed to the whole lot of them. Not such an easy thing to do, with his older siblings spread as far as the Yukon. Since the family resided only down the road a teeny bit, we stopped by with fresh-baked casseroles, bread and the like several times. There being such a long wait for the kin to reach home, the wake was now in its fifth night. Way too long for even any decent summertime.

"We attended to say the Holy Rosary and lament the Litany of the Saints for ol' Mr. Meltier. By then, because of the extreme heat, the decaying body could hardly be seen for the swarming, buzzing, lazy flies. At that point, they finally flung overtop the open end of the coffin, two layers of fishnet. On the sixth night, the last wake night, with all the kin gathered to bid their final adieus, the following events can only be described as astonishingly grizzly! Keep in mind, most corpses weren't embalmed back then. No money for such fussing.

"The summer's blasting temperatures finally reached fever pitch when poor 'ol Mr. Meltier's fermenting body came 'a crashing through the bottom of his now rotted-out coffin. It was a scene of disbelief, mayhem, shock and then silence for what seemed like an eternity. And just then and there, with the help of a few reluctant men, he was picked up in one fell swoop and rushed off to the cemetery for immediate burial. At midnight. Without a priest! Unheard of in these parts. To this day, Mr. Meltier is remembered for the history he made."

It was after hearing her tell a round of such stories, in 1992, that one of

Mom's regular callers, young Robert Frenette from up the road a bit, penned this poem to her.

OUR STORY LADY

I sit down and ponder my soul
How did it feel to be moved
By one with such spirit and zeal?
She opens her door and she opens her heart
To a lifetime of stories, of love and strong will
Her eyes start to twinkle as they roam to the past
Even bad stories have Margaret's kick and panache
Her eyes are full of the seas and the lands she's passed
Knowing Margaret upon them, a bright light was cast.
For us going to visit is no task
For our spirit and heart she'll delight
And our senses when leaving will widen.
Now I'm saddened that our visit is over
But sadder I'd be if visit I hadn't.
I'll walk out the door, richer than before
And treasure her always
I will.

A rainy boat tour of Percé Rock.

(L to R) Paul Menard, Mom and Tom. 1996

Ten

Opening Windows of the Mind—Mom's and Mine

Times change. Sometimes a tiny bit at a time. Perhaps the reason so much did change in our house was because Mom, very early in her life, made frequent changes. Her leaving the small village of Jacquet River in the 1920s to broaden her life by working and studying in Boston was an early step. Maybe the most rebellious change had to be when she attained the legal separation from her husband, even though everything she was taught and everything she had lived and believed told her, "No! We are married until death do us part!" I remember vividly just how profoundly painful it was for her to accept responsibility for her decision to separate from him and make a new life, and to abstain from her "religious communion" that had so sustained her in the past.

Another profound decision that changed her and all of us was the day she left us all for a year to study to attain that hairdressing licence. She knew it was going to be the only way she could support us. But leaving us in the care of anyone else must have hurt her deeply. Mom was no stranger to mulling stuff over and coming up with tough decisions. But there was one change about to come, and I didn't know how she would take it. I was twenty-four years old when circumstances forced me to disclose my dark daunting secret.

I returned home for a summer visit from the University of Dayton, Dayton, Ohio. It was a blistering hot August day and the image of Mom standing in her shop, arms high in the air, wearing that familiar blue and white-checkered shoulder-draped dress remains vivid to this day. On top of the summer's heat, the hair dryers hummed nonstop while Mom did over a dozen heads for a weekend wedding. The tense bride held her long sparkling veil in her lap so Mom could style the woman's hair perfectly to fit, while the nervous bride's mother mopped her daughter's brow. I knew the scene, so I got down to brass tacks without adieu, washing and hanging towels out to dry.

Late that night, the air still smelling of perm solution and hair spray, I opened the doors and windows wide to catch any cooling breezes, while Mom set out two extra- large batches of bread ready to be shaped and baked. One was brown raisin and the other was fluffy white potato bread. She was expecting them all for a summer visit: Uncle Paul, Aunt Ruth and the kids, along with my older brother, Billy, and his family.

Chatting nervously, somehow Mom had sensed that I was preoccupied by something. She walked over to me and tenderly placed her arm on my shoulder.

"Dear Tommy. In the long run it'll work out for the better with your leaving the seminary. God knows, that's no easy way to live a happy normal life."

Mom's out-of-the-blue statement stunned me. Since arriving home, I'd said nothing. I muttered, "But, Mom, I haven't officially left. Father Superior knows my intention and he suggested that during the summer recess, I reflect carefully on my decision to leave the priesthood studies. Though I have decided to leave, I'll still complete my theology/philosophy degree this year."

She busied herself slicing the raised bread dough into small buns. Then while shoving a set of readied pans into the oven, she said quietly, "I could tell that you never got over the breakup from your high school sweetheart. But that'll pass and in time you'll meet the right girl and settle down to a happy family life."

I guess on hearing that, I just blurted," Good God, Mom, sure the breakup hurt, but in heaven's name, there's more to it than that!"

"Now dear, don't get upset. You don't necessarily understand everything there's to know about love. We all make mistakes. Believe me, you'll have no trouble finding the right girl."

I thought, oh my God, this conversation's out of control, so I jumped out of the chair and near yelled, "Mom, I'm not leaving the seminary over a girl! Believe me, that is the reason I joined the seminary. The priesthood was the ultimate escape route for men like me."

"Well dear, don't fret. My good friend, Ted Cannon, was in love with my sister Tookie when he left for the seminary. Then, just weeks before his ordination, he said he realized that he just loved women too much, so he couldn't become a priest."

My gut turned over on that one. A sickening wave of trepidation swept through me. Say a prayer, I thought. That gave me the courage to gently take Mom's hands in mine and look straight into her eyes. "Mom, this isn't about girlfriends. I'm not leaving the seminary for a woman. I'm leaving the seminary because I love a man. I am a homosexual."

Though I have experienced tragedy, sadness and drama as a child, nothing prepared me for Mom's sudden reaction of throwing herself into a chair, holding her head and lamenting, "Oh, my dear God! What did I do wrong? Where did I go wrong? I nursed all my children except you and Mary Sue. Oh, for sure, God's punishing me for not staying with your father…"

I didn't know what to say. She sobbed uncontrollably. Yet, even in that blur of pain and confusion, I realized that somehow my honesty had given me newfound courage. It wasn't until some time later that I began to understand how that night opened both of us to deeper mutual trust and a journey of self-reflection. No, Mom didn't get it like I wanted her to understand and accept. Why, at that time, I was scarcely aware that I wasn't even remotely close to accepting my own homosexuality. This was the late 1960s and few even knew handles existed to our closet doors. That took me the next ten years to understand and accept. So how in the name of God could Mom get there any faster?

But through her bewilderment and tears that night, she kept repeating to me, "Dear, dear Tommy, I love you no matter what. This is hard for me to understand but it doesn't change the little boy I loved so much and will to my dying day."

The rest of that visit home flowed in the normal pattern of relatives and neighbours, the beach and swimming and fun with visitors in between Mom's appointed heads. However, for the rest of the time, we avoided further discussions about homosexuality. Even then I knew how fortunate I was. A fellow student had recently shared with me how his parents had told him to "never again show his face at home," after telling them of his homosexuality. Outright disowned. Mom couldn't be capable of thinking such, let alone not loving all of her children above and beyond anything in her life.

There followed countless discussions, which included at various times my sister Susan (Mary Sue), with Mom and me, together with my partner, Paul Menard, or just dialogues between any two of us. The detail is not as important as the difficulty for Mom to shift from thinking that she herself had done something wrong. From there, her own logic eventually took her to believing that I had somehow gone wrong.

In struggling through the journey from head to heart, she knew there was never anything wrong about my birth or Susan's or any time thereafter. Instead, over the many discussions and—I am sure—the hours alone when she mulled over this "announcement," she eventually came to understand that it was "wrong thinking" about differences that got distorted. That is, just because something or someone is "different" in some way, we tend to think something is wrong or bad. Well, that's common enough.

We came to agree that believing that homosexuality is somehow wrong or bad follows the same line of distorted thinking as those early teachings of, "Those Jews, they killed Christ," "Negroes have no souls," "Protestants will never make it to heaven." Without reflective questioning about such assumptions and beliefs, these distortions push their way to being "right" in our thoughts and our actions.

Another common statement that we discussed was the idea that one should never get into conversations about religion, politics or sex. Well, why not be open to learning about different ways of believing, different ways of governing and living? By opening our minds, our hearts and our ears to really listen to other ideas and opinions, the opening of such windows could replace mere tolerance with appreciation and understanding.

I recall Mom agreeing with a smile that she felt that Phil Donahue and Oprah had opened windows for her. She constantly spoke about Oprah. Oprah's television show had often moved her to tears. "You know," she offered," I guess that gay parade you took me to in Key West made me think that those gay parade drag queens were really not so much differently dressed than the Knights of Columbus or the Shriners in their parades. Or even the pope, cardinals and bishops, laden in silken, jeweled vestments, pointy hats and purple slippers weren't all that different either..." Her voice trailed off as she got lost in her musings.

Just think: there's hot and cold, hard and soft, light and dark. And those are just the extremes. What about all the warm grey areas? Certainties and absolutes belong to those who believe that there is only black or white but nothing in between. I pointed out to Mom, too, that her life was the example of how I learned that living is a fluid experience of an evolving understanding through shades, shapes and sizes of everyday living. Like supper didn't really mean the kitchen table, because supper could be around a beach bonfire, on a grassy hillside, or enjoyed between a musical singing and dancing evening.

One afternoon, visiting relatives from Boston came calling to see Mom. Mom's grandson Brent was there with his girlfriend, Tara, as well as I and my partner, Paul Menard. After the commotion of hugs and kisses, Mom proudly introduced, "This is my grandson Brent, Billy's oldest, and his girlfriend, Tara." Then without hesitation she continued, "and this is Paul Menard, a friend of Tom's."

Later, after all the relatives departed, Paul and I prepared a dinner of steamed fresh cod and boiled new potatoes. Mom baked a pan of sticky buns. When we all got situated comfortably sipping tea on the veranda, I turned to her and said, "I'd like to say something about what you said earlier today." It wasn't hard to see Mom's apprehension in her stiffened shoulders. Of course, who wouldn't feel defensive with an opening like mine? As was gradually becoming newly sensitive behaviour for me, I abruptly changed my tone and approach.

"Mom, sorry about that. You didn't do anything wrong. Rather, it's about the way you introduced my partner, Paul, to the folks today."

Mom's shoulders relaxed visibly. "Dear child, I know that Paul's your special friend, I love him like a son."

"Mom, why is it so hard to call Paul, 'Tom's partner?' "

"Well, I never called Emile my partner. We were together thirty-five years. He didn't seem to mind. It's just the way things were. Once you got married around here, the names stuck for life. To be a part of what existed, you played by the rules. That meant, for me, Emile could only ever be a friend. Nothing else."

But then, looking fondly at Paul and me, she added, "Why couldn't I see how much you and Paul were hurt by my calling you just friends? I'm not blind; I see the gentle, loving relationship you share. This is not a promise, but a pledge that I'll do my best to introduce Paul as your partner from now on."

It took time and many thoughtful conversations, but I knew Mom had shifted from mere accepting to understanding when I noticed a framed picture of me and my partner displayed in the parlour on top of the piano. Every day Mom sat at that piano.

A cousin had said to me, "I would never tell my mom and dad I'm gay. That would hurt them. Why would I do that this late in life?"

First, I had to acknowledge that whatever my cousin did was strictly his business. However, I also recognize my birthright to exist. My being gay is not something I chose. It's just what I am. I can't imagine that I hurt someone else just because of who or what I am. No, in hindsight I should have realized that Mom just needed time to work it all out in her own mind as she had done with other issues so often in the past. Were I to have known how she would respond, I'd've told her I was gay long before I left home. Now I wonder how I could have so underestimated another's ability to understand—especially my own mom.

With my sister Susan and my partner, Paul Menard, I travelled to New Brunswick for Christmas every year. In all fifty-some years, I missed only one Christmas with Mom. Each year, I averaged two to three months of visiting time with her. The Christmas visit was always about two and a half weeks. In May, I got home for Mother's Day. While there, I organized a spring cleanup to shake up the flowerbeds. That would take two or so weeks. Summer months brought me there twice, with a wrap-up fall visit to winterize the property. The important thing is that we had lots of time to be together and to take time to really share our thoughts.

Some winters, Mom visited with Paul and me for a month's stay in Miami Beach. Every now and then, Paul and I drove home to pick her up for some special trip. She loved riding the "Rolls." Like a queen, she knew the moves, gliding in and out of the backseat without a wrinkle. She could have happily stayed at the Atlantic City Casino complex, playing one-arm bandits and listening to Sammy Davis Jr. for weeks on end.

There's not a subject we didn't chew on. We had abundant opportunity to bump into and wade through anything a person could possibly think. Nobody got struck by lightning or heart attacks by our discussing stuff, be it talks about Monica Lewinsky, O.J. Simpson, the ozone layer, Mother Teresa, vegetarianism or Boy George. I might add, the intensity got raised occasionally when our conversations pierced a few shells protecting previously cherished beliefs and assumptions delving into self-worth, intimacy, sexuality, fear, religion and chauvinism.

On more occasions than I can remember, Susan, Paul, Mom and I talked often about our understanding of God. "Evolved understandings" would be an apt description of our conversations. But no matter the changes and shifts in Mom's beliefs and understanding, she remained a Catholic right to the end.

"My dear," she'd say, "that's my faith, what carried me through life I'll never give it up." Yet so much in how she viewed her religion did change. Like what Vatican II ushered in during 1963: changing the Latin to English, and dispensing with the necessity of eating fish on Friday—previously, to have eaten meat on Friday would be counted as mortal sin. Even Sunday's attendance to Mass got shaved to Saturday, with a lot more leeway other than another "mortal sin."

Eventually, Catholics could more easily purchase annulments. That was something to which only the very wealthy previously had access. Along with those changes in the Catholic Church, Mom thought sooner or later they ought to ordain women priests, permit priests to marry, integrate more religions and "allow gay priests to come out of the closet because it only makes them do things dishonestly the present way."

But she still had difficulty with guilt. Even to the end, she felt guilty over not having lived with her husband "until death do us part." She said to me, "It's just something I can't get over. I grew up that way, what Mama taught me that the Church says. Because of this, I'll have to suffer more, because I know you've got to earn your way to heaven."

"But," I responded, "don't you think you've suffered enough, that you've done enough good to earn peace?"

Again she said, "No, dear, this is my way. Before I pass through to wherever that is, I'll need to do a little more." Then added, "You just can't get from one place to the next without a stopover."

Growing up in the far northeast of New Brunswick, I realize now that our neighbourhood had its own peculiarities that we just took for granted. What constituted a big change for us was when folks got to shifting to "orange pineapple ice cream" instead of "maple walnut" on their weekly Sunday-afternoon outing. Most homes with pianos never got the feel of warm blood; the piano was just a 'specially nice piece of furniture. Many of us were pennywise with words: you could barely get a "yep" or "no," let alone a "maybe who knows" from most neighbours. The only talker in our community was the parish priest, and I stopped listening before he even started. Because the entire Church service was in Latin, I could never figure why he didn't also preach in Latin. Our community did no trail-blazing, so when Elvis and the Beatles came along; they all surely thought hell couldn't be far behind.

Once again, Mom thrived on being different. The way she listened so thoughtfully to others, often made them open up and share more perhaps, than they would have with other folks. She was really always open to learning deeper and wider about anything and everything, and as versed as she was in her beloved church music, Patsy Cline, Louis Armstrong, Lena Horne, Peggy Lee and Elvis all found themselves spinning out their music in our house. The piano in our home got a daily workout, to everyone's enjoyment. Those stacks of 33s, 78s and 45s remain in mint condition. Sounds and voices of strings, horns and piano in soprano, tenor and bass filled our space. Day in, day out, these notes got played and stored in my memory bank. Heck, even though we rarely left the Bay de Chaleur, by the time I moved away, I at least knew there was a "Gay Paree," "Blue Danube" and a "Jamaican Bay." I don't recall many others in our neighbourhood being that adventurous with music or anything else. Life just shifted along in much the same ways as it always had.

No question that expressing myself so openly that summer evening so long ago, opened us into deeper and more reflective discussions. No question too, that Mom's openness and obvious pleasure in learning and discussing new ideas probably gave me the courage to speak as I did. Some issues that we touched early on took longer to sort through, but there was no question that the windows of our minds were opening.

We Could Always Share Our Ideas and Feelings

In the midst of the daily rough-and-tumble as provider, Mom also found time to pursue something else that was totally new for her. Besides writing poems and notes in her journals regularly, she also sketched and color pencilled. One

Friday afternoon I got off the school bus, and Mom stood waiting by the roadside to tell me she was hitchhiking to Campbellton. Since at that stage I was the main "child cook" and "house organizer," she wanted to be certain I telephoned to order grocery supplies for Saturday delivery. To pursue her "totally new" interest, she had registered for a five-day oil painting class. Every bit the responsible child, I remember saying, "But what about your hair appointments?"

Yes, she had thought of that, and asked that one of us telephone and reschedule them. That, I believe, was when painting got born into my life and maybe something else—the pleasure of opening windows to let in fresh ideas. Like everything, Mom gave away all her paintings. Good thing she gave some to me. That year, I remember my high school teacher, Sister Sophie, telling me, "You have a most unusual mother, special and unique. Who else has a mother who can play piano and organ, sing, write, paint and be a full-time mother and father, all at the same time?" Sister Sophie had long since moved on from Belledune, but continued to visit Mom, often staying overnight. She kept in touch right up to Mom's end.

I also realize now that long ago I should have known that Mom and I could always share our ideas and feelings, had I but reviewed not just our words that travelled through phone calls and face-to-face conversations, but also through the letters she wrote. Letters that mostly got written over days, so they read like a book. In reading her letters, I could visualize the physical descriptions she detailed. From the beginning, I saved Mom's letters and cards. As she saved mine. She always encouraged and inspired me with positive, motivating, nurturing and sometimes humorous messages.

> *Thank you, I really appreciated your card. You seem so far away (Dayton, Ohio, studying) but then, I so look forward to seeing you. May 12, 1969*
>
> *I attended (still learning at age 65) the Beauty Couture Seminar at Bathurst Trade School, still can pick up many good tips of my profession. April 3, 1974*
>
> *Always take time to relax my dear, all work and no play makes for a dull boy, and that goes for this girl too. October 1975*
>
> *I love you—forever and ever. December 1976*

Remember to bend a little, even if it hurts. 1981

I admire the way of life you have adopted and put into practice. Want to know something? I love you very much. 1982

At a dance, a man asked me if I liked "dancing close" and I was in a crazy enough mood to say, "Oh, yes" but I really don't as while dancing I like to fantasize like I can do it like Ginger Rogers, but when you don't have a Fred Astaire, you do what's next best—-have fun, eh? October 23, 1984

You too Tom can still grow, because you and I know that faith is the watering can for new life. When the earth is sufficiently fertilized, the moisture and sun takes care of the rest, so like with our souls. 1984

I admire your strength and determination, and your sharing, caring and goodness (not a mean bone in your body). Just remember as long as you can hang on to a shred of faith you will conquer everything that has led you to question the adversities that befall each and every one of us. June 1988

I confess I could be resentful at times but I do say for myself, by trying to overcome the situations that arose, it gave me more strength of character and the gift of acceptance. It's God who's done everything in life for me. I do possess a love of my children that I didn't know could exist. And you are the salt of the earth and my dear Tom, I always said you were destined for greatness, which you are. Your Mom who loves you. 1988

Diligence is the mother of good luck. Knowing you and the efforts you put into practice throughout your life, you will succeed in any path you must follow. 1989

Your judgment and accurate intuition will be with you. I love you, Tom, until the end of time. 1990

Thank you for the support you so generously gave me. It is your very own self when you have been home or abroad, your dear face, sometimes sad, mostly serene! How well I know there were times when it was I who should have been showing the cheerful and happy side of me. Wish I could promise to do better, but promises were made to be broken. I do know it's not a promise I'll be making but a declaration of the tremendous heartfelt love for you that helps me to go on. I believe you were born to be a "great" person and so far you have been. Our greatest glory is not in never falling, but in rising every time we fall. 1991

Those who marvel at the beauty of the world in summer will find equal cause for wonder and admiration in winter. In winter the stars seem to have rekindled their fires, the moon achieves a fuller triumph, and the heavens wear a look of a more exalted simplicity. February 18, 1982

Lately, I've been in a few poker games, so far it's been a zigzagging affair. I'll have to win next game, enough to say I'm square. 1992

Tom dear, start out today with faith in your heart and climb 'til your dreams come true. 1992

I realize I can't thank you enough for your love and caring all these years gone by. But you must have felt the love I have for you. June 14, 1993

I had to come home without you because you didn't gain enough weight after you were born. Ten days later I went down to the hospital and came home in evening on the bus. I remember like it was yesterday, because I was so happy. I love you Tom. April 1996.

Dear Tom. Whether the road is rough or smooth, when you look at that "new moon" don't forget your special wish. I always did and aren't I lucky? 1997

Birthday—Dear Tom—I think of you today as that boy of mine who grew up to be steadfast and helpful through hard and good times. With all my heart I ask—Please God, stay with Tom and me. I will be grateful eternally. I love you Tom. 1998

There is no question or doubt in my mind that Mom evolved in her thinking from "catholic" absolutes gradually towards seeing life and the world as more complex and realizing the necessity of understanding its shades and depths. And I know that rubbed off on me too.

Mom's last Christmas at the homestead.
1999

Eleven

All Alone—Who Loves Mom?

Nine Kids—Then There Were None

You could say we're an interesting bunch. None of us are in jail or sleeping on park benches. As the saying goes, "We all turned out pretty darn good." We at least appear to be a contented lot.

For starters, all of us today are talkers. Nothing shy about any of us. We'll be first to grab your hand and heartily greet you. Be it Bill, Gene, Paul, Ann, Gail, Mary Sue, Henry or myself, you'll quickly notice our intense personalities. Our approach, like Mom's, is to burrow into whatever the task or conversation. Even in entertaining and hosting, we can handle a crowd with food and flow as she relentlessly did throughout her years.

A family as large as ours is bound to have differences. The gap from Bill, the eldest, to Mary Sue, the youngest, was seventeen years. In a sense, that could be enough to make strangers. The vastly different early environment between the firstborn and the last made for different influences and impacts on us too.

In recent years, I have realized that the emotional effect of Dad's alcoholism caused greater injury to our later family life than it had earlier. The disease of alcoholism gets worse with the years. At least my older siblings have a few fond memories of our father. Those of us who came along later have not a single good memory of him. I was left with only terror and nightmares. I think that because of all these changing family dynamics during the progression of Dad's alcoholism, we're not all going to see and understand through identical perspectives. Then too, each of us has his or her own personality. I don't pretend to speak for all my siblings.

The two eldest, Billy and Ann, inherited the "I am responsible" characteristic. Billy worked and helped Mom from the beginning, and he carried through afterwards for years sending money home to help Mom. His generosity put some of the flour in our bins. Ann, our surrogate mother, learned early, even as a child, to care for a family. At eighteen, she left the nest, already experienced in changing and washing the shitty diapers of Gail, Gordon, Henry, Mary Sue and me. Ann had formal child-care responsibilities under her belt looking after us before her own graduation as a kid. Ann, too, generously mailed monthly cheques to Mom, helping in our financial support. When we talked about this, Ann added, "But we still got to play. And we always had to be careful what we did around Billy because he'd be certain to tattle on anything we did. Billy could be quite cagey and sneaky!"

Once the older siblings were off, and Mom's hairdressing salon opened, our financial condition improved. About then, Paul took his turn helping us financially, and his dollars were much appreciated by Mom. Paul, known as the "silent Yokum," quietly went about his business. Mom always said that Paul made no waves as a child and got into no trouble.

It seemed that Gene always took the blame for whatever happened at home. He was an easy target for everyone to point the finger at because he just accepted things without complaint. Mind you, Gene was known by everyone to be quick in raising his fists. As kids, his was the hot temper, mine was fitful. I never understood it, but when young, Gene somehow always found himself right in the middle of trouble. And it was Henry, the rambunctious one, who caused some of the trouble. He was always looking for a fight, though he was not in the least bit vicious, and didn't really have a bad temper. "Looking for attention," Mom said, "because they didn't get enough from me and they certainly had no attention from their father."

Gail was the studious one but made time to take over the potato peeling and the washing machine after Ann joined the Air Force. She also got to socialize. Well-liked, Gail was the sought-after "blonde bombshell." Where Ann had little time to party, Gail got in her share of beach-party bonfires. Henry and Gail graduated at the top of their classes. Both burned the midnight oil studying. And Gail went on to become a registered nurse.

Months after Gordon was born, rheumatic fever and polio permanently damaged his brain. Encephalitis. At six he became too much for Mom to care for. With no other choice, because of our family's financial and emotional condition, she placed Gordon in a mental institution, where he stayed until he died at age eighteen. In those days, they didn't permit visiting rights to siblings, only to Mom. For her—and I know this from all our talks—the decision to commit Gordon was the most distressful in all her living years. She felt as though she had buried him alive. Over the years of so many regular hospital visits, she would remain heartsick and broken for days after. She never got over Gordon's illness, hospitalization and death. She went to her grave feeling guilty for not having done enough to keep and save her son.

At the bottom of the heap of kids, Mary Sue and I got lots more spare time to play. Gratefully, I washed no diapers. Each of us probably inherited characteristics from both ends—a touch of "terminal seriousness" and a touch of the "good humour." When we became teenagers, with Billy's help, Henry, Mary Sue and I got to work at Ontario Hydro even while we were studying.

By 1952, five of us—Billy, Ann, Gene, Paul and Gordon—were no longer home. That left Gail, Henry, four-year-old Mary Sue and me with Mom. None of us made it to Harvard or the Massachusetts Institute of Technology (MIT), not that we didn't measure up intelligence-wise. After finishing high school, Bill acquired a commerce certificate at New Brunswick's St. Michael's, while Ann joined the Air Force. Gene became an electrician. Paul joined the Air Force and later studied at what was then Toronto's Ryerson Institute of Technology (now Ryerson Polytechnic University). And he worked throughout his career for Ontario Hydro. My brother Henry graduated from engineering, did a stint at graduate school then joined the workforce. Got to tell you, Henry received and rejected a scholarship to study for his master's degree at MIT. I completed a university degree and was in graduate school for a time. Mary Sue received her teaching degree at St. Thomas University.

Quite something how both older brothers, Bill and Paul, made such successful careers with Ontario Hydro. That was Bill's only job. And he reached the top of the company's pecking order as a construction auditor before he retired at age fifty-five. The three years following, Bill bought and then profitably sold a grocery convenience store back home on the Bay de Chaleur. Paul did a patriotic stint with Canada's Air Force Radar Unit. Like Bill, he reached the top of his ladder in construction surveying before retiring at age sixty-five. As an electrician, Gene travelled, I think, to almost every major city in North America, though every bit as often visiting their local casinos and watering holes as well.

Henry, the mathematician, became the top-dog engineer for Cape Breton's largest newsprint plant. As said back home, Henry had hundreds of men underneath him.

Gail's had many careers. First as a nurse in Bathurst, New Brunswick, then in London, Ontario, then in Santa Barbara, California. She loved pediatrics. Probably why she married. Once her own kiddies grew tall, Gail purchased a franchise for The Second Cup. For five years of sweat, she made a ton of money, and then sold it for another bucketful. Not surprising, Gail outdid every other franchise at cleanliness, order, staff development, retail sales and profitability.

Susan's checkered career, stretched from teaching school, real estate management and sales, owning and operating three franchises of The Second Cup, to developing Provincetown's best, and one of the largest, bed-and-breakfast inns. She bought an eight-suite historic inn and developed the adjacent property into a seventy- guest establishment over the next years. Recently, she sold that and is looking for a new career.

Ann left a successful Air Force career to marry Art, an Air Force officer. In order to marry an officer, she had to leave, as she had yet to achieve officer status. Ann would have, no doubt, received her commission. Her European stint got her an invitation to attend Queen Elizabeth's coronation in 1952. Not bad for a down-home girl. For several years, with Art as aide-de-camp to Canada's Governor General Massey, Ann often found herself amidst Canada's powerbrokers. "That must have been expensive fashion wear," I said. "No," Ann replied. "I sewed all my own gowns."

Parcels and Poems
Even though her children had flown the coop, believe it or not, Mom contin-

ued to bake, bake, bake and preserve, and to pack those monstrous boxes of care packages for us to share with our friends. And she never let up on sending them to all of us no matter where we were living. On a regular basis, in the mail, these large boxes arrived filled with gumdrop cakes, mocha balls, oatmeal fudge and date-filled cookies, scotch cookies, homemade white and whole-wheat raisin breads, along with bottles of her preserved wild-strawberry jam, peach and plum jam, pickles, beets and home-canned lobster and clams that she and Emile, her friend of so many years, canned by the hundreds in the late-summer season. These boxes would be followed by another parcel containing her very carefully foil-wrapped meat pies, along with some special darned, knitted or sewn gift.

There's one special parcel from Mom that my sister Ann will never forget. "In the summer of 1966, a large box arrived by post from Mom, which included fresh stocks of summer savory with the instructions 'Hang to dry.' At the time, my husband, Art, and I were in the middle of an Air Force transfer to Europe, and we lived in a seventeen-foot trailer in Trenton, Ontario. So the summer savory was put out to dry on the clothesline while we took off for the day. But that day in Trenton saw the storm of the summer. On our return, nothing was left on the clothesline, but we were now living in a savory- seasoned trailer park."

Mom could have managed any packing company. I've never seen the likes of it. Nothing ever got smashed or broken. Mom just never did anything half-assed. On top of all that, she always took the time to write special prose or a verse that suited each one of us, even when we ranged in ages all the way up to our sixties—she knew we were still kids at heart.

Finding a Way

That did it. Nobody was left at home—only Mom and the big house. She was living alone in the house—Emile lived twenty-six miles down the road in Bathurst. Now she faced, perhaps in a different way, her "failed Catholic marriage vows." In her mind, she now had proof that not having lived up to her vows of "marriage till death do us part," her loneliness without the children was her punishment.

Just think! All her kids got fed, clothed, educated and were on their way. She had performed miracles in providing us with safety, shelter, food and such a wonderful diversity of life experiences, surely it was now her turn to relax, bask in the sun and smell her lilac trees. Now in her early sixties, it would seem that she deserved a break. At least, a gentle slide into the golden years. Time to breathe easy and kick back a little.

Not to be. Like her marriage, her sixties still didn't deliver easy street. Her first retirement year after rearing her children got a start akin to the sheriff's visit twenty years earlier when he nailed up the sign on our house, "County Tax Notice Bankrupt Sale." That bankrupt notice referred to our back taxes owing on the house and our unpaid grocery bills. Fresh into her golden age, here's the notice Mom received from her insurance company, cancelling the house insurance.

March 30, 1970

Dear Mrs. Culligan. Because of the age of the building we require an electrical certificate done by a qualified electrician to prove the work has already been done and advise on the plumbing as well....

In the previous twenty years, all her earnings had gone towards looking after the day-to-day things. We all know the list: schooling, clothing, medical needs, food and fuel, along with upkeep essentials that gobbled every red penny. Not a dime to spare. We still had the well, deep in the basement, but there were times in spring, after the snowmelt, that we couldn't use the well water and other times when the well just went dry. The roof was beyond repair. The veranda floorboards showed their wear. At no time in those days could Mom ever think of major repair.

During this period, when I was still at university, there came an update from Mom. She sent me the insurance notice with these words: "Now, Tom dear, don't you worry about the insurance because I'm not. I've always found a way and it'll be no different this time."

Believe it or not, she did find a way. Mom started a new business. That was her solution. Can you imagine? Long past her prime—she was no spring chicken. Now in her sixties! As she said, "My hairdressing job just couldn't make what I needed fast enough, so I've got to work quickly to make big bucks."

It wasn't like she ever stopped working the neighbours' heads, she simply hung out an additional sign on the house: Hotel. She filled the house with boarders. She rented the five empty bedrooms to workingmen. For near two years, she ran a hotel, hairdressing salon and did her monthly government

Dominion Bureau of Statistics job as well for one week each month for twenty years. And she did it all without help. No extra bodies. Around the clock, Mom shampooed heads, cut and set hair, baked bread and pies and sticky buns too, made roast and scalloped potatoes and God knows what else. There was no letdown on scrubbing. The house stayed clean and polished as always.

As usual, she gave her all. Her boarders paid well. Mind you, they demanded a lot. Not only did she feed them a gigantic breakfast of egg, bacon and oatmeal, they also insisted on a huge lunch pail filled each day, to keep their hunger at bay until their main meal at suppertime. They were the team of engineers and surveyors from the Saint John, New Brunswick, Marine Company, building the Belledune port. As Mom said, "I could take it all, for in less than two years, I knew full well it would all soon come to an end. What made it worthwhile was the bulging cash envelope at the end of each Friday's supper."

How I so remember my Christmas at home that year! The boarders had gone home for Christmas week and this was Mom's one weekend off. Once she completed the hairdressing part, she had three days free. Still, she baked into the wee hours of every night, making sure we had our Christmas delights just like always.

The insurance got renewed. Along with all new wiring, new roof, additional plumbing, rotten boards replaced, and Mom even got a new well. Yet even with the freshly minted money, she had to borrow some extra from the Bank of Nova Scotia. That just meant she'd keep right on trucking.

Filling the Emptiness

Mom tried to get used to being at home without any kids while still having to work hard to pay the bills. Physically, mentally and emotionally, during this transition time, working as a superwoman left her drained and lonely. There was just way too much for her to do. In the midst of this, she swung into high gear as "Mamère," devoted grandmother to all her twelve grandchildren and eight great-grandchildren.

This was now about the 1970s, with Mom in her mid-sixties, and when we adult kids were just beginning to be able to respond financially to her needs. Though my older siblings, Billy and Ann, gave very generously while we were younger, their financial support had dwindled by the 1960s as their own family responsibilities grew. From my understanding about this time, Mom was overwhelmed by loneliness, financial insecurity, guilt, weariness and uncertainty.

That Christmas was the very first time I noticed that she was drinking heavily. She told me later that the drinking filled all these needs and her sense of emptiness. Alcohol was her crutch. It dulled the pain for her.

Dad Waked and Buried

Mom got herself out of that scary financial insurance crisis herself, with some help from the bank, but another tough blow was when Dad died Christmas of 1975. His alcoholic days had caught up to him. He'd been living in Toronto most all the years after being tossed out of the province by our sheriff in 1951, and except for the two times he showed up in our driveway in those first years, he never returned home again. In New Brunswick, you would have thought that would free Mom. Unshackle the marriage grip. But a strange mix of feelings engulfed her during and following this "finalization."

The news we got was that he had died of a heart attack, but the details only came out later. Dad was drunk and driving the car, along with my brother Gene who was also drunk. They were on Highway 401 coming back from the Woodbine racetrack in Toronto, when he had a heart attack and died instantly.

When Dad died that December, the older siblings wanted him "waked and buried" back home in New Brunswick. We all asked Mom for permission and she agreed. And so we did just that. It was a two-night wake and full funeral at Belledune Church. Even though I really didn't want to have anything to do with this, it was my oldest brother, Bill, and I who made all the arrangements.

While the intentions may have been good, the results were not. We felt later that we could have done without that "at home" event. Gene, despite attending with his wife and four kids, stayed on at the house for almost three weeks, and every bit like Dad had been—violent, raging and drunk. It was, all in all, an agonizing experience and one that Mom and the rest of us had been removed from for years. To top it off, the Culligan relatives attending the wake went on and on about their long-beloved and missed cousin, Charly.

We did what we thought was right, but we could have done without the New Brunswick Charly Culligan wake and funeral. (In 1980, Gene stopped drinking and has been living a happy, sober life since. A blessing and, I might add, an even happier and prouder Mom, for her son's powerful example of sobriety).

Covering Catholic Anxieties

"Yes, Charly was gone," Mom said, "but that didn't make my seeing Emile, a divorced Catholic, any less sinful."

A reasonable time after Dad's death, the divorced Emile asked Mom to marry him. "My God," Mom said, "after all these years, me looking after my children by myself, why would I marry another man now?" No question, she liked Emile and enjoyed his company. Emile's musical talents were a match for hers, and what a great couple they made on the dance floor. At about this time, she told Emile she wanted only a platonic relationship from then on. She told me that she drank "to cover her Catholic anxieties."

By the end of the 1970s, Mom had turned seventy. Her drinking progressed. Under these conditions, the results couldn't help but affect everybody in close contact. Sometimes the siblings exhibited worse behaviour than our now-alcoholic Mom. So her drinking increased, especially during our family visits. In spite of this, as always, she remained a nighthawk, and still managed to produce her multiple baking and preserving provisions for siblings, grandchildren and visitors.

It Was Getting to Me

However, I did find the humorous side of my last Christmas with Mom while she still drank alcohol. In a way, it makes loving sense to always find a touch of humour even in the worst of times, and I even eventually came to understand and accept her alcoholism after I learned about Alcoholics Anonymous just as a family member of an alcoholic. That helped me to clearly separate the Mom I knew and loved, from what this disease was doing to her. Looking for humour was my way of maintaining my sanity, rather than getting caught up in misery. I guess, ultimately, it's my ability to see the bright side of life.

So it was that once again, I was able to remember Christmas Day, 1978 with some humour. Mom had still prepared and roasted the turkey. I set the table, this time in the oak-panelled dining room, and we included lots of candles for Christmas atmosphere. Of course, we had Bing Crosby crooning "I'm Dreaming of a White Christmas" and other songs. Susan and I got everyone to the table. My older brother, Paul, had made it home that Christmas too; Emile, as usual, took his place. My brother Henry and his wife, Cathy, and their three very young boys came up from Cape Breton. All was well, with a family setting right out of a movie. We had music, lights and food, while outside snowflakes swirled in the bitter cold. It just doesn't get any better.

As everybody was seated, Susan and I served the plates. Mom sat on the side rather than on her usual armchair at the head of the table. It was late, probably about 8:30 p.m. That meant lots to drink beforehand.

But even from Mom's short walk as she left the kitchen, I noticed the staggering, so I helped her into the chair she chose, very gingerly. Earlier, she had given us one of her crying-jag stories yet again. Now only two places had no full plates of food, so I quickly disappeared into the kitchen to fetch the dinners.

When I returned to the dining-room table, I saw only the top of Mom's head. She was face first in the turkey, potatoes and gravy. I never forgot that scene, even though we quickly cleaned up. She took no interest in eating that night. She only drank wine.

Words got said that really made no sense, because there are no words to lessen or alleviate alcoholic symptoms or behaviour. Instead, all those words thrown at the drinker are much like throwing gas on a fire. The results inflame an already worsening situation. In the end, all you get is an emotionally charged atmosphere where no happiness, serenity or understanding exists. Only compassion for the alcoholic loved one can help.

It seemed that it all fell on her at once—being alone at home, feeling guilty about her relationship with Emile and fearful always that she had not lived up to her Catholic marriage vows. Then there was the insurance notice and financial woes, and finally Dad's wake and funeral. She had gradually made the shift from a drop of gin in her cup of black tea for "relief and comfort" to a drop of black tea in her gin, albeit still in the teacup.

In a conversation with her after I discovered her pouring gin into a cup of black tea, I recall just how troubled she was about my concern. It took me some time to connect her uncharacteristic erratic behaviour with alcohol until I stumbled upon her pouring that gin. Later, I found a Gordon's Dry Gin bottle hidden behind the yellow sugar tins behind the pantry door.

For several evenings before that discovery, I was aware that Mom slurred her words, but I just thought she was tired. Her sudden mood changes scared me most. From what seemed out of nowhere, she started to sniffle and then cry, bemoaning her life in self-pitying monologues.

"You don't know what it's like, living like this. Oh, I ought to know better.

Not even see him. God's getting back to me after all these thirty-five years of keeping company with Emile…"

Night after night she repeated these reproaches over and over. "What will take away this pain? Oh, I know folks don't approve, but what am I supposed to do? Bury myself?"

With a heavy heart, I struggled to the decision that I had to talk with her about the alcohol drinking and the unusual behaviour. I also observed that her previous energy, bounce and song were missing. I was seeing Mom in a totally different way, almost like a stranger now. I became apprehensive and uneasy. Suddenly during the morning, I heard my own voice asking her, "Mom, how are you feeling?"

"I suppose the question is about your mother having a drink or two more than usual?"

"Well, yes, that's part of what I'm wondering about."

"And just what do you mean by that?" she retorted defensively.

Somehow calmness came over me. "Well, Mom, over these recent nights, you appeared drunk after cup after cup of tea with gin. Every night you cried. Like crying in your teacup, literally. Something's really bothering you. Because your constant references to your past life and God's punishment have to be about your years of seeing Emile and your 'Catholic status.'"

I gained courage as she looked at me, wide-eyed. "Why don't you marry Emile? Get rid of all this shame and guilt due to this Catholic marriage vow thing? And just forget what others think and say?"

That broke the dam.

"You have no idea, my dear. I've been Catholic all my life. That will never change. I cannot marry Emile because he's a divorced man. I made my bed; I'll be the one to lie in it. Yes, I admit to taking a few more drinks to escape. Even in the earlier years, I took a drink at the dances with Emile to cover up. Oh, for a time that helped me face the people. Even forget! But to myself I'd think, what will take this 'thing' away from my heart?"

My head was really spinning then. I'd probably always been aware of Mom's religious Catholic-guilt upbringing, but really never understood how immense her spiritual suffering was. Looking at her, it seemed that the talking had taken some of the strain from her face. "But Mom, aren't you afraid this drinking will get worse?"

Because of what she did and said, I'll never forget that morning. The kettle was whistling away on the stovetop as we talked. Then she picked up the dented tea tin, grabbed handfuls of loose tea and dropped them into the old granite tea mug. Slowly she poured the bubbling water. The steeped tea looked bluish-black while tiny bubbles crackled around the rim of the mug. Carefully she poured our cups, then walked into the pantry with her cup.

My heart sank with a thud. "Oh my God! She's gone again to pour gin into her tea!" I thought. I just felt paralyzed. After what seemed like an eternal wait, with my feet glued to the floor, she suddenly appeared, her tea in one hand and with the other, offering me a plateful of her sugar doughnuts. I guess my relief upon seeing the doughnuts, must have returned my pulse, pumping blood down to my feet, because suddenly I could move them again.

She placed the plate on the table, then slowly walked over to the sink window and looked out over her beloved ocean.

In a near whisper she said, "Dear Tommy, don't you worry about me. I'll never drink as your father did. Before that could happen, I'd stop. I've known heartbreak, despair and sickness in my own life as well as in other's. Through my faith I've gotten out of worse conditions. This will be no different. And as you'll learn, dear Tommy, in your own good time, nothing in this life is equally the same for any two people.

"Some folks live to a ripe ol' age. Others don't make it past fifty. I plan on staying around a lot longer.

"It doesn't matter that you think I should put aside my guilt. As long as Charly was alive, I was still married to him in the eyes of God. I made the vows. That's what it means to be a Catholic.

"There are times I still hope a couple of drinks will let me forget. Dear God, now I know that no amount of alcohol changes anything. No, dear. Have no fear, I'll not go the way of Charly. I'll stop drinking first. This is between me and my God. I'll find the way as I've always done."

Mom's drinking caused no cars to smash, no windows to break, nor did she throw any radios or chairs against doors or walls. She never even knocked over a glass that I am aware of. Years later, thinking back on this morning, I asked her when she first noticed that she had a drinking problem.

"Well dear, I remember playing cards for penny ante with Mary Sue and some others. Mary Sue lost and when I saw her fallen face, I laughed and said,

'Mary Sue, if it affects you that bad, you shouldn't play for money!'

"But then as I started up the stairs, Mary Sue began to cry, and when I asked what she was crying about, she said through sniffling and tears,' You have a drinking problem! We're going to have a drunken mother too!'

"Tommy, that startled me. Having my youngest say this alarmed me to thinking—what am I doing with drinking?"

After that experience, Mom became increasingly aware and self-conscious about her drinking. But it didn't stop.

"Oh, I knew it was getting to me. I just delayed admitting such. Instead I thought, damn it to hell, so what? I was bold then. 'Sure, I'm drinking and it's no goddamn wonder,' I'd say to my dear friend Marion when we'd have a drink together. She and I would confide in each other. What would we have to look forward to without a drink? I thought my drinking gave me nerve, yet I knew that if I kept on drinking, my own remorse would make me feel worse."

Even after Dad died, her guilt intensified and she continued to drink gin. Except now she graduated to a glass filled with gin and a splash of water. No ice cubes. Over the years when I visited for weeks at a time, she never drank in the daytime and not even every night. But on the nights that she did drink, her bemoaning of terrible woes and "nobody really understands" progressed to deeper and deeper sadness. Tons of tears fell. Her "poor me" jags persisted to 1979 when she joined Alcoholics Anonymous.

Many times over the years I expressed my sincere gratitude to Mom for thereby relieving me of additional devastation from his alcoholism by her brave and courageous decision to remove Dad from our home. I was often a witness to the ongoing wreckage in many homes throughout our community as the result of drunken dads. Denial was the common cover that those families used in "keeping the family together." Though it's entirely each family's business, I saw, and still see, the harm inflicted by alcoholism on spouses, children and older adults.

Alcoholism must be the most cunning, baffling and powerful disease because of the very way families remain oblivious to the escalating and devastating cycle that the disease reproduces. Generation follows generation in the name of love. It's a love that calls itself protection, "Say nothing!" "It's nobody's business!" Silence and denial at all costs!

Looking back again over the years, I guess that Mom's sixty-ninth year had to be her worst in drinking, what she called the "pity pot." But it's never too late to change. Hope really is eternal. The best example of this is that Mom did eventually find sobriety. Though her worst drinking lasted only about ten years, it was painful for her. She was seventy when she decided to join Alcoholics Anonymous and thereafter enjoyed twenty-one years of sobriety. She founded the first A.A. meeting for our entire area.

Throughout the 1980s, Mom attended major A.A. conventions and spiritual workshops in New Brunswick, Montreal, Toronto, Hamilton, London and Barrie. She loved the attention and made a host of friends through her open kitchen, pots of tea and teacup readings, and her baking was shared with lots of alcoholics, sober or not. Mom especially sought out the womenfolk she knew had been suffering from miserable drinking problems. They in turn loved her. At Christmastime, after she sobered up, lots of folks she had worked so hard with to "help sober up for even a short duration" stopped by her home with little tokens of their appreciation and love for her.

Over these years, Mom still kept company with Emile as a friend. Concerned, I once asked Emile how he had felt about her drinking, and he would only say, "Your mother can get a little nasty when she's had way too much, which became more frequent, but other than that, it doesn't bother me." How true to form for Emile. He said little of the personal level. Never heard Emile minding anybody else's business.

Mom finally closed her hairdressing salon near the end of her drinking. A full-time mother gets no pay. Neither during nor after, as in Mom's case. As a self-employed entrepreneur, she didn't have the luxury of buying into the Canadian government's pension plans or even whole life insurance. At the end of her road with the "providing for children" responsibilities, there was no husband or man's pension to kick in.

Though Emile was generous over the years, frequently buying groceries, fixing furniture and the odd thing and even handing over cash to her occasionally, he never really provided for her or our family. In all my years as a kid, teenager and through university, Emile never gave me so much as a penny. Nor to any of my other siblings. It wasn't his job to do so. Mom provided for us, not anyone else. In a sense, his and Mom's thirty-five-year relationship was strange because Emile visited, ate and slept over countless times. But the way he lived his life, with moderation and with carefully learned skills, served as an important example to me.

In his ninetieth year, Emile died while cleaning the snow off his car. Folks who hurried to help him had found a seafood chowder still stewing on his stovetop, being prepared, to bring up to Mom's, for their dinner that night.

We siblings grew even more generous in our financial support for Mom. Her last twenty-five years were financially secure. Yet, she had one heck of a hard time accepting our financial generosity. She faced a real challenge trying to accept that others were now helping her. She even felt guilty about it. Many times, I tried to gently explain how my giving to her now was only natural, and that it was a sharing of resources. And after all, that was no different from what she had done all her life. I reminded Mom many times that it was her giving that made possible my ability to give now.

Mom at her beloved piano. 1999

Twelve

Three Priests and Silence When it Ends

Most years, Christmas at our house was pretty much the same, especially when it came to Mom's participation in playing the organ and singing for Christmas in the church. Twice it happened that it was very different.

While Christmas brought Mom's busiest time for Margo's Beauty Bar, it also brought her obligations to contribute her musical talents for the church. Somehow, she managed to handle both. Just like the farmers, who never let a sunny day pass during the fall without taking advantage of good weather to cut the hay, trash the oats, or dig potatoes—so too, Mom saw to it that no one ever got turned away during Christmas and New Year's holiday weeks. She squeezed in appointments for everyone who wanted one, because she knew that January delivered few heads.

On Christmas Eve, Mom worked her darnedest to get her last customer out of the house by 10:00 p.m. She wanted to be sitting at the church organ by 10:30 p.m. for that last-minute choir practice. On this particular Christmas Eve, I stood in the kitchen ironing my red soutane and white surplice altar boy's outfit to wear for serving at midnight Mass. When 10:30 p.m. ticked by, Mom still had two women under the dryers and she was combing out her twentieth head for that day.

Father Damure, the Jacquet River Parish priest, had arrived to pick her up. Mom played the organ and sang in the Jacquet River Church, while us kids continued attending the Belledune Church. Our Culligan village belonged to the Belledune Catholic Parish, so our family attended Catholic school and church in Belledune. However, because Mom was born in Jacquet River, the neighbouring Catholic parish, she started her organ playing at that church and continued doing so until she stopped being their organist. So, you could call us a church-going split family.

Most times, Father Damure's picking up Mom didn't cause a problem, because he'd be back at the church sacristy by 10:30 p.m. for sure. Besides, the drive back gave them time to review the night's music-cued agenda.

Except this time was different. It was 11:30 p.m. and both Father Damure and Mom were still not at church. Her final customer remained in curlers. We were all somewhat nervous because we'd passed the stage of talking Christmas lights, while Father Damure waited it out at the kitchen table, still in his over-coat and winter boots. My younger sister, Mary Sue, grew real anxious over Mom making it even later. Finally, Mary Sue, unable to contain herself, said, "My God, Mom, hurry up, we're now going to be late for midnight Mass."

Father Damure just chuckled and said, "Mary Sue, don't you worry about us being late for midnight Mass, because nobody can start without the priest and the organist, and that's me and your mother."

Like a bride and groom, Mom and Father Damure were indeed the central players for Christmas Eve Mass. Though they arrived late that Christmas, nobody was much the wiser as to whose heads caused the delay.

Up to that day, except for her short stay in Boston, Mom had played the church organ near thirty-five years. At fourteen years of age, she accompanied her mama on the church organ, continuing the long line of Firlotte church organists and soloists. Mom got cemented to the church like a pew. Just like her sisters Tookie and Camilla, their music studies enabled them to play and sing Latin Gregorian Masses for the dead, for weddings, ordinations, feast days and even for Sunday Masses. To the end, Mom remembered every Latin line and verse. Be it the "Ave Maria," "Dies de Rea," "Sanctus," "Kyria" or "Gloria."

From inside her belly while pedalling the ol' church organ, Mom taught each of us Latin and the organ notes. "While I was pregnant," she said, "all of you got to hear and feel Gregorian in full delight. And all in happy times."

The Next Christmas

Life does at times seem cruel. Especially when people go out of their way to hurt others because of judgements. In a mixed-up way, that's what next happened to Mom, the Christmas of 1964. She got thrown another curve to deal with. After the usual Sunday organ playing, Father Damure drove her home after Mass. Instead of just leaving her off as usual, he asked to have a chat with her in the house.

Once in the kitchen, he told her his task at hand was one of the most difficult he had performed since his ordination. He was direct. He said she could no longer be the church organist because a group of parishioners demanded she be removed. The reason given was that she was known to keep the company of another man, that being Emile, while being separated from her husband. Now it was two issues that compounded the fact that, in Catholic eyes, she lived in sin. This branded her as an outcast Catholic.

Close friends, both she and Father Damure were devastated by this turn of events. But his hands were tied by the parishioners' demands. He had to deliver Mom's head.

The choir gave a going-away, thank-you party for her at our house. Arthur Arsenault, the choir director, cried, as they all did when they presented Mom with a card and gift. I remember the party seemed more like a funeral.

That event delivered mean stuff, especially from our school-bus mates. My siblings and I were taunted by "Look at the whore's bastards." Those nasty comments came not from strangers—our own cousins delivered them! Mom said nothing about the parishioners' removal of her as organist. She never talked about how she felt. Neither did we. The conversations and the feelings took years to unravel.

Amazingly, Mom never gave in to her attackers with comments or actions. Yet the personal blow dealt deep damage inside. Her dedication to the Catholic faith fabricated increasing guilt over what had occurred. Unfortunately, she interpreted the punishment that had been demanded by the parishioners, as "I'm guilty because of my unfaithfulness to my marriage vows." From that experience, she took on their scorn, accepting it as God's punishment   and this long after her separation from Dad.

In the 1960s, our community was still ruled by Roman Catholic dogma. Even though I could see there was no loving sense of what was done and said, there were no human relationships that could even consider thwarting the authority of the Church. It was a black-and-white matter. Mom's life, as was ours, got lived from confession to confession. We all lived through a scale of sins— venial, mortal to cardinal. Even with priestly penance and absolution, there really was never any escape from being in a constant state of sin.

At Sunday Mass, all the parishioners were on display. Those who did not walk up to the communion rail were guilty of mortal sin. And we knew that were we to die of mortal sin before confessing, we'd be going straight to hell. Little leeway was made for a brief visit to purgatory. Under that kind of public stress and judgement, many of us made it to the communion rail without confessing. And after a period of time, that all just buried into deep guilt. Since the priest controlled God's mercy with ill-fated confessions, somehow the real meaning of God got lost in the interpretation.

But Nothing Lasts Forever

After a few years, a new parish priest arrived at Jacquet River along with a bunch of new declared changes after Vatican II. Father Trudel was the new guy. Mom found him to be friendly when they met during parish events. Church organists were few and far between, as were the dwindling churchgoers. Times were a-changing.

One morning at tea, Father Trudel came knocking at our door. He asked if Mom would come back as church organist. Wow! For her, that request was like being handed a million dollars. Church music was her identity. Indeed, she agreed. But even though at first she cautioned that it could only be part-time, she committed to play organ for funerals, weddings and special church events just as always. She never accepted any pay for these services. Any contribution received from families for funerals and such were donated to the Church.

"Going back to the church organ was easy," Mom said. "That's my life." The large practiced choirs were a thing of the past, but she readily blended in with the new music. Guitars and brass were added instruments to their regular Sunday Masses. The one big thing that remained the same, Mom said, "was that people always get married and they die, and that gave me plenty opportunity to bang out my Latin favourites."

And it was exactly in that manner in which Mom received another joyous gift. One Sunday, Mom was playing the "Ave Maria" for communion music, when she noticed Father Trudel leaving the altar rail. He was carrying the large golden chalice while walking directly to her, seated at the organ bench.

He stopped by her side, picked out a host and said, "Margaret, receive the body and blood of Christ," to which Mom replied, "Father, I cannot receive because I'm not confessed," to which Father Trudel replied, "Margaret, I'm telling you, through the almighty power of God, you've long been absolved of all your sins, and I'm giving you Holy Communion."

That's just how it happened.

After years of torture and self-doubt over her marriage vows, Margaret returned to the Holy Communion she had so longed for. As for Father Trudel, he gave no ear or voice to any parishioner's gossip or criticism.

Many years later when Mom was ninety years old, though she had played organ at home daily, she no longer played at church. Her parish pastor was on a leave of absence and the last priest to fill in for him was Father Parker. This was the same parish priest who, thirty-five years earlier, had warned her that since she was not only separated from Dad but was also seeing Emile, he felt that he had to refuse her Holy Communion because of her "known sinful state."

After Mass that Sunday, Father Parker asked if he could come over to our house to visit. It happened that I was also home at the time for a two-week stay and I still find it tough to believe what happened next.

Father Parker was no sooner in the house than he got down on his knees and begged Mom's forgiveness for what he had done and said to her thirty-five years earlier. She immediately lifted him up with a big hug, assuring him she'd never held anything against him. They talked and talked and tears were falling while drinking tea and eating sticky buns that she had just happened to have baked fresh and warm.

What happened next is a reminder to not put off to tomorrow what you can do today.

Days later, Father Parker dropped dead from a heart attack. However, he hadn't departed before leaving Mom the gift of a lifetime. His visit helped her to slice off a gigantic piece of guilt that had become embedded over with years of steeped Catholicism.

I suspect that had Mom lived another year, she might have cast off all guilt.

And Silence When It Ends

Wouldn't I love to stop those hands of time for just a little longer? It's true, I am surrounded by death, but it's not morose. In a natural way, dying takes its place. First leaves, then a branch, and later the whole tree. Usually it all happens silently. Grass greens, turns yellow, wilts and then is gone. Bright daisies, yellow and white, petals fall left and right, until nothing's in sight. Gardens full and lush drop their stalks by fall. Salmon just know to do the right thing. Caterpillars turn into butterflies, and then flutter gently away. Logs in a fireplace hold their weight, and then dissipate, ash, earth, gas, sediment, sparks and skeletons, all signs of involvement to evolvement, and the cycles of life where death is just a part.

One thing ends so another can begin.

Sparkling fire. Lit candles. Shining stars. Streams of sunlight. Crawling ants. Croaking frog. Stirring wind. Scampering squirrel. Ruffled feathers. Smiling child. Honking horn. Whispering voices. Drifting smells. Chiming bells. Clicking heels. Smacking lips. Lapping waves. All this tells us there is life.

But there's also rot and decay that feeds the seeds that give us food. We never know exactly when something begins or just where it all goes. But we feel the emptiness and silence when it ends.

Watching over Mom those last few days, really, I didn't know where it all began. Or who or where she even was in the spaces in between. Instead, I got to feel what I could never see in those spaces between when she was with us and when she drifted off. Like the leaf that dropped, and even the branch that fell, I was still certain it was a tree, and as sure as I was, I knew that it was my mom, even while her voice trailed off.

Even in death, Mom left us intact. No final instructions. No regret. We sat around. Stood beside. For six preciously gifted weeks, we absorbed her silent love while she took leave for another shore. Call it a gift. These last weeks were in the Gatineau Hospital. Small and new. Perched on top of the mountains. Seeing for miles, I'd point beyond to where New Brunswick was, while looking over the Gatineau River, snaking its way through the valley below. This all could have been Switzerland in another time—the place resembled a mountain resort. And I've got to believe St. Ann herself must have trained the staff. Gentle and loving, beyond the call of any duty.

Those last six weeks, she couldn't eat. The stroke had left her very weak. Gently, Gail, Susan, and Paul, my partner, and I lovingly fed her through a straw, drops at a time. It was all with laughter though tears dripped through the spaces between.

"I love you," she said softly to us. And in turn we said, over and over, again and again, you are the love, we know you love, you've given us love, we've always felt your love—for you are God's love.

Although I'd hugged and kissed Mom often in the past, I did something I had never before done. I stroked my mother. Held her hand and rubbed her shoulders and massaged her neck. Wiped her mouth and moistened her lips. Sponged her lids and washed her limbs. Changed her linen and powdered her cheeks. Paul did her hair, brushing her curls and spraying them carefully. Gail, Susan, Paul and I repeated this scene over and over and over.

We wheeled her around and around the grounds like a queen in a fancy reclining wheelchair, pillows everywhere to buffer her brittle bones, thick white cotton blankets up to her chin. Put a bouquet of white daisies on her lap, just to notice a small army of bugs crawling up her sleeves. She never said anything while we were swatting them off, maybe she never noticed.

Mom would even entertain us with short stories, spoken lively in an Indian dialect. No doubt Pelagie was near, all smiling, laughing, deciphering a few words here and there. Part Indian, Great Grandmother Pelagie Culligan's spirit seemed on Mom's mind and tongue those last days. Pelagie, like Mom, were kindred spirits in sharing food and clothing to anyone in need.

And sometimes, we played the orchestra—softly, rhythmically, with voices, brass and violin. Because music was always part of her scene. How she loved to listen. Indeed, she sang. She could recall the sounds, so she hummed and tongued to the notes. Her face shone, smiled, twinkled and winked many a time. For she knew we were all playing for time.

And Mom knew well the race was at its end.

Finally she said, "Right now, it's taking too long." That's quite something, for it didn't take long after that for her to slip silently to the other side.

I have not ever witnessed a transition so beautiful. How could death be so peaceful! We now know it, because we saw it. We were all there: Gail, Susan, Paul and I holding hands, head and feet. Feeling the shift of her leaving. Until her last soft breath, she had eyes so blue and bright. They were twinkling with delight, looking straight up into the skylight. As we whispered her God's delight, Mom gave us one last sign of her own delight with a squint with all her might, then ever so softly, closed her eyes with a last breath of fresh air.

Sure enough, it was there. Bones and flesh left behind. We cried. We smiled. Somehow we just knew that the tears and the smiles were the "in between." Hers and ours, all were the same. After all, she never left us. The lack of movement gave evidence that something's missing, until, that is, we hear it and feel it in each other. She's not gone. She's our middle or somewhere at our end, only to give us our beginning once again.

Later on, after Mom's dying, my brother-in-law, John Partington, who held vigil alongside us with Mom, said of her, "I was struck by the bipolar complexity of her nature as I experienced her, as well as my own ambivalence towards her—love and respect mixed sometimes with resentment and mistrust. On careful reflection I believe the latter had more to do with me than it did her.

"In her good years and in her last few months and days, Margaret's personality reflected a spectrum of characteristics. Publicly she was energetic, cheerful, fun loving, interested in others, generous, caring, accepting and open.

"But there was also the lurking underside of her faintly veiled judgemental nature, including a self-serving hidden curriculum.

"You sensed she wasn't satisfied, and perhaps she felt nothing could ever satisfy her. In the last year and a half, her multilayered nature became more apparent. Most memorable for me was her disappointment, bitterness, anger and suspicion.

"But closer to the end, her positive tendencies reasserted themselves. She became forgiving, thankful and grateful. Her love and appreciation of the world of music, flowers, trees, sky, weather, wind and poetry returned. Then at last, I could feel her connect with me and with others in an unconditional loving way, which I found just wonderful. It gave me hope for the possibility of my own metamorphosis."

An image John says he will hold on to is Mamère gardening: "Bum up, bent double from the waist, legs dead straight, and head down for hours in the perennial flower beds under the grand maple trees out front. Every morning after tea drinking, Margaret would faithfully zip outside to dribble little streams of cold tea on the struggling cedars, battered from the brutal winter winds. They eventually flourished. As did her African violets too, from dribbles of tea. I wonder still, was it really the tea? Or what the tea leaves said?"

Mom's determined stance carried through all she did, adjusting only to the task at hand, be it beach tricks, brushing out heads, rolling pastry or bottling strawberries.

We Noticed Small Differences

Who can predict a crisis? They sometimes come like a sudden summer storm. Whenever one comes, it can leave you confused, bemused, frustrated, agitated, irritated or even misunderstood. One and a half years before Mom died, she had quite a serious stroke. Even after her hospitalization, you would think that nothing had happened. Or at least that's what we all thought. She wanted to go on as usual. But gradually we noticed small differences.

I kept hoping nothing was different.

I think we call it denial. Such as me believing her to be fully mobile. All the previous Christmas holiday years, Susan, Paul and I loved every minute of time we had with her. They were fun. Filled with meals that we cooked for her—quite a change from all that she had always done for us. Days filled with play and contented nights of dining, music and movies that lulled us to sleep.

Our last Christmas together was the only one I ever complained about. We all grew agitated. At the time, we all figured we had good reason to be upset. Mom acted strangely. She refused to wear a sweater, even though the winter fell to near forty below. No matter what we cooked, "Surely there's something better," she'd say. Whatever we did, she couldn't be satisfied.

No question, my patience wore thin. After Christmas, we all scattered, leaving her to fend for herself—really all by herself. Even though we knew that because of the stroke she ought not be left alone, we also knew that just before Christmas she had fired all the staff my sister had hired in the fall. But we all left anyway.

Two months later, attending a conference on recovery for family members of people with addictions, I listened to a woman telling of her mother's condition.

She was a ninety-year-old lady who'd had a stroke affecting her cognitive powers, leaving her unable to cope and almost unrecognizable probably to herself and for sure to her family. The woman went on to explain that although her mother was really fearful, she pretended to look after herself. In fact, they discovered to their dismay that she no longer could even prepare a meal. Not eating, not resting properly, her mother became irritable, unreasonable and shaky.

I sat there stunned. My God! It was exactly the same as Mom! I thought of our Christmas. I called my cousin back home to have him check on her. Sure enough, he said that Mom was unable to look after herself. Oftentimes, he noted, she didn't even know night or day.

Then I said, "Bobby, surely that's got to be wrong. Because only last week, Mom told me she cooked a stew with four different meats."

"Oh no, that's impossible, Tommy, your mother has no food in the house, and besides, she wouldn't even know how to work the stove, let alone use the toaster or plug in the kettle. I suspect she survived on store-bought cookies, crackers and ginger ale. They were all just a simple matter of tearing open the packages when she remembered that she was hungry. The last meal she ate was the chicken I roasted in the oven."

That was so hard for me to believe. With every phone call to her, she'd be telling me just how much she'd been eating. Bobby reiterated that not only was Mom not cooking or eating, she had also stopped answering knocks at the door.

After hearing that, we made it home to New Brunswick fast. From that moment to her death near fifteen months later, we never ever left her alone.

A fine day at the beach

Mom and Tom. 1998

Thirteen

Letters To Mom

$\mathcal{D}$ear Mom,

Happy Birthday! Can you believe another year? And yet you left us not a year yet passed! This would be your ninety-second year of birth. Putting you in your ninety-third year.

Over the years, I have written cards, sent gifts, and had you visiting our home in Florida for your February birthday celebration. Like last year. You arrived here with Gail and John in the evening of your ninety-first birthday. We celebrated with a late-evening meal right in the Florida room, where I'm presently sitting and writing this letter to you. We took pictures. Susan was here. She fetched you folks from the airport.

My God, hard to believe that was a year ago. But how shocked we all were when, after a few weeks' visiting, you fell. It happened in this very room as you stepped down from the living room to enter the Florida room.

Somehow we got you to Mount Sinai Hospital, almost three hours later. But none of us could believe the diagnosis that you had broken your hip. You only complained of pain when you moved—it all happened so fast. And then surgery right the next morning. Imagine, you were put under, cut up, and your bones connected with screws! And you were ninety-one going into your ninety-second year.

Mom, how quickly you healed. That same day, you stood and moved some steps. We knew there was some pain, though you were so good about it all. To think you stayed in the hospital for near a week, and then they flew you back to Ottawa, to the Gatineau Hospital, for recovery. Though I didn't see it, my sisters told me that the attendants had tied one of your arms to the side of the bed and said that this was to keep you from getting up and out of bed. Really, it was to prevent you from trying to walk on your own and possibly falling and breaking the other hip. I hear you did recover quickly that time.

But I also remember when you broke your hip the second time that same year in May, and lay in the Hull Hospital in Ottawa. We wanted you to be near Gail and John's home in Gatineau for your convalescence. But it was not to be. We were all so shocked when, after a full recovery from the first surgery, you tripped over the doorstopper in the hospital's recovery section, fell back, hit your head, had a stroke and then broke the second hip. Again hospital staff had tied your right arm to the bed, but that was so you wouldn't pull out the intravenous needle stuck in your left arm. I untied you. I took the tie out. You never tried to pull the needle out, though your hand went there. I told the nurses not to tie you up again. I saw how restricting that was and I knew how you felt about that. I was appalled. No need for such force.

Although I've written cards and given you gifts for your birthday in the past, I've never written a long letter. Somehow I want to do this now.

What can I tell you, what can I say that I've never said before? How can I say anything differently? How do I say "I love you"? How does anyone say "I love you"? How can I demonstrate or even express my appreciation for all that you've done for me? What's "appreciate"?

Mom, so often I've argued over issues with you—like homosexuality, religion, community life in Belledune and your choices—but rarely have I really listened. Most always I know that I was intent on making my point. I had an agenda. I needed to scream out in some way that I knew more and that I knew better. Too often our conversations were of me trying to convert your ideas. My communication was one-sided.

Well, there were exceptions, like the conversations that I taped with you. I purposefully wanted to capture your words. Guess I finally realized that silence and an open kind of listening were required to encourage your answers to my questions. Somehow it took me all this time to grasp that gleaning knowledge and information from your thoughts and feelings about your life meant that I had to really listen. I'd need to remain quietly attentive. Before, it was only rarely that I consciously listened and communicated with humility instead of trying to formulate responses.

Wow, Mom, that's something. Well, that's something for me!

To think my whole life, I rarely gave you a chance to be yourself and just talk openly about your feelings and life experiences. I was usually ready to react and set to filter what you said. Often trying to preach to you just so you'd know how smart and spiritual I was.

Mom, this is not to victimize myself for saying these things now. Instead, I guess I'm only trying to see the truth about myself. It's only now that I am recognizing how it was with me, realizing just how I communicated. Well, I've come to the point that for me to live in good conscience and with the capacity to move to the next moment life offers, I must face the truth about myself. Perhaps today these acknowledgements will help me in future relationships. Now I need to say other things.

I remember, in letters over the years, I've thanked you for what you've done for me. How you sacrificed so much to provide for my well-being as I was growing up. I thanked you for the determination it took to separate from Dad when I was only six years old. Your courageous decision resulted in my having a violent-free environment for the rest of my years.

I remember your always saying to all of us, "To your own self be true!" More important than what you said, it was the way you lived your own life that told me—though you never flaunted your beliefs and independence, you let no one walk over you. Your head was always high above the community. You were always a part of the community, continually giving of yourself and yet never losing yourself in the process.

There was no half of you in one place and another half some other place. Mom, you never sat on any fence. And you gave me the ultimate freedom: the choice of being myself. I am you in the way you always lived. Though I've rarely thought about your gift of honesty and sensitivity, it is the greatest of all gifts that you've given me.

Perhaps that is why, when, in my twenties I discovered my homosexuality, I found the courage to tell you and the family. I took the risk. Even though this was still in the 1960s—early in the gay movement—I instinctively knew that I had to be true to myself. No matter the pain, anxiety, misunderstandings and anger that could erupt in the midst of my coming out, I did come out as a homosexual when doing so still remained a physical and emotional threat. In fact, it remained frightening to "come out of the closet" until the 1980s. Tragically, still today, employers in the majority of American states can legally fire men and women solely on the basis of their identifying themselves as gay.

Mom, you never ran from anybody or anything. There was no mouse in you. You demonstrated independence and integrity, self-respect, self-esteem and self-worth. Confidence was a suit you wore naturally and well. It showed and it glowed.

From you I learned that this was true independence. You have always been a woman who took responsibility for her place as a fully participating person in the universe. Not some half rib from another. In nobody's shadow. Instead, you always walked straight, upright and forward. All of this you gave to me. Though in the earlier years I didn't understand this gift, it was somehow working within me. In the midst of my own journey of recovery from the effects of living within the family disease of alcoholism, this strength of character that I inherited from you pulled me through those dark times.

I stopped writing yesterday. This reminds me of many letters received from you over the years, because some morning you'd get started doing some cooking chore or a neighbour would pop in looking to have a chat and the teacup read, and your letter to me would be continued the next day. Some of your letters got written over several days. Up to this moment I'd forgotten that and here I am doing the same thing!

And I've even kept all those letters and cards from the 1980s and 1990s written to me by everybody for over twenty years. How exciting it will be to go through all the boxes of past mail and sort out your cards and letters to me. I did write some long letters to you over the years, and perhaps there still are some back home.

Yesterday, I wrote you of the greatest gift of "independence" you gave me. Certainly these many past years you've said during your telephone calls to me,

"I love you, Tom, like I love all of you." Often you've said, "It's you children who have ever only counted, meant everything in my life." Yes, you've said, "What would I have ever done without you children, you're all so so good to me, especially you dear, dear Tom." I've heard you say that many times these recent years.

Mom, that's how I understand "love."

The greatest gift you ever gave me is and always was love. If love means having done everything a person possibly could do to provide for a child's welfare or well-being as you did for me, then love is the greatest gift given to me.

I think about how it would be, Mom, for you and me to be talking together today. Would I be listening—really listening? Or would I still be intent on trying to tell? Persuade. Give me a hint. I want to listen. Really hear you. Yes, I have tapes now of your recorded voice. I look forward to listening again to them all because I think now that I will be aware of when I've been "manipulating the agenda" by inserting my expectations and who knows what. But I will try again to really listen.

Mom, let me tell you, this letter is about love. Of my love for you. No matter what my words, expressions and questions in this letter, I love you with all my heart. I love you, Mom. Thank you, Mom, for you. For everything. Especially for your patience with me. For letting me be me. All the time, for sure you never interrupted me. Just let me go on. And on!

Mom, I don't mind telling you, I'm crying, sobbing, tears are soaking these pages. They're from me. From my heart and my soul.

I feel again the way I felt the night before I drove you away from the house in New Brunswick for your last time. It was left to me to convince you to leave the house and to live in a full-care retirement home of your own choosing, hopefully in the Ottawa district where you could be close to Gail and many other relatives in the area. Your doctor had told us that you could never again be left all alone because the continuous small strokes were disorienting you. We saw that. There'd be days when you couldn't pour boiling water to make tea, or even remember how to take the toast out of the toaster. Other days seemed okay.

The person that was you just seemed to come and go.

We'd taken turns staying with you in your home, but we had to move ahead eventually. Each of us had our own lives and couldn't remain with you in New Brunswick. We did find the perfect retirement apartment home in Ottawa, with your approval, and furnished it with all your own stuff from the New Brunswick home right down to your African violet plants. But we know that you never really liked it. It was just too late for you to make that kind of adjustment.

The night I had to drive you away from your home, I cried. Wept. That was while you went upstairs to take a bath, just after you had been sitting there crying. And I didn't understand. Only sensed your frustration, over you not being able to tell me earlier of not having had your hair washed and done. Or how something was going on inside of you, as you were about to leave your home that you loved so much. The days beforehand when you just sat, sat, sat and stared. Knowing something was happening. Knowing that every wall and floor and piece of furniture in the house was speaking to you of the countless memories that wove together—thread by thread—creating the fabric of your life.

It's now too late. How I would love to take you back to your beloved home. Right now—to hold you. Sit with you. Be with you. Say nothing. To let it happen. Feel the moment.

Are you now shedding light into my soul? Helping me? I can tell that you are with me, aren't you? Still in this room—but no, in my heart and my head. You're smiling—that's your face—and even holding me.

Oh my God, I can touch me. Touch you. Feel you. You are opening something in me. My drenching tears wracking every muscle of my body and mind.

There's a sort of relief in the subsiding tears. No regrets over these tears. Instead—relief, release, even soothing. Cleansing. More like a dam that trembled, rumbled, then blasted open. I'm proud now of my flooding tears. Helping me. Delivering me joy and serenity. No sadness. Sheer joy. My God, Mom, how wonderful to really feel.

What can I give you for your birthday in this your ninety-second year? Your body does not go on any longer. No longer here alive. You left your body. I was there. Witnessed your final breath. I watched you, with your eyes so wide open, held by such a soft open face, as you let out your last breath. So quietly. Gently. Peacefully. And you shed that last tear from the corner of your eye. Gone from us.

Paul and I sat in the room with your body for three hours afterwards, waiting for them to come and take you away. We knew you had left your body. There was no question Paul and I were looking over only flesh and bones. That's what amazed me. How fast it all was. One moment you were in this body, a part of this flesh and bones and sounds, movements and air. Then, ahhh, and you were gone. Though not lost. Immediately I recognized you in me and Gail and Susan. Your existence in that room held me captive.

Today is your birthday. And I'm talking about death. Dying as I saw you. It seemed like you waited all day for Paul and me to come and be with you until you made your final exit. I say final because the body died. No life left. But I know that your spirit lives on inside me. I don't know how or where, but what you made of me is really you—living on. Believe it or not, Mom, you're still living in me, in Gail, Susan and the others.

I need to return now to what I am going to give you for your birthday. How do I give you the right gift? Perhaps it's this letter.

You loved poetry. That reminds me—Neil, your grandson, wants the poetry you've written. He wishes to record your poetry in song. What a gift. I shall make copies of your poetry for Neil. Yes, that would give delight and joy to your heart and soul. Having your grandchild write the music and production of your poetry into song. I will do what I can to help Neil accomplish this as a birthday gift.

My, how you loved and respected land. That had to be what enabled you to hold on to our own property through even the worst financial disasters. You never once considered abandoning our home and land on the Bay de Chaleur. It was your blood.

That's what I think convinced me to keep the house going financially all the years. I was and I am a part of your foundation. One of your growing roots. That, and some sense of earth and water. Maybe it's the salt—the salt of the earth! Always, the saltwater and air is—for me—both of faraway places and of home at the same time. The beach at home has been my anchor. The beach of the land and home you loved.

Mom, what did you see, so often looking through the kitchen window? Down at the bottom of the brown field there was the blue water and seagulls and crows. And in their time there were the rows of potatoes growing, and oats, barley, hay and clover. Sometimes ships were passing, and small boats out fishing. And near the end of the field the wild strawberries bloomed and grew on the edge overlooking the sand. You picked each one so gently, lovingly. And we did all the eating—you never ate them—enjoying that special sweet seedy strawberry taste. Were you thinking of all that as you looked out?

In staring motionless, out the window, what were you looking for? Sometimes I thought that I knew. But then, you'd slowly move away and your attention would shift to the limp brown leaf on your African violet, and then to a fresh little bud peeking out from under another soft leaf. Nothing in nature missed your look, lacked your touch.

Mom, here I am, caught between your dying and remembering your living. And I'm ready to listen, really listen. Wanting not to miss a thing. From now on, I'll be trying to get it right the first time.

Your loving son,
Tom

Mother's Day, Sunday, May 13, 2001

Dear Mom,

Happy Mom's Day!

Did I miss last year? You were recovering from hip surgery from your visit to our Florida place in February, and somehow I knew you had changed. I didn't recognize the same mom. The one I knew had gone—though not completely. I do remember you playing the piano and how it took you time to find your fingers on the keyboard. Although it was cumbersome and awkward for you, I kept encouraging you to play for me. The more you tried—in time—some of those ol' familiar pieces sounded out.

But I'm both ahead and behind in sequence. What I need to share with you is about last year's Mother's Day. You were on the recovery floor in the small Gatineau Hospital. I was not able to telephone. Or was it because I couldn't face reality? I think Susan continued to telephone, and finally reached the nursing station. They would go to get you and put you on the telephone.

I got to see how that worked the second trip around, of your recovery from the next hip break. Over those six weeks you took telephone calls from Susan, Henry and others. You listened. Seemed to register recognition. For certain, you were alert to who was on the phone. When Susan sang those songs to you, you tried singing along. Even twinkling your eyes. Sure showed you recognized your baby Mary Sue's voice—Susan and you always had a special bond.

Sitting here on this day, my thoughts so mixed up with memories of other times. I'm noticing the green, white and blue glass rocks that Gail, Susan and I plucked from the Bay de Chaleur shore as we walked along the water's edge, silent with our own thoughts. That was the afternoon after we buried your body.

Rumbling thoughts are in my head now too, remembering you for so many other Mother's Days and wondering now how or why I didn't write or even call last Mother's Day. And what of former Mother's Days? Often I drove or flew home to be with you for that special day. Was it often? Or is it that I just wished for often? Somehow it was always cold in early May in Bay de Chaleur. Still we would get those brilliant sunny blue skies over the heavy white-crested waves sweeping along the dark blue ocean waters.

And we'd say, "Boy, is that east wind ever cold!" Those raw sweeping winds would whip up along the newly ploughed fields. Even the freshly ploughed earth gave contradictory messages of inevitable death but also of new life to come. Like standing beside a freshly shovelled grave. But the helter-skelter seagull motion of the wind over the field swept me back to the present, and to this frozen fresh day. Even the crows got into the action. They always reminded me of life. Strange, though, how often those thoughts were tinged with loneliness. I think that's because of you, Mom.

For so many years, while slowly driving away from your house after one of my visits, all the way back to Ontario I could hear this *caw, caw*. And I could see their cruising black bodies sweeping over the backyard, signalling yet another goodbye.

My God! Crows are synonymous with you, Mom. Just like the whistling train. The other night, sitting quietly, and with the darkness dropping over the lake and only the sound of calling loons, suddenly there it was—the *juy, juy, juy*, and with that long *toot, tooodooot, toooot, toot* in the distance drawing closer with more whistle calls and echoing through every bit of night, bouncing off the pine tree-covered hills onto the lake top and up into our opened Muskoka-room windows.

The train whistle was calling me home to the backwoods. Even now I can feel myself drifting up the Culligan rail tracks in the blackened night like a flying giant, waving my arms out over our home, our bay and our village. And there, all of them are standing at the train station, and I can see Granny, Aunt Alice, Shirley Culligan and you saying, "Our summer's over, another year gone by, how lonesome. It won't be long before the flurries are flying."

How often have we all heard "You never appreciate what you have until it's gone." I remember my cousin Ursula telling me that after she lost both her dad and mom in the same year. Also Cousin Anita telling me how much she missed her mother, Frances, even after five years. And her telling me, with tears in her eyes, to enjoy my mother while we were so fortunate to have her still with us. Yes, maybe that sounds so trite. Yet, so darn true!

Mom, I know I said this in my birthday letter to you that I would just love to be able to sit with you again, not having to say anything, especially not interrupting you, offering no contradictions, no opposition, and not a negative comment. Only just to listen to you again. To appreciate your magic and your power and that wisdom from your lifelong collection of pain, suffering, joy, creativity, inventions and bright presence in all our affairs.

Mom, more than anything, I need to hear your voice. Mom, tell me something. I'm asking you but I know it's too late now. I read your letters yesterday. That last letter you sent me. I only noticed for the first time—just yesterday—that you had dedicated your journal diary book with many of your poems to me. "This book I will dedicate to Tom, my son, and hope you can recall some memories and get the feeling of love I harboured for you. Mom."

Mom, you heard me. I just went to your diary. Of you telling me how much you loved me. Maybe I ought not ask questions like, How can we not understand and have this appreciation in our lifetime? Why do these feelings emerge so strongly after you're gone? All the times of your own tears, when you recalled sorrow over your mother and losing your son Gordon, I just wanted to fast-reel it speeding ahead. Not listen. Not learn. Why was that? Does it matter? It's in the past. Or perhaps these tender memories are for awakening my understanding today. Maybe this is really just a journey to my heart on some other level—this time, a journey of understanding.

Not about perfection! I accept. Me. You. Our relationship. I'll carry your message of love and caring forward. I'll toot the whistle for you. Mom, your name will resound, bounce and echo among the tall pines, ocean waves, flying crows and rolling hillsides.

What's coming to me now is this overwhelming sense of thankfulness. Mom, you gave me strength, even though your gift was filled and filtered through weeping tears. Yes, I loved and will always love you. I have been beside you all my life, and was with you to the very end. I know that you always understood my devotion, caring and appreciation.

My, we had some great times. Especially the last ten years, on so many visits. Paul, Susan and I loved having Christmas with you. The meals were special. The two to three weeks were a mix of cheerfulness, music and singing, entertainment and a peaceful sense of warm togetherness. Rarely did any of us have differences. Only on that last Christmas—but we never knew or understood how much you were physically declining in those months.

I remember you saying, "I don't feel old, still feel young, I see myself as still a young person, just as though I were the young girl of yesterday." You were ninety when you said that. Well, guess what? Though I'm fifty-six now, I feel like Tommy, the little boy in the red V-neck sweater with a bit of a lisp—just a little boy in large-sized shoes and larger hand-me-down clothes.

I suspect my needs are basically the same now as they always were, but grown-up talk simply covers them up. Somehow too many of the little-boy feelings of wonder and emotion get ploughed under by the makeover job of growing up. Assuming responsibility overwhelms our minds and engulfs us in a world of terminal seriousness. But just as I get to keep the same heart and the same eyes from my childhood, I can still own the same little boy. Love, fear and all that stuff never really leave us. Mostly they just get buried. And usually buried alive. Kicking alive. Sometimes mortally wounded us, and destroying so much of our present.

How difficult to see you, Mom, as child or a young girl or even as the adult you were before I knew you. But I know that written all over you were the letters M-O-T-H-E-R. It's a feeling like stopping at the door of a home but not entering and therefore never seeing or really knowing what's inside. Maybe I only looked into the windows occasionally as I passed by in my own busy life.

Is there a prescribed way to treat Mother's Day? Besides wearing a red or white rose, or taking you to Danny's Diner or Swiss Chalet, or perhaps writing and sending a card? Flowers? Candy? Or is it the time to replace kitchen appliances? Gifts of dresses, purses, hats and diamonds.

But I can clearly picture you in the garden. How you loved gardening! Always digging up your perennial beds. Adding to the mixture of yellows, blues, violets, reds and whites. You seem bent over more than straight, with your head facing the earth. There you are, pail in one hand and the other mixing in your favourite growing formula—RX15. You came back into the house at the day's end with blood crusting all over and mosquitoes and black flies sticking onto you. You were like sticky flypaper! Puffed up and out, probably hurting but, it always seemed, scarcely aware of it.

As often, in your last two years in your own home, when you were eighty-nine and ninety, you'd stand very still, staring very quietly at the wonders of all that work in the garden beds. You had your own strongly held reasons for soaking the earth just as the sun was setting—but also just when the mosquitoes were biting.

You never considered giving up on your flowerbeds, the lawn, the house and the kitchen, or yourself, right up to the end. Even the day before we drove away together from your house for the last time, you talked of wanting to cement the basement floor again. Getting rid of the cracks. Painting it up fresh. Be sure it smells fresh. Cut down the dampness. You worried about those things because, after all, it was your home. Who else would have such thoughts? It didn't matter how much we argued that all was fine. No need for such additional work. You knew better and you said to us, "Let one thing go. Eventually all will wither, go and collapse."

And I'm thinking of our Culligan home. It's only a building, true, but that's never been my thinking. Everything's on loan and I am accountable. So it's how and what I do with what's been given to me so freely. Not to let anything rot, decay or crumble. Instead let me do my best to nourish the home and the memories.

But you were wrong on one thing, Mom. We did let you go gently on your way, but each of us knows that your memory will never wither, will never go and will never collapse.

Until the crow flies,
Love to the end,
Tommy

Sunset over our back stoop. 1998

Fourteen

For the Rest of my Life

O n one of my last visits with Mom, something very special occurred. The experience changed how I now relate to people.

On the way to that visit, I accidentally left my tape recorder at the airport on the way home to New Brunswick. So, instead of taping, I made copious notes during and after our conversations. This made for different dynamics. Because of the journal writing that I did each day from memory, tape recording enabled me not only to hear, but also to really listen to her voice and words, and later to reflect, which in turn inspired me to direct deeper questions to her. It is from this reflective probing and writing that I now have learned lessons for the rest of my life.

I knew that I wanted to begin by saying, "Mom, suppose *Time* magazine was interviewing you and asking you to tell people—from your life experiences—what could engender happiness and prosperity in their lives, what would that be?"

But somehow, instead, I found myself asking her a different question, and realized that it was something I'd always wanted to know. "Mom, is there any one book that influenced you the most?" The story that she revealed to me that afternoon stunned me. It was surely divinely touched.

At the time, we were sitting in what used to be the outdoor wraparound veranda of our Culligan home that is now glassed in from top to bottom. The walls of glass made it seem as though we were sitting right in the field of clover on the shore's edge. The beating and smashing of the waves wafting through the open windows punctuated our conversation, and I could taste the salt air with each sip of tea. Earlier that day, I had painted that very scene that was now all sound and scent. Perhaps it was in the silence of painting that scene that I knew more profoundly than ever before just how much Mom was so a part of this salty air.

I watched her then, stand up and stretch, breathing deeply the air from the window nearest the ocean—as she loved to do—and then start her story.

"While I lived in Boston as nanny for the Garlands, we summered on the ocean. That last summer before returning to Canada, they rented a beach house in a place we'd not been to before. It was there that I walked the beach daily and fell in love with the ocean.

"Some distance up the beach stood a steepled lighthouse and a small cottage. Rain or shine I walked there every day where I sat on the lighthouse steps to read and memorize my Shakespeare sonnets (which she could still recite by heart) and write my daily journal. I knew even then that writing washed the soul like tears heal the heart. And that writing would be partnered with my piano playing as a solace for life.

"From that time, the lighthouse vividly stands as my beacon for faith and hope. For me, the lit sanctuary lamp, like the lighthouse, shines its light for safety and comfort. Before I returned home from Boston to help Mama with her pregnancy, I promised myself I'd carry that lighthouse beacon with me always as the sign of faith and hope that can never be extinguished.

"You asked which book most influenced me? My heavens to Saint Ann, it's that the entire world is small indeed. Let me tell you there are no coincidences in life. You'll discover how everything eventually comes together and makes sense. Clarity only arrives at our most calm time, usually after living our worst storms. I say to you that Og Mandino was like my kinfolk—like old Grandmother Rubber."

My ears pricked up at her mention of Og Mandino. A great writer who sold millions of books worldwide—and I had read every single book he wrote! I didn't say anything then, but listened to her as she continued reminiscing.

"Og Mandino's books, *The Greatest Miracle* and *Greatest Secret*, combined the best ages of wisdom passed on through centuries. His books share how each of us can find the secrets that lie deep within our heart and soul and that help to bring us to the stillness so we can really hear and be able to listen to our own heart and soul. Therein lie the answers we so desperately seek.

"Did you know where Og Mandino lived and worked? In a recent biography on him, I discovered that Mandino's writing studio was the same lighthouse where I read sonnets and wrote during my last summer as nanny. What's more astonishing is that he called his writing studio a 'sanctuary!'"

Talk about being knocked off your chair! Sanctuary! Mom's most sacred ritual was always to pray while lighting her church sanctuary lamp. On hearing her say this, I recalled this event. Some time ago, I attended a book workshop because I knew that Og Mandino would be there. My purpose was to meet and speak with him. His books were a huge part of my deliberate study to learn about business, as well as life. During the workshop, he and I came together and chatted. Rarely have I been so taken by another person as I was with him. All the international fame had not jaded him; he was a gentle, warm and soft man.

I said to him, "Of all the books I've read and studied, it's yours that most motivated and inspired me to excellence in all I sought to do."

As he held my hand in his, he said, "Tom, I feel I've known you all my life. Perhaps we've been together somehow before."

My God almighty! Of course we'd been together. Both he and Mom had shared the "sanctuary" of his lighthouse and both wrote of faith and hope all life long. In some profound way, they were connected on the same path. To think this man inspired millions through this same beacon of hope and faith is simply awesome—combined acts of two spirits that produced their miracles and presence that lingered forever on the lighthouse steps. Mom would often say to me, "Dear, when I light the sanctuary lamp, I feel united with every burning sanctuary lamp throughout the world, with a feeling of faith and hope in abundance."

Mom's reading Og Mandino's books and her Boston ocean experience were not coincidence. Neither was mine in seeking out Og Mandino.

"All energy is meant to unite, always making its way, and no snow plough, manipulation, or any show of force will prevent nature's course," Mom said to me thoughtfully.

During the days of that visit, we talked and talked, cried tears and laughed and drank teacup after teacup after teacup. We did finally get around to my " *Time*-magazine happiness and prosperity" interview question. And I believe the simplest way for me to share her answers would be to summarize each point that she made. Of course, I'm the lucky fellow because I've had the blessings of Mom's gifts working in my life for years. Quite imperfectly, I might add, yet divinely.

So here's Mom's recipe to happiness and prosperity. These really are simple fundamentals, yet they have worked through the ages. What's written here are words that just say in good old-fashioned Maritime speech what all the ages of wisdom—the Ten Commandments, the Sermon on the Mount, the Torah and Gandhi's teachings—have expressed to us. But in Mom's own words.

For the Rest of Your Life

1. Above all else—EXERCISE.

Do something each day to move your limbs. Have all body joints exercised. Stretching works—from head to toe, left to right, up and down, until you feel elastic. Gardening helps stretching. Walking, jogging or swimming even for twelve minutes will do it. Just be mindful to relax when being physical, then it's exercise. A recent morning I was telling myself, "Come on Maggie ol' gal, you can do it, just get yourself out to the flower beds and the rest will just follow." And sure enough it does. I don't even notice the time, weeding, digging and transplanting, and before you know, it's way past my lunchtime.

2. Develop the habit of BREATHING DEEPLY.

Focused deep breathing and slow exhaling is meditation. As did the ancient monks. No matter what pops into the mind during your breathing exercise, don't struggle with it, just return to your deep breathing. Focus. This will clear your mind. And body. Oxygen sure beats any pills. Supplies energy for any physical or mental task. So often, dear, folks come to me frightened, anxious and many with real panic over their marriages. I'll always first say, "Take a deep breath, dear, all the way into your stomach and hold it there." And we'd repeat that several times. With that, everything's changed.

3. There's no better prescription than a SMILE.

No matter the trouble, always wear a smile. Yes, be brave in time of problems and put on a smile. Even a forced smile will deliver positive results. At the minimum, a forced smile rids you of a sour, troubled look. Keep smiling, it becomes a habit and contagious—worth catching. Just look around and watch for it. When you smile, the world smiles back at you. It's our choice to be happy or not, by simply choosing to make a habit of smiling.

4. My heavens, cheerfully GREET EVERYBODY!

Remember dear Miss Nobody on your daily path and lend a greeting. Especially an extended handshake—it lifts you and the other upwards to heaven. In acknowledging, recognizing and greeting another, we build self- and mutual respect. This cannot help but lead to self-confidence and self-worth. All creation is divine. And so it is for you and me. Blessed it is when we acknowledge so in each other.

5. Open your mouth and SPEAK CLEARLY.

Lift your head high, keep your back straight, look the other in the eye and articulate clearly what you have to say. Please, no mumbling. No slouching. Folks will take note and interest when they hear and understand. This alone can get you to the top of the class. Even to the very shy, I say, start by at least looking at the other. And start with one word. Remember, practice makes perfect.

6. ACCEPT results in serenity and maturity.

Why struggle? It's rarely about who's right or wrong. Being right and dead's not especially fun. Graciously accept compliments, success, abundance, rejections and disappointments. Allow others the dignity of their own decisions and results with acceptance. And live your own life to the fullest. At the very minimum, look in the mirror to start. Then say, "I accept myself."

7. GROUNDED! That's where your feet should be.

Find your connection to nature. Try your best to open all your senses: eyes, ears, mouth and feelings to be in touch with Mother Nature. Think about how all growth occurs then fades, and ultimately decays. Yet is reborn from its own rot and decay. Keep it simple by using your nose to smell, eyes to see and observe, mouth to taste and your whole body to feel the environment. When I've been the busiest, I remember to say to myself, "Stop, look and listen!" Pretend you're at a railway crossing.

8. Always err on the side of GENEROSITY.
Forget what you've given, so that you'll never miss it. Do everything reasonable to clothe and feed the helpless. Generosity always gets multiplied. Of course, the most difficult part of this is to remain anonymous.

9. Through all circumstances, keep your INDEPENDENCE.
Above all, keep an independent conscience. Strangely, it's only through a selfish program of building courage, strength and serenity that you will be of any value to others. Lose your independence, and you'll flounder and be tossed like a captain lost at sea. A strong faith and hope will engender independence. Compromise and improve in every area of your life except for your evolved understanding of the living principles of faith, honesty, trust, humility, love and gratitude.

10. Learn how to IMPROVISE.
Find ways to make something out of nothing. Look at what you have from every possible angle, then examine again, and improvise from that perspective. Observe nature in how freely it grows abundantly to nurture us. Use it freely. Travel outside your own circumstance to observe and utilize what's available to help build your dream. I am living proof you don't need much money for whatever you want in life.

11. In whatever you do, exercise ENTHUSIASM.
Passion. Be passionate in whatever you do. Go talk to some person who exudes passion. Enthusiasm will move mountains. Energy begets energy. People love positive upbeat energy. Most importantly, just put yourself out there—again and again. Replace fretting and worrying with enthusiastically trying again. Results simply take care of themselves when you're enthusiastic. Eventually enthusiasm

will win. It just can't help it.

12. Open the window to your soul and mind with WRITING.

You just start with a word. Yes. Words. Whatever comes to your mind. Write it down. Don't edit a single word or thought. Write every day. Suddenly, the words become sentences and the sentences become paragraphs. Paragraphs become plans, dreams, goals, visions, organizational structures, solutions, profits and God knows what. In writing, you develop a relationship with a most valuable friend. Writing, like music, saved my sanity. It's a sounding board that delivers answers, questions and solutions.

13. FAITH will carry you all the way.

Never, never give up! Persevere through every single obstacle and you'll reach your goal. Have unshakeable faith that you'll be provided for to work through each single obstacle that lies in your path. Trust that you're receiving everything you need this very moment to do whatever you know needs doing. Find a power greater than yourself to believe in. Be it the sun, some wisdom, the god of your understanding or Mother Earth. Believe that abundance and prosperity is your divine right. Faith does indeed move mountains. Resources are there right at our fingertips. Should there be any one thing I can tell you, it's this: Believe with your heart and soul that you're never alone, that you're being looked after every single moment of your life. Hold on to that thought, especially during your darkest moments.

14. Don't be afraid to DREAM.

It's okay to start small. One tiny step at a time. Build momentum towards your dream. Whatever! Anyone who sincerely acts enthusiastically on his or her dream—it will inevitably come to pass. Be not ashamed of your dreams. Imagine. Create. Think of it as yours. Nothing stops that kind of power. Think of the many possibilities and claim what is to your liking. Whatever the reason, some folks, just plain as the nose on your face, bold face tell you your idea is crazy. Well dear, I say no, it's them that's crazy, even foolish, to knock anybody down.

15. Be resolute until you find the SOLUTIONS.

Turn over every rock until you find what you're looking for. Be curious. Ask questions. Research. No matter the task at hand, most always the information you need is free. Exhaust every source. Reminds me of the "let your fingers do the walking through the Yellow Pages" advertisement! No matter the goal, task or dream that you seek, someone's already been down that path. Go seek them out. Folks just love to tell you of their success, their way, and the secrets on how they got there. It's all for the asking. Don't be shy. Go to any length to find out and to build what you want in life.

Mom still had more to say. "Now, we all heard when you stop making mistakes, you've stopped trying. So my way of thinking is that the more mistakes you make, the more you're trying, which ultimately leads to the solution. Thus success!"

Breezy bonfire with Mom and
Mary Sue. 1999

Fifteen

Sharing Stories of Mom

After Mom died, hundreds of folks wanted to share their stories of her. Many sounded familiar because of her public persona in the church. For quite a few, she had piped them into church with her organ music for their baptism, first communion, confirmation, graduation, wedding and any number of family funerals. For many others, she may have been hairdresser, teacup reader, jam maker, wonderful cook, poker player, dancing twelve-stepper and perhaps above all, a loving mother, grandmother and friend.

But how can I have the last word when so many others are pressing forward?

When we visited, we often retired to bed long before your mom. Sometimes I don't think she even made it to bed. At ninety years, we marvelled that Margaret wasn't afraid to stay in that big house alone. I think, though Margaret loved company, she preferred the isolation and welcomed the solitude her last years provided. In her kitchen cupboards and jam closet, enough food was stored to last, I'd say, at least five years.

Deany Johnson, Mom's first cousin

~

No matter where or when we ran into her, Margaret always had a beautiful smile and gracious greeting.

Ann Cronin, cousin from Massachusetts

~

My boys loved when Margaret came visiting. Always had time to pay attention to their interests. I remember her once with James, sitting there with him and listening to a whole tape of 'Mr. Dressup.'

Theresa McDonnell, neighbour and Mom's good friend

~

When my oldest child, Joanie, was born with a mental handicap, Margaret gently encouraged me with loving attention. We became even closer, because she fully shared of her own little boy, Gordon, affected permanently from encephalitis and later dying from polio. Many times our tears intermingled in shared sorrow. Margaret's great love for her family and firm faith in God was ever present. I don't think I will ever meet another person like your mother. She was pure joy to know.

Clara Flanagan, Mom's longtime friend and hairdressing customer

~

Gail and I were playmates. I spent nearly as much time at your house as I did ours. What a wonderful place, making taffy, french fries, jumping off the veranda roof into snowbanks and getting to sleep in the warm half of the house. Margaret was out a lot trying to earn money. She had no money to spare but never made me feel that I wasn't welcome. I don't know anyone else with such generosity and hospitality. Margaret had a beautiful voice, not just in song, but in her manner of speaking as well.

Carolyn Thornton, cousin from Boise, Idaho

When I was young, babysitting for your mom, she'd let me bake cookies and squares for the kids. Now, I wasn't much older than the ones I looked after. Over the years, we had delicious meals at your home. With a pot of tea, she served up a pan of her hot sticky buns for dessert. They didn't last long. Then, Genevieve, Joanie, Maureen, Lee and myself would reminisce with your mother late into the night.

Cousin Mary Kay Adele from California [visiting family Culligan relatives]

⌒

I often listened to Margaret as she played the organ and sang in church. As a matter of fact, she's the only thing I remember from sitting in church all those years.

Alton Roherty, neighbour and owner of original Culligan gas station and garage

⌒

My wife Susan often shares her visits to Aunt Margaret's with me. She tells of the legends of Margaret's life in her magical house, the all-night poker games of gentlemen friends and a freezer full of lobsters from who knows where.

Michael Priddy, first cousin Susan Boudreau's husband

⌒

My mom used to say, "Margaret will never be a rich woman, for she would give it all away." Along with being a very generous woman, she was also a woman of strong faith. When I brought her communion, Margaret was truly in the presence of God. It used to do my heart good to see her.

Bobby Culligan, next door neighbour, cousin and Mom's dependable friend

⌒

A vibrant person who shared whatever she had with everybody. We never left her home empty-handed.

Gene Cronin, cousin from Massachusetts

⌒

The last time I saw Margaret was at the hairdresser's. She came over to my chair and sat down. Then she sang, "Silver Threads Among the Gold." So like her to the end, thinking of others—my hair is almost pure white and she was encouraging me still. Margaret's beautiful poems, music and song, excellent cooking and courage are legendary.

Clara Flanagan, Jacquet River friend

⟿

I learned over time that Mamère's character was not limited to a few simple attributes. As well as being, disciplined, heritage oriented, articulate, family loving, and a God-fearing woman, she naturally had the knack of making people feel good about themselves and towards their other family members. She had nothing bad to say about anybody. This became more apparent as I got older and listened to her talk about my aunts, uncles, cousins and other kinfolk. When young I didn't appreciate how talented she was. That came later after hearing her sing, play piano and organ and read poetry. I realized I came from someone truly unique.

Mark Culligan, grandson

⟿

My life's most treasured memories are of the years I spent in Belledune getting to know your mother. She was intuitive, sensitive and a very caring person. We spent many hours at the ol' piano. What a lovely voice! After spending time with Margaret, I always left lighthearted and confirmed that life was worth living.

Dortha Ultican, Boise, Idaho

⟿

I first met your mom when Paul Boudreau, Susan's dad, was in the hospital for that terrible three weeks after his surgery for pancreatic cancer. Somewhere in this chaotic process your mother arrived in town. She'd come to see her brother Paul before he died. It didn't take Margaret long to figure out the stress, anxiety and sadness that flowed through that home. She announced she was moving in. Didn't ask permission. She knew where she was really needed.

"Even though she was dealing at that time with her own grief watching her much-loved brother die, she reached out of herself to help us. Your mother baked loaves upon loaves of bread; a tabletop full of pies and bottomless casserole dishes kept appearing. She even cleaned the house from top to bottom.

"Still, Aunt Margaret took the time to make a pot of tea, sit down and listen to us talk. She didn't try to dominate conversations or take anything over. She was just there for us—a great comfort. And I felt very close to her through the entire experience. After Paul died, she remained very involved throughout the funeral and the family gatherings that drew us together for comfort."

Michael Priddy, first cousin, Susan Boudreau's husband, Missouri

During one visit, we were upstairs getting ready for Theo's (Culligan) funeral. Mamère came running down the hallway from her bath, partially covered with a skimpy towel, with boobs swinging. When I tried to duck my head and cover my eyes, she laughingly said something. It meant she wasn't afraid to be seen like that and that everything was okay. I was struck by her openness.

She and Gail talked freely in the kitchen, about menstruation, Kotex pads, health situations, bowels or just name any list of unapproachable topics. These were words and topics that were never uttered nor discussed openly in my family home. Nor anyone else's of previous experience.

And life with Margaret was dramatic. Filled with ups and downs. Everyone would be waiting downstairs, shined and ready to go, be it a dance, to Mass, an ordination or a funeral, when suddenly from upstairs you'd hear her say, "Where did I put that pearl necklace, those black high-heeled pumps, the small black purse?" For others, it could be a frantic crisis, but not for Margaret.

She was never to be hurried over her ablutions. She'd take her lengthy bath and pick her outfit, leaving all to the very last minute. And just when you'd believe she had the outfit on, off it would come to try on anther. No matter what the cost in time and energy to her and others, Margaret always appeared looking spectacular, gliding out to the car, the reigning queen lady that she was.

John Partington, Gail's husband

I found Mamère at peace with the universe in the 1990s. She showed positive energy and it felt good to be in her presence. It was contagious. Mamère was always more than her physical self. She was a way of looking at life and living.

Brent Culligan, Mom's grandson

For me, at times, Margaret was like a god. I survived my crisis with the help, nurturing and encouragement of your mother. After I got through the lunch crowds in my restaurant, I often called Margaret to come visit. She loved to eat and I loved to cook for her equally as much. She was a power of example in courage and strength for women all over.

Elaine McGregor, Mom's down-the-road friend

Tom, I've been thinking a lot about Mamère. The other day, Holly, one of my twins, was sitting in my lap and told me that I smelled different. Well, I was wearing a shirt that Mom had given me, so I said that I probably smelled like Gramma Gail. But Holly answered, "No!" She thought that I smelled just like Mamère! I don't know why she made that connection, but I was grateful for Holly's thought. It made me feel sad realizing that my children won't know firsthand what an extraordinary woman Mamère was.

After Holly made her comment, she looked at me with wide eyes when I said that I missed Mamère and Holly told me softly, "I miss her too." Hugging Holly, I told her that Mamère was watching over all of us.

I didn't know at the time that Sadie (the other twin) had been listening. Because two days later, Sadie asked me how Mamère watches over all of us at the same time.

Here's what I told Sadie and Holly: Of the many joy-filled memories of Mamère, the one that stands out is of her singing to me when I was eleven years old. She and I were in her bedroom, just sitting on the bed when she took my hands in hers. She told me that she sensed a deep sadness in me, and said how much she wished for my life to have happiness. Mamère then sang, "Let the Sunshine In." I always felt that she truly knew and accepted all of me—and really loved me. That's why I sing that song to my children now, but instead of singing "My mother told me something," I always sing, "My Mamère told me something" and it's true. It's my children's favourite song.

After that story, I told Sadie that Mamère takes turns looking down on each of us. Tom, I only hope that it is my turn right now, and that she's smiling as I write this to you.

Kari Partington, Mom's granddaughter

Her approach to discipline was a stern voice with a well-informed and experienced lecture in how and why we do things her way in New Brunswick. She cared about what was going on in my relationship with my father because she cared so much about him and the well-being of our family. She was adept at pointing out my good and bad characteristics, and not afraid to let me experience the feelings that come with the bad stuff as well as the stuff on cloud nine. She also had a captivating effect on my girlfriends with poetry readings and piano singsongs that lasted all night.

Mark Culligan, grandson

When our family moved into the Culligan community in the early 1950s, we'll never forget how it was your mom who welcomed us. Being the only French family to live here made for a difficult situation. Mom and Dad always talked of your mother with fondness and praise for friendliness and acceptance of us.

Rose Gerard, up-the-road neighbour

Margaret was the one person of all of the Culligans who treated everybody alike. We really counted with Margaret. Godfrey and the boys thought the sun rose and set on your mother. While some ignored us, your mother gave us the time of day. And I know how often she brought homemade cooking to Godfrey and the boys after I left.

Alice Carrier, down-the-road neighbour

My sister believed Mom was plagued with a guilt complex that distracted her views on a number of subjects, and that her high expectations of everything made it so that no one could please her. But Mom's greatest strength was her perseverance and stamina in facing responsibilities under the hardships of being sole supporter while keeping our family together.

Ann Titus, Mom's daughter

Towards the end of your mom's life her mini-strokes hit her hard, occasionally making her sick and depressed. One such night, Bobby and I visited her at the house and found her very low. Shortly on our way as we drove her to Dalhousie Hospital, she began to sing—and sang the entire half-hour trip. She could even uplift herself, but Margaret really just needed to be with people.

One evening when Tom (Mary's husband) and I were returning from a walk—it was just a short time before he died—Margaret met us on the road in her car. She had had company in for a lobster dinner and they had gone home too early. That is, too early for her. She wanted company! She invited us down for lobster. Tom never ate lobster, so we declined. She insisted, so we ended up walking home and getting the car to go down to her place.

We spent a memorable evening with her piano playing and singing. Tom loved to sing. She loaded us both down with lobster, she found trout in the freezer for Tom, squares left over from her dinner and then got an audiotape of Rose Marie Devereaux's organ playing, all that for us to take home!

Mary Young, Jacquet River friend

⌁

Your mom reminded me of Katharine Hepburn, poised and dignified, exuding inner strength.

Faye Johnson, Mom's Ontario cousin

⌁

We've all heard the advice carpe diem. Margaret lived life that way. It didn't have to be frenzied activity, she always seemed to know that "seizing the day" sometimes meant a lovely walk on the beach and other times enjoying a lively party. Margaret had a passion for life.

Carolyn (Ultican) Thorton, Idaho cousin

⌁

Margaret never forgot us at Christmas, with her delicious gumdrop cake. She'd bake these cakes in October—how well I know because of the cases of gumdrops she'd purchase at our store. After the cakes were baked, she'd be sprinkling them with wine over weeks. At the holiday season, she delivered them to us and I guess just about everybody else in the area. To this day, no matter how special is the gumdrop cake I offer my boys; the remarks are always "It's nowhere as good as Margaret's!"

Theresa McDonnell, Jacquet River friend

⁓

Your mom and I had a past—I've always remembered our fun together. One of her Florida winters was spent with me in Key West when we occupied the condo next to Tom and Susan, smack on the ocean at the southern-most point of the United States. Both of us were every bit fascinated and entertained by the parade of drag queens and the leather scene of Duval Street. We rated that winter a "ten out of ten" remembering the fun, laughs and just crazy behaviour we permitted ourselves.

Your mom had said to me, and I agreed, that there just didn't seem to be the usual rules people pretended by. There was a freedom being on Key West.

Adeline Flanagan, lifelong friend of Mom's from Jacquet River

⁓

We were somewhat of two peas in a pod. Besides from being Tom's godmother, I was his mom's regular poker chum. Lots of all-night sessions over the years playing poker at my house, at Aunt Annie's house or Hicky's. We cooked, fished, hunted, played, laughed, cried and travelled together for eighty-some years. Your mom and her good friend, Emile, together with Walter and me in those way-back years brought home the bacon more than once. We'd return from hunting or fishing camp loaded with assorted wild meats for the winter supply.

In our fall hunting trips back in the woods of Benjamin Portash's, Margo, Emile, Walter and I ate our meals of boiled potatoes and herring from a cast iron pot that got cooked over an open fire. We hunted right along with the men, bringing home moose, deer, rabbit and partridge for the Christmas meat pies.

Win or lose, after playing poker all night at Hicky's, I'd go back with Margo to her place and she'd play the piano.

One time, she and I went on a Caribbean cruise. I got blistering sunburn and had to stay put in our cabin. When we crossed from Central America, the trade winds got so rough, I stayed vomit-sick for two days. Margo nursed me, fetching liquids for me to drink and looking out the porthole watching for land, since all I could think was, "Please God, just stop this ship!" Thank mercy

God I got better. So your mother and I played the one-arm bandit all night long for the last two nights. On board, Margo was a genuine missy, made friends so that everyone admired her.

She leaves a big empty space with her being gone. I miss her and think of her always.

Yvonne Daley, my godmother, Dad's double first cousin, from
Benjamin River, N.B.

It doesn't matter which side of the kitchen table they're on. Be it serving or sitting, they're always ready for a spot of tea. That's how it always was in Mom's kitchen. Mary McCarron was sharing tea with me some time after Mom had died. Only this time we were on the porch.

"Good God almighty!" Mary remarked as she sipped from the blue-flowered china teacup, "you wouldn't know Margo's gone, drinking this cup'a tea. My Tommy, I half expect your mother will start up on the piano any moment or maybe call us all in to sit at the kitchen table for a poetry reading from one of her books.

"I think what I'll remember most always about her is her standing in front of the high window by the kitchen sink towards the ocean view, without so much as a bend to her neck, so like her own mother. Margo would read the weather out of the splash of the waves and the passing cloud formations.

"And you know, after Margo told me the cloud formations, I'd rather listen her up to her predictions than remember what each cloud meant!

"I'll never see this kitchen without your mother standing by that kitchen-sink window. Your mother and Aunt Pina (Momo) will be with us always to comfort and heal us."

Mary McCarron, Dad's double first cousin from Jacquet River

A HEAVENLY MESSAGE
The angels came silently,
And carried her on high
To God's heavenly home
Above the azure sky.

They said,
We have brought this mother to you
With all the sufferings
That she went through
Her name is written in your book of gold
And all her good deeds that were left untold.
You will miss her sweet smiling face
For no one could ever take her place
But you too will live for evermore
To walk with her on that heavenly shore
Where there is "Eternal Peace"
And no more pain
The place where all will
Meet their loved ones once again

Clara Flannagan

Backyard birdhouse

Afterword

When visiting with Mom, nobody left the house empty-handed. Way long after all of us kids flew the coop, she just went on baking and preserving as though her house was filled to the brim with people. Folks always left our house with a piece of Mom. Be it a half or full gumdrop cake, a loaf of home-made potato bread, a bottle of those tiny wild-strawberry preserves, a handwritten copy of one of her poems, a ditty on the piano or even one of her favourite sweaters or some clothes.

Just sharing Mom's story would be one sandwich short of a picnic, as they say back home, were I not to give you something as we take leave.

Since much of her enjoyment and solace also came through writing poems, here are a few of her cherished favourites. Though she recited Shakespeare sonnets by heart, I don't believe she composed her poetry thinking in terms of popular techniques or metrical composition.

These poems just poured out of Mom's heart and soul. They reflect her passion for her children, people all around her, and Mother Earth beneath her toes.

THE BAY DE CHALEUR

The Bay de Chaleur is long and wide
Mighty rough when a storm comes up
Quebec and New Brunswick on either side
Sometimes warm and often cold
Beaches sandy and others with stone
A place of work and fun for everyone
And this can't be said of everywhere!
The fishing's varied for one and for all
Herring, mackerel, codfish and sole
Lobster and salmon, clams and oysters
Mussels and scallops 'til fall
We're lucky one and all
For smelt, ice broken, we fish through a hole
They come and they go, and some bide awhile.
This is our life since our forefathers came.
Oh, the Bay de Chaleur is long and wide
But we love it best in the fire's glow
As we sing and we dance from side to side
Watching the sun dip slow and low.

February 1972

I LEARNED TO QUESTION, "WHY?"

There was a time when I would pray
On bended knee and every day
The words learned at Mama's knee
Would cleanse my soul and set me free.
But then I grew and time passed by
And I learned to question, why?
When I would dwell on earth and sky
In awesome wonder did I see
The birth and growth of every tree
To crown and nurture in the field
The untold wealth that it did yield.
The sun, the moon, the stars give light

To all on earth by day and night.
For life goes on and if well spent
Comes our journey's end without lament.

1970

STRAIGHT FROM OUR HEARTS

We travel near and travel far
To meet with people here and there
The day with sun, at night a star
And then came our dreams from everywhere.

Ellen's the woman I dare to say
On this fair night she came to dine
Beautiful and in a wondrous way
Held me spellbound like rare wine

The words we spoke might well have been
Straight from our hearts because we knew
The world of strife and book and men
We could teach each one, not just a few.

I want to live that I might really be
All I hold so dear and more
The words learned at life's knee
Form a wealth of lasting lore.

May 12, 1975

TOMMY

It was June wild roses, garden and more
When I carried and waited so lovingly for
My precious babe, so a part of me.
Each day would dawn and nearer would be
The time to prepare and ready for birth
Oh! Joyous wonders for all on earth
One would think and rightly so

After reading this verse with all apropos
I was waiting and well on the way
For child eight was coming any day.
Might well others learn from their life and their way
How one and all should care so much
Then along with me to sing with joy
A lullaby sweet to Tommy my boy.

1945

MUSIC FOR THE HEART THAT BEATS WITHOUT A SONG

Music hath charm but not for one
With sorrow unsurpassed.
But who can know that heart
That beats without a song
Might well have quickened to belong
And loved by the very one
Whose word would dust
The heartstrings in that human bust
The day and night must come and go
To each his own as waters flow.
The paths that wind through life's full time
The straight, the narrow, the sublime
Can hold to her for one and all who pray
And live for all from day to day.
Then let all hear the strains of music sweet
That guide the way of dancing feet
With steps that falter nevermore
Until they reach that other shore.

February 1971

MARY SUE

Susan came to us in summertime
In early hours of the morn
No poet with this verse of rhyme

246

Could write the words that would adorn
This babe I held with pride and joy.
I loved you then and love you now
You are you, will always be
In all life's trials come what may
The cloudless sky, the stormy sea
Wanton waif, the sad, the gay.
I've treasured and blessed the day you were born
But let it be for someone else
To take your place
When time and tide have won the race.

1948

GOOD TO BE ALIVE!

I like to wish upon a star
Walk a trail that goes afar
Feel the crunch of crystal snow
The frosty sting that makes me go
Stepping faster as spirits rise.
Feeling the urge to fantasize,
I say out loud, "It's good to be alive!"
To laugh and cry, to share and love,
Ever grateful to my God above
And all on earth who helped me
Try and try for that serenity.
After acceptance comes peace
Of mind and will to find—
I've gained the long sought treasure.

1986

ENJOY THE FLEETING MOMENTS

Put yesterday behind you
It's gone and won't come back.
And we cannot see ahead
Far down tomorrow's track.
So enjoy the fleeting moments

That come just for today—
The sweet song of a bluebird
And the morning sun's first ray
A warm and loving handclasp
And welcome letters in the mail
A bunch of fragrant violets
Warm rain splashing in a pail
Each day has something special,
Some joy or souvenir
It might be gone tomorrow
So enjoy it while it's here.

1986

KNOW THAT I CARE
Down to field of green, dish in hand
To feed the birds from sea and land
A patch of clover caught my eye
So bent to look, and thought I'd try
First one then two and up to ten
Four-leaf clovers I plucked and then
Wished for my kin so many things
Like happiness and health with love to spare
And hope that everyone will know that I care.

1988

WHO LOVES MOM?
Who loves Mom? Oh, we all do
And with all her faults to mention a few
Someone must tell her!
But who? Don't let it be me!
But maybe you?
It might be a problem she could conceal
But at times a word would reveal
That from that cup she drank to feel
Everyone was genuine and real.

But that was something overrated
With words like "disgusted" and "deflated"
Assigned to Mom and her behaviour
Whom they'd looked up to as a saviour.
Who loves Mom? Oh! We all do.
They're on their own
While I'm alone
They need time to think
How Mom stood by and in her way
In what many would think was so astray
Would loudly proclaim to say
Let it be you or let it be me
Your conscience as guide should set you free.

1973

TODAY IS THE DAY GIVEN TO US

The night is long with time to reflect
On all of life's journey,
To have laughed, loved and cried
Is what counts most today.
The works penned by us could take much time
As days have passed and we do recall
The memories, some vivid some dim.
We must dwell on the graces received from Him.
Today is the day given to us
For spiritual progress, not perfection.
Partners are we to reach the top
Of that glorious home on the mountain
To rest.

1980

REACHING OUT

Now a song in my heart as the sun shines bright
And dawn appears to dispel the night of worried dreams
That haunt and fill our lives

Like boats on a storm-tossed sea.
Mother Earth wakes up and so should we
When in sight of the harbour not far away
God waits with outstretched hand
Loving us, forgiving us, without demand.
Then hark! What does my soul say?
You are safe now and don't forget
God helped you and you must proclaim
That wondrous message A.A. is the name.

1982

DAY AFTER DAY
Our Bay de Chaleur in winter
With widespread snow-covered ice
Where beyond and beneath does still
The moving waters of gray and blue
The seagulls have gone? Well, maybe a few
Slowly winging and dipping from shore
To drop to the rock that they might fulfill
The search for the mussel or fish that will
Help them live the long winter through.
Taken for granted—"Just birds!" some say
What with their plumage of white and grey
Lovely in flight, so graceful in dive
Their noisy chatter and siren-like call
Makes me rejoice and feel grateful
Day after day
That the wonders of God will forever survive.

1989

A PART OF EVERY HEART WILL LINGER HERE
Oh, we love your summer cottage,
As we join you here today
And we will not forget,
Though we be far away.

In your little summer cottage,
Every voice will bid farewell
And shiver off in twilight
Haunting, like the vesper bell.

One day a hush will fall, and our footsteps all
Will echo wall to wall and disappear.
And as we sadly start our journeys far apart
A bit of every heart will linger here.

In your little summer cottage,
Here we met and learned to know
That through the years we'll see you
In the sweet afterglow.

1970

To Henry and Cathy's Children, Christopher, Barry and Neil

A VALENTINE POEM
(Sent with a box of homemade baking)

Our birthday can be such a big celebration
And as we grow up and learn
That more is in store
For the lads who seek education
Doing their best each day of the year
In the choice that is made—be that as it may
The three R's with music to boot
Let's give three cheers for Valentine's Day
With the goodies it brings to loved ones away.

February 14, 1985

A card with box of goodies to John and Gail's children

> *The Easter bunny looked around*
> *The eggs all gone but then he found*
> *Missy Hare had joined the race*
> *With mocha balls to save their face.*
> *Happy Easter!*
>
> > *Love, Mom. 1978*

To Gene's children, card with baked goods

> *These sweets were baked with loving care*
> *For dear ones when I can't be there*
> *Lucky me that you are mine*
> *So—can I be your Valentine?*
>
> > *Love, Mom. 1978.*

Card written to Mom's niece, Susan Boudreau, with a gift for her marriage to Michael Priddy

> *To dear Susan and Michael*
> *April showers bring May flowers*
> *To deck the many fields and bowers*
> *And Mother Nature's mystic way*
> *For seasons past does seem to say*
> *Rejoice and come along*
> *It's time to sing a wedding song*
> *For Michael and Susan when vows they'll speak*
> *With binding love to help them keep.*
>
> > *Love, Aunt Margaret, April 1, 1978*

Mom's last visit to the beach